Key to Emerson – P.17
"caducous" P.81
Harold Bloom P.90

Thinking and acting are parts of a single action

The whole is in the fragment

We need to see the transparent that
underlies, gives order to &
unifies all reality: The hidden laws
beneath the apparent chaos.

Transparency is revealed thru damification—
see p. 88

writing is fragmentary pursuit of the whole
vs. recording of facts or expressing
ideas.

Criticism = science (P.130) – the existence of
limits & boundries

The Emerson Museum

The Emerson Museum

*Practical Romanticism and the
Pursuit of the Whole*

ॐ ॐ ॐ

LEE RUST BROWN

HARVARD UNIVERSITY PRESS
Cambridge, Massachusetts
London, England
1997

LIBRARY OF CONGRESS CATALOGING-IN-PUBLICATION DATA

Brown, Lee Rust, 1956–
    The Emerson museum : practical romanticism and the pursuit of the
whole / Lee Rust Brown.
        p.   cm.
    Includes bibliographical references and index.
    ISBN 0-674-24883-X (cloth : alk. paper). — ISBN 0-674-24884-8
(paper : alk. paper)
    1. Emerson, Ralph Waldo, 1803–1882—Knowledge—Science.
2. Literature and science—United States—History—19th century.
3. Literature and science—Europe—History—19th century.
4. American literature—European influences.   5. Romanticism—United
States.   6. Landscape in literature.   7. Science in literature.
8. Nature in literature.   9. Romanticism—Europe.   I. Title.
PS1642.S3B76   1997
814'.3—dc20   96-44959

For John Hollander

Contents

Abbreviations

CEC *The Correspondence of Emerson and Carlyle.* Ed. Joseph Slater. New York: Columbia University Press, 1964.

CW *The Collected Works of Ralph Waldo Emerson.* Ed. Robert E. Spiller et al. 5 vols. to date. Cambridge, Mass.: Harvard University Press, Belknap Press, 1971–.

EL *The Early Lectures of Ralph Waldo Emerson.* Ed. Stephen Whicher, Robert E. Spiller, and Wallace E. Williams. 3 vols. Cambridge, Mass.: Harvard University Press, Belknap Press, 1960–1972.

JMN *The Journals and Miscellaneous Notebooks of Ralph Waldo Emerson.* Ed. William H. Gilman et al. 16 vols. Cambridge, Mass.: Harvard University Press, Belknap Press, 1960–1982.

L *The Letters of Ralph Waldo Emerson.* Ed. Ralph L. Rusk (vols. 1–6) and Eleanor Tilton (vols. 7 and 8). New York: Columbia University Press, 1939–.

PN *The Poetry Notebooks of Ralph Waldo Emerson.* Ed. Ralph H. Orth et al. Columbia: University of Missouri Press, 1986.

TN *The Topical Notebooks of Ralph Waldo Emerson.* Ed. Ralph H. Orth et al. 3 vols. Columbia: University of Missouri Press, 1990–1994.

W *The Complete Works of Ralph Waldo Emerson.* Ed. Edward Waldo Emerson. Concord edition. 12 vols. Boston: Houghton Mifflin, 1904.

The Emerson Museum

Introduction:
The View from the Notch

To find an American romanticism independent of Europe's, it is best
to begin in the mountains, among the sharp peaks and edges from
which all romantic pursuits take their bearings. The spot I choose is
in the White Mountains of New Hampshire, at a passage once known
simply as the Notch. That handy, understated New England term
hardly prepared travelers for the violent impression of a "narrow
defile, extending two miles in length between two huge cliffs, apparently rent asunder by some vast convulsion of nature." So it was described by Timothy Dwight, president of Yale College and the grandson of Jonathan Edwards, who made his first trip through the
Crawford Notch in 1797. His account of the passage, published later
in his *Travels*, helped to establish the Notch as one of the high places
in the canon of American landscape.

> The entrance of the chasm is formed by two rocks standing per-
> pendicularly at the distance of twenty-two feet from each other: one
> about twenty feet in height, the other about twelve. Half of the space
> is occupied by the brook mentioned as the headstream of the Saco,
> the other half by the road. The stream is lost and invisible beneath
> a mass of fragments, partly blown out of the road and partly thrown
> down by some great convulsion.
>   When we entered the notch we were struck with the wild and

solemn appearance of everything before us. The scale on which all the objects in view were formed was the scale of grandeur only. The rocks, rude and ragged in a manner rarely paralleled, were fashioned and piled on each other by a hand operating only in the boldest and most irregular manner. As we advanced, these appearances increased rapidly. Huge masses of granite, of every abrupt form, and hoary with a moss which seemed the product of ages, recalling to the mind the "saxum vetustum" of Vergil, speedily rose to a mountainous height. Before us, the view widened fast to the southeast. Behind us, it closed almost instantaneously, and presented nothing to the eye but an impassable barrier of mountains.

It is not hard to see why President Dwight felt that he, like Aeneas at Delos, had been admitted into the rocky temple of the god. Readers familiar with eighteenth-century theories of the sublime will recognize the mind's initial effort to grasp an intimidating scene by common standards of measurement, in feet and by halves—an effort that fails once Dwight passes through the stone portals into the Notch itself. There he must deal with the inhuman "scale of grandeur only." Dwight tries to make sense of the scene by seeing evidence of a designing hand, but once again the huge scale of things refuses analysis into regular units: reality presents itself only in abrupt, ragged, piled-up fragments. To explain this place as a whole, Dwight must invoke not the synthetic handiwork of creation but a more recent event of human and geological catastrophe. The Notch can only have been formed, he surmises, by the convulsions attending the Deluge: "Nothing less than this will account for the sundering of a long range of great rocks, or rather of vast mountains, or for the existing evidences of the immense force by which the rupture was effected."[1]

Nature instructs us according to our dispositions, and Dwight considered his diluvial hypothesis to be both good Calvinism and sound geology. The English naturalist Charles Lyell, who held in view a longer and more uniform schedule of geological change than Dwight's, would later have no trouble attributing the formation of the Notch to the steady work of water draining through the granite into the Saco River.[2] Yet Dwight's story of a sudden deed of destruction is a better picture than Lyell's of the imagination's struggle to comprehend a special pass of experience that by nature overwhelms normal conceptual frameworks. With his images of instantaneous closure in one direction and a rapid widening of prospect in another, Dwight describes a mind that is halted, captivated, while in another sense set free and hurried onward by powers it hesitates to recognize as its own.

When Thomas Cole came to New Hampshire to paint the White Mountains in 1828, he noted a visionary effect comparable in scale to Dwight's experience, but different in nature: "We now entered the Notch and felt awe struck as we passed between the bare and rifted mountains that rose on either side thousands of feet above. The clouds had by this time partially abandoned the mountains but some were yet whirling round and round the sky nursed pinnacles. The sun shone brilliantly and the clouds and shadows moving swiftly over the sides of the mountain contributed much to the grandeur of the scene."[3]

If Cole's first impression of the Notch seems less fragmentary and more continuous than Dwight's, it is due to the circular movement of clouds and to the lights and shadows that rush across the vertical clefts of the mountains. Such movement unites the scene, just as freely abandoned thought may find itself able to do, because somehow it shares the power of the larger resources of sun and sky. Surely there is something impious in this; for the creative and destructive energy that Dwight imputes to a terrible deity, Cole momentarily claims for his own supervision. Cole is not afraid to look up; indeed, he could as well be on top of a mountain as at the base of a mountain. Dwight's historical scheme of explanation, on the other hand, participates in a horizontal line of vision, one that must negotiate its path through ruined forms. Dwight has it on authority that life is itself a dash between two vertical interventions; his passage through the Notch dramatizes the way human history wanders between cataclysms, in the aftermath of the Deluge and in the foreground of the apocalypse. Cole's vision, however, refuses the bearings of past and future in favor of a present prospect full of the authority of boundless power. It anticipates a point Emerson would make repeatedly in the coming decades: that nature's chief value, for all its ruins and narrow passages, lies in its capacity to introduce us into "the present, which is infinite" (*CW* 2:168). Standing in the Notch, Cole feels no need to repair to history or scripture in order to bring broken things together. The reason for what he sees or fails to see in nature is in his own eye.

The Notch of the White Mountains was a spot that brought home the terms and vistas of imagination for any number of Americans in the nineteenth century. To the most ambitious travelers, this involved bringing home the burden of European poetry and aesthetic theory; and the distance between Dwight's and Cole's passages is a measure of how far what is now called romanticism had become naturalized in the New World by 1828.

It was not just local colors but the intellectual breezes of Coleridge and Wordsworth that animated Cole's infinite present in the Notch. The energy whirling around his "sky nursed pinnacles" was an American manifestation of the disturbing yet unifying "presence" sensed in "Tintern Abbey"—"A motion and a spirit, that impels / All thinking things, all objects of all thought, / And rolls through all things." This fresh sensibility did not exclude or diminish the drastic force Dwight had found evidenced in the Notch; the invisible world pressed just as fiercely on romantics as it did on devout Protestants. In Cole's passage, however, the romantic difference appears in the way that power coincides, at least for a moment, with Cole's own deed of vision. The sky nourishes the mountains, the mountains release the clouds—and the whole circuit of meaning becomes more than a matter of reflection: it is somehow enacted, consummated, within his eye's circumference.

Like Wordsworth, Cole devoted himself to nature as a whole rather than as a limited set of conditions and localities. Hence Cole's visionary power was inspired by places such as the Notch, but because he carried the terms of transport wholly within himself, it was not bound to any particular place or time. As Emerson wrote in his epigram to "History,"

> There is no great and no small
> To the Soul that maketh all:
> And where it cometh, all things are;
> And it cometh everywhere. (*CW* 2:2)

This constructive Soul is common to every individual regardless of context; thus Emerson's "everywhere," translated into practice, becomes "anywhere." Cole's vision comes into its own as both American and romantic by finding itself liberated from the dictates of historical, even of geographical, placement. "That earlier, wilder image," as William Cullen Bryant named Cole's original resource, was entirely portable, and strong enough to profit by all manner of foreign sophistication. Cole could take it with him to England and Italy, as he soon did, and bring it back to America without loss. "Thine eyes shall see the light of distant skies," Bryant wrote to his friend in 1829, "Yet, Cole! thy heart shall bear to Europe's strand / A living image of thy native land, / Such as on thy own glorious canvass lies."[4] Cole could transport the American image intact because of his power to "bear" it—suffer it, bring it forth again—from the heart, which in its devotion to the whole sense of nature made up the original for all his canvases.

This mixture of imaginative independence and practical mobility stands out as a major feature of the romantic dispensation for Americans. At the same time, independence and mobility were themselves practical responses to new American conditions. The distance between Dwight's and Cole's accounts of the Notch reflects essential changes in the American scene between 1797 and 1828. Dwight traveled in a barely inhabited area; the crude road through the Notch was so steep in places that ropes were needed to draw up horses and wagons. By the time of Cole's visit, however, the old road had been replaced by an incorporated turnpike; and Ethan Allen Crawford, grandson of the pioneer farmer who had sheltered Dwight in his log cabin, was now proprietor of a comfortable inn advertising guided tours to the top of Mount Washington.[5]

Romanticism needed a certain degree of cultivation in its wild places, which nineteenth-century travelers could find with relative ease in the Catskills, the Adirondacks, and the White Mountains. These accessible preserves of remoteness lay nested within the American region most given over to manufacture and commerce, a region whose interior was well serviced with transportation routes (first turnpikes and canals, soon railroads) and whose integration could be seen both in its expanding literary life and in the way religious and political passions, when their time was ripe, spread instantaneously from one locale to another. In such a context, the desolate spots of the Northeast were bound to acquire something of an aestheticized, pastoral charm. To the increasing number of writers, painters, and tourists who came to see it, the Notch was not unlike parts of the Alps or mountain settings in Cumbria or Wales. Its savage opening lay entirely inside the anatomy of familiar terrain; it was a sublime threshold between domestic zones, a deep romantic chasm, but, before that, a highway for crossing into the Connecticut Valley.

Still, the Notch was an American place; and to pass through it in the first half of the nineteenth century was to be possessed not only by European influences but by a crucial national difference. "We in the Atlantic states," Emerson said in 1844, "by position, have been commercial, and have . . . imbibed easily an European culture. Luckily for us, now that steam has narrowed the Atlantic to a strait, the nervous, rocky West is intruding a new and continental element into the national mind, and we shall yet have an American genius." Easterners "by position" enjoyed a special advantage. In local spots of sublimity such as the Notch, their experiences of uncontained vision reflected geographical and literary passages already incorporated within traditional boundaries. As Americans, however, they were also aware of the stunning newness only recently abolished in the East but still existing in the West. "We must regard the *land,*" Emerson continued, "as a commanding and increasing power on the American citizen, the sanative and Americanizing influence" (*CW* 1:229).

Even in New England, wild prospects still owned the aura of the open-ended American reality that now lay in the western frontiers, in what Bryant called "The unshorn fields, boundless and beautiful, / For which the speech of England has no name."[6] Given the controversy and promise generated by the new western states, and even more by the settlements in Texas and Oregon, this extra sense pressed at least as hard on Americans of the Jacksonian era as it had on earlier generations. So while their views of the eastern mountains drew color and integrity from similar views imported from Europe, they were also moved by the presence of a wildness that was both earlier and more immediate than ever, an incipiently national wildness that dwarfed the settled regions of the land. Out there in the West, the grandeur and solitude suggested by places such as the Notch extended over a whole continent. Old means of formal enclosure, whether political or literary, met their own limits in regard to this new reality, for the passage west was so unbounded as to render passage an end in itself. Americans across the Mississippi were moving toward no domestic outlet; rather they moved the whole nation toward an unprecedented historical outcome that, as those at home in the East were bound to see, was even then conjuring all the elements of catastrophe and new birth.

Nothing could be more American, and at the same time more answerable to the demands of romanticism, than the West. As Emerson said, the western aura of the land "intruded" into the national mind to counteract or "Americanize" strong influences from abroad. Of course, romantic influence also had intruded across a straitened Atlantic, offering Americans such as Cole, Bryant, and Emerson new ways to outgrow their parochial horizons. On the other hand, the West's "continental element"—for Emerson not just a place but an immaculate ideal of continence thrust out aggressively or defensively from within America—offered a prospect for that growth opposite from the obvious direction of imitating European models. "Who shall dare think he has come late into nature, or has missed anything excellent in the past," Emerson asked, "who seeth the admirable stars of possibility, and the yet untouched continent of hope glittering with all its mountains in the vast West?" (*CW* 1:136). If Americans could see themselves growing into the terms of an earlier, more original prospect of nature, then they could afford to welcome all the materials of foreign import and domestic sophistication.

This double intrusion of romantic influence and continental prospects would hardly have shaped American art and literature as it did, however, if the romantic import were not already, by nature, more than European. Romanticism enabled Emerson and others to raise cosmopolitan yet native standards for American expression because romanticism's true scope was global, its ultimate interest concerned the whole of things rather than one part or another. In spite of the efforts of English romantic poets to give their vision a local habitation, and so to develop a counterspirit within its diffuse and universal tendency, their strongest moments of realization, like the sunlight in Turner's paintings, always threatened to drown all particularities of place and time. Even the monumental fixtures of nature were not immune to the eye's higher powers. "I gazed upon thee," Coleridge wrote in his "Hymn" to Mount Blanc, "Till thou, still present to the bodily sense, / Didst vanish from my thought: entranced in prayer / I worshipped the Invisible alone." Romantic vision was most at home in just those scenes and events where traditional outlines of identity tended to vanish: vast prospects, revolutions of geological and human history, thresholds between wakefulness and sleep, organic metamorphosis and the transmutation of elements. It was this unlocalizable, mobile sense of power that made romanticism, for Americans, an import not so much appropriated or conformed to but discovered within the capacities of the self and empirically affirmed in confrontations with native place.

But let me return to the Notch, which, like any impressive showing of nature, becomes an index to the imaginative possibilities of those who visit it. Timothy Dwight saw it as a monument to the historical rupture between human and divine realities. Thirty years later, the Notch was available to be experienced as a scene of convergence, much like America itself. It was a place where the domestic conveniences of New England met the renewed sense of openness and promise generated by the West. And it was a place where romantic capability, the mobile power Coleridge called "the shaping spirit of imagination," realized itself in the living image of the land. Since it derived from the bearings of the heart as much as from nature's impression, this image was bound to include more than the Notch, more indeed than any particular place. Even for New Englanders, its unsettled center lay west of familiar territory—somewhere westward within the individual viewer as well. Looking out for that center, whether one did so in the wilderness, in homebound reflection, even in foreign travel, meant looking toward the future.

～ ～ ～

Ralph Waldo Emerson was gravely in need of a place such as the Notch when he came there to face his "hour of decision" in July 1832. He was twenty-nine years old, in what then would be considered the middle of life's journey. Regarding his professional career, an unwary observer might have agreed with his younger brother Charles that "the prospect seemed brightening & enlarging before him" (*L* 1:353). Emerson's education and family history had led him naturally into his office as junior pastor in the old church of Increase and Cotton Mather. He had sat on the Boston School Committee; and he served as chaplain to the state senate, just as his father had done before him. But Charles also knew that his brother's inner world had come to pieces. Emerson still grieved for his wife, Ellen Tucker, dead from tuberculosis for a year and a half. His brother Edward was in the terrible last stages of the same disease (Charles was to die of it, too, four years later). Emerson's own health had been poor for years—eye trouble, rheumatism, incipient lung disease—and now a more pointed anxiety was threatening to eat away what remained of it.

Emerson had always been of two minds about the ministry. Since the death of his wife, however, he had come to feel intolerably trapped by it. The problem had more to do with Emerson than with the church, for only in a secondary sense could his dissatisfaction be put down to doctrinal issues; nor could he claim to be unduly restricted in his work by the church elders. Surely the career of his teacher William Ellery Channing demonstrated that the Unitarian ministry offered as broad a professional framework for intellectual life as one could reasonably hope for.

Emerson's problem was that his own massive, indefinite ambitions could never find an outlet within the guidelines of any given profession. These ambitions were by nature romantic, a factor that underlay his insistence, all along, on identifying them with the vast open-ended demand of America. They had first been expressed in his earliest journals, records that Emerson later recollected were intended to create "a sort of Encyclopaedia containing the net value of all the definitions at which the world had yet arrived" (*JMN* 7:302).

From the start, Emerson's writing practice was driven by an ideal of unbounded expression no less grand than the ideals that had driven the projects of Coleridge, Wordsworth, and Novalis. During his sea passage home from Europe in 1833, after he had come into the prospect of his future work, he described this ideal as more of an instinct than a conscious aim: "That which I cannot yet declare has been my angel from childhood until now. It has separated me from men. It has watered my pillow; it has driven sleep from my bed. It has tortured me for my guilt. It has inspired me with hope. It cannot be defeated by my defeats. It cannot be questioned though all the martyrs apostatize. It is always the glory that shall be revealed; it is the 'open secret' of the universe" (*JMN* 4:87).

It gives one some sense of the demanding scope of Emerson's not-yet-declared "angel" to remember that Goethe had famously called *nature* an "open secret." Emerson's angel had always been the prospect of his work, a prospect he could not bear to think of as anything smaller than nature itself. At the age of sixteen, he had secretly conceived the enterprise of his journals under a similarly open and comprehensive title, "Wide World." It was more than coincidental that the fifteen volumes of "Wide World" ended when he began his divinity studies in 1825, exactly the period when he temporarily lost his sight in one eye. For Emerson, being a minister was always like seeing with only one eye. As it turned out, he had to leave the ministry, and America itself for a time, to restore his vision to the angel's standard—that is, to the standard of nature, which, as he already knew on the ship home, was going to be the title of his first book.

But Emerson's undeclared angel was more than the prospect of a book: it also included the inner territories of his life. As he wrestled with questions of responsibility in 1832, he was possessed by the crucial idea—at once a leap of faith and a practical criterion—that his real efforts, whatever their issue, could only originate in what he called "self-trust." Even as he worried that his youth was dwindling away, Emerson became increasingly sure that authority derived only from the fresh dictates of individual life, including its entire range of idiosyncrasy, contradiction, skepticism, and annihilating revelation.

Self-trust was a principle that left no room for mixed allegiances. Emerson traced it in the history of Protestant dissent; but he discerned it just as clearly, and in a way prophetic of his own growing resolve, in Wordsworth's poetry: "His noble distinction is that he seeks the truth & shuns with brave self-denial every image and word that is from the purpose—means to stick close to his own thought & give it in naked simplicity & so make it God's affair not his own whether it shall succeed" (*JMN* 3:306).

To Emerson it was clear that sticking close to his own thought meant, in practical terms, renouncing conventional pathways and abandoning the issue of his success or failure entirely to fate. He could not know, however, what he was entrusting himself to beyond the immediate force of his denial. It might be said that he compounded his romantic literary ambitions, which he had continued to nourish through reading and journal writing, with the venerable and dangerous Protestant concept of the inner light, and that the result could only lead him to a negative impasse. Or, more simply, it might have been that his world had gone hollow by 1832—that the possibilities it presented to him fell miserably short of his desires, and that his commitment to those desires finally voided his more conventional obligations. In any case, it was a major turning point in Emerson's life, and ultimately in the life of American literature, when anxiety, illness, and disciplined insight led him to decide that the profession of his fathers was too small for him.

The story of Emerson's abandonment of the ministry has become a familiar one, perhaps too much so. His later success tends to create a providential narrative that conceals the actual blankness and uncertainty of his decision, which he undertook without any clear path to follow. The deadly route of despising himself in a false but secure role would have been far easier than breaking out into an unprecedented way of living and working. "It is the worst part of the man, I sometimes think, that is the minister," Emerson wrote in a journal of January 1832. He then changed the sentence to read "It is the best part of the man . . . that revolts most against his being the minister" (318). The strength of Emerson's "worst part" was reinforced by the uniform pressure of his family, his need to make a living (Ellen Tucker's modest estate was frozen in litigation with no end in sight), and the fact that he was already possessed of the most liberal conventional platform for communicating his thoughts to an audience. Nevertheless, he was revolted, mentally and physically, by the preestablished role he was playing: "The difficulty is that we do not make a world of our own but fall into institutions already made & have to accommodate ourselves to them to be useful at all. & this accommodation is, I say, a loss of so much integrity & of course of so much power" (318–319).

Emerson's first steps toward integrity and power lay in accepting the revolt itself as his own "best part." A few weeks later he wrote: "Every one makes ever the effort according to the energy of his character to suit his external situation to his inward constitution. If his external condition does not admit of such accommodation he breaks the form of his life, & enters a new one which does" (324). He had no practical idea of what his new "external condition" was going to be. At that point, there was nothing for him to rely on beyond his long-deferred ambitions and the private resource of his journals. All he had was his protest, which he mainly directed against himself, and the sheer openness of the future, which offered no known or appointed ways into it.

He contrived to stage a limited version of his protest in early June, when he wrote a letter to his church asking for changes in the rite of the Lord's Supper. He could hardly have been surprised when the church committee turned down his proposals. In other hands, dissent of this sort might have generated one more fork in the manifold schismatic history of American religion, but Emerson used it only as part of a framework for private action. The real ceremony of sacrifice was to be his own.

Looking over Emerson's career makes it clear that he often created ritual occasions for his private and public turning points. The previous March, he had brought his grief for Ellen to a head by opening her entombed coffin and viewing the year-old remains (she becomes much less of a presence in the journals after that event). During his

stay in Paris in 1833, when he received the revelation of the nature
of his future work at the Muséum d'Histoire Naturelle (known also
as the Jardin des Plantes), Emerson claimed to experience the episode as a marriage ceremony, a comparison he often reverted to in
later discussions of natural history. His 1836 manifesto *Nature* and the
Harvard addresses of 1837 and 1838 were all invested with the aura
of ritual initiation, as was his long-resisted entry into the antislavery
cause in 1844. Each of these ceremonial occasions had deep fore-
grounds in solitary work and deliberation, and in each of them Emerson self-consciously overturned a previous view of things and introduced a new set of prospects and responsibilities.

The lengthiness of Emerson's ceremony of revolt in 1832 reflected
the grave difficulty of the decisions involved. The process began formally with his letter of protest. Its well-known coda came three
months later, when he accounted for his resignation in his farewell
sermon, "The Lord's Supper." But it was during his summer trip to
the White Mountains that the crucial moment of his renunciation
actually took place.[7] Emerson's biographers can hardly be blamed for
skimming over this event or bleaching it out into theology, since moments of absolute discontinuity, of rupture between past and future
ways of life, resist efforts to fit them into a smooth explanatory sequence. As Emerson notes in "Experience," "Every man is an im-
possibility, until he is born; every thing impossible, until we see a
success" (*CW* 3:40). Certainly much can be gained in the way of continuity by sifting through Emerson's emotional life and sorting out
his theological vexations during his brief career as a minister; but if
his writing, taken as a whole, teaches us anything, it is that the meaning of critical events such as his decision at the Notch cannot be
accounted for by their prehistories. However elaborately we build up
toward them, our moments of abandonment come when we "do
something without knowing how or why" (*CW* 2:190): they share
more in common with things to come than with things past. So Emerson's deed is best judged in light of its consequences—or, leaving
those for future chapters, in light of the bare form of his departure,
a form suggested by the wild place in which he found himself.

After receiving the negative but respectful response from his
church committee on June 21, Emerson left Boston along with his
brother Charles. The trip turned out to be a mixture of society and
solitude, of retracing old paths and confronting striking new reali-

ties.[8] The brothers spent the last week of June with relatives in Maine before pushing on as far as Conway, New Hampshire. At that point Charles started back home, leaving Waldo by himself "under the brow & shaggy lid of the White Mts. boarding at a comfortable little house of a private family—His health . . . improved—His spirits pretty good."[9] Emerson remained alone at Conway for several days longer, hoping, as he wrote in his journal, that "here among the mountains the pinions of thought should be strong and one should see the errors of men from a calmer height of love & wisdom" (*JMN* 4:27). He returned to Fryeburg, Maine, to deliver a sermon on the following Sunday. Then, in the company of his aunt Mary Moody Emerson, he traveled northwest and crossed through the cleft of the Notch. By its western outlet into the Ammonoosuc Valley, they lodged at Ethan Allen Crawford's inn, as Thomas Cole had done five years before.

Once again Emerson hoped for heightened perspective: "The good of going into the mountains is that life is reconsidered; it is far from the slavery of your own modes of living and you have opportunity of viewing the town at such a distance as may afford you a just view." He was still straining "to solicit the soul," to "propitiate the divine inmate to speak . . . out of clouds & darkness . . . He who believes in the reality of his soul," Emerson went on, "will therein find inspiration & muses & God & will come out here to undress himself of pedantry & judge righteous judgment & worship the First Cause" (28–29).

For his reading at the Notch, he had brought, significantly, William Sewel's history of the Quakers and the current issue of *The Edinburgh Review,* which contained Thomas Carlyle's anonymous "Corn-Law Rhymes" review. The example of the Quakers, with their devotion to personal illumination and their aversion to ritual forms, suggested arguments Emerson would later make in his farewell sermon. From Carlyle's essay he copied into his journal a sentence that pointed ahead to "The American Scholar" and "Self-Reliance": "Imitation is a leaning on something foreign; incompleteness of individual development, defect of free utterance" (28). Given the pass Emerson had come to, what now seemed "foreign" was not the message from overseas but the Unitarian church of his fathers. Estranging himself from the familiar meant making himself strangely at home in his own native instincts, which were themselves foreign to his established situation; and this removal into romantic capability was supported equally by the scenery of the Notch and by the unsettling persuasions of "my Germanick new-light writer whoever he be" (45).

On the opposite side from Carlyle and the Quakers, a certain ritual symmetry was provided by the presence of Emerson's beloved aunt Mary. Of all his family members, she remained the most stubborn and articulate defender of religious orthodoxy, even as she pursued a life of extreme individualism. For months she had been urging her nephew to persevere in his ancestral profession, to leave a name worthy, as she said, of being "enrolled with the Mathers & Sewalls of that venerable City" of Boston (*L* 1:353). One can only imagine the arguments and imprecations that Emerson heard from Mary on their trip together. But Carlyle's voice, which spoke to his own "best part," was stronger: "He that has done nothing has known nothing. Vain is it to sit scheming and plausibly discoursing: up and be doing! If thy knowledge be real, put it forth from thee: grapple with real Nature; try thy theories there, and see how they hold out. *Do* one thing, for the first time in thy life do a thing; a new light will rise to thee on the doing of all things whatsoever."[10]

So Emerson went into the wilderness along with both advocate and adversary. The result, like a natural cataclysm, was to be neither resisted nor accounted for. Aunt Mary saw it coming and returned home chagrined after a single night at the Notch. During the next day, Sunday the fifteenth, Emerson stayed indoors and made up his mind:

> A few low mountains, a great many clouds always covering the great peaks, a circle of woods to the horizon, a peacock on the fence or in the yard, & two travellers no better contented than myself in the plain parlor of this house make up the whole picture of this unsabbatized Sunday. But the hours pass on—creep or fly—& bear me and my fellows to the decision of questions of duty; to the crises of our fate; and to the solution of this mortal problem. Welcome & farewell to them, fair come, fair go. God is, & we in him. (*JMN* 4:29)

It seems fitting to all that converged at the Notch—domestic convenience and sublime scenery, foreign literary ideas and native insights—that Emerson records his "hour of decision" as taking place indoors, at a homey way station, rather than alone in the woods or on some bare summit. The event's peacefulness, like that of a long-awaited death, follows from ceremonious preparation. Emerson pictures himself confined in a kind of waiting room, with the grandeur outdoors obscured, the horizon drawn in. Expectancy freezes the scene, as if his very openness to the oncoming crisis still retained the form of his prior resistance. The human company is indifferent. Time both creeps and flies. And when the moment of letting go finally arrives—"Welcome & farewell to them, fair come, fair go"—it does so as a quiet affirmation. "Nothing can bring you peace but yourself," we hear at the end of "Self-Reliance"; "Nothing can bring you peace but the triumph of principles" (*CW* 2:51).

The next morning, freed and invigorated by his decision, Emerson climbed alone to the boulder-covered summit of Agiocochoock, the highest point in the White Mountains. It had been renamed Mount Washington the year after the Revolution, and Emerson looked out from it across the other peaks of the freshly constituted American landscape: Adams, Jefferson, Madison, Monroe, Franklin. He was really looking west of those founding names, though, toward his own wide-open prospects. These would require another year or so to come into practical focus. In the meantime, after formally resigning his charge, he traveled to Europe and met (or looked over) some of the foreign eminences—Landor, Coleridge, Wordsworth, Carlyle—who had inspired and sustained him during his crisis of renunciation. He crossed back to America with new views on the aims and methods of his writing practice; and these came into preliminary focus in his first lyceum lectures in late 1833. The lectures addressed themselves to a new kind of divinity study, natural science, which, as Emerson had realized in Paris, was the one discipline capable of uniting the massive ambitions of romanticism with the boundless scope of the New World.

Settling in Concord in the fall of 1834, Emerson greeted his past and his future: "Hail to the quiet fields of my fathers! . . . Henceforth I design not to utter any speech, poem, or book that is not entirely & peculiarly my own work" (*JMN* 4:335). Then, with remarkable confidence, he started bringing his work up to the standard he had committed himself to at the Notch—bringing it into line, in other words, with his own, and his nation's, not-yet-declared nature.

ꝏ ꝏ ꝏ

The process of abandonment and affirmation that came to its climax at the Notch confirmed a certain model of action for Emerson, who later insisted that the more often we bring ourselves to such passes, the more alive we become. "In proportion to the vigor of the individual," he says in "Compensation," "these revolutions are frequent, until in some happier mind they are incessant, and all worldly relations hang very loosely about him" (*CW* 2:72).

As "revolutions" suggests (the geological metaphor had not yet gone dead in the word), Emerson considered his critical moments to be more than changes of mind. They were also *events* of effective transition, real events both suffered and enacted, and involving practical as well as mental costs and advantages. Despite his popular reputation as an idealist, close readers of Emerson will find him steady in his refusal to put thinking and doing into separate boxes. "The triumph of principles," however it may happen, involves more than merely philosophical confidence; its eventuality includes concrete deeds and situations, and its results always appear as expanded powers of action. If we let ourselves be guided by the active, practical element that persists through all Emerson's arguments, we will see in his writing not just a sequence of strong ideas but a way of working that takes precedence over every particular realization. How he pursued this way of working is my main subject in this book.

For Emerson, reasons and consequences cannot be set apart, even when, or most especially when, those consequences are hardest to predict. In "Circles," he warns that "the masterpieces of God, the total growths, and universal movements of the soul, he hideth; they are incalculable. I can know that truth is divine and helpful, but how it shall help me, I can have no guess, for *so to be* is the sole inlet of *so to know*" (189). The decision at the Notch, bare and provisional as it might seem, was Emerson's first masterpiece, the first deed of a total nature that he had yet undertaken; and as such it yields a livelier index to his future concerns than any theological demurrals he may have made along the way. Certainly this deed was unique in bringing about a revolution in his entire framework of commitment. Then again, it was also an initial instance in an open-ended series of such events in his life, each one experimental rather than conclusive, and each one balancing loss or repudiation against an investment in new prospects. More often than not, as he says in "Spiritual Laws," these critical events arrive without fanfare, in the silence of meditation and ordinary work:

> The epochs of our life are not in the visible facts of our choice of a calling, our marriage, our acquisition of an office, and the like, but in a silent thought by the way-side as we walk; in a thought which

revises our entire manner of life, and says,—"Thus hast thou done, but it were better thus." And all our after years, like menials, serve and wait on this, and, according to their ability, execute its will. This revisal or correction is a constant force, which, as a tendency, reaches through our lifetime. (93)

One of Emerson's most central and difficult claims is that deeds of total revision, which at great cost break up and reconstitute our investments in the world, give us our only real grounds for living. His own challenge was to make such events into the measure of his work. Somehow he had to do this for his work to become, in turn, the measure of his life. Bringing the practices of life and writing into line with one another meant cultivating the "constant force" of "revisal or correction," and for Emerson that meant returning to Notch-like passes of experience again and again.

These passes recurred in grand formal revelations, such as the one he recorded at the Jardin des Plantes, as well as in more local revelations deriving from everyday life, as in the moment, detailed in *Nature,* when he experienced a "perfect exhilaration" while crossing the bare common at Concord. They recurred in the effort of surmounting personal disasters, which he suffered in the deaths of his first wife, his two brothers, and his firstborn son; and they happened in various reorientations he undertook in response to the pressing new issues of his time. Most important of all, they took place in innumerable moments of crisis and decisive insight achieved in the constant practice of writing.

Emerson devoted himself to creating a discipline in which "the masterpieces of God" could take effect repeatedly and in such a way as to shape the very body of his work. To see how this was possible, one must discard the image of revelation as a billowing afflatus or an otherworldly rapture. Elevated as they often are, Emerson's crucial moments always bring about a revision of prospects bearing directly on work to be done. They make quite precise incisions between past and present; they stake out the distance crossed between old forms and new possibilities. It can even be said that they include a confrontation with historical and conceptual limits comparable to what Timothy Dwight experienced at the Notch, for the vistas that come into view must be negotiated across the ruins of a forsaken past.

Emerson acknowledged his own need to make such ruins as he settled down to work in Concord, a place full of ancestral traditions. In an 1834 journal entry that would reappear in "The Over-Soul," he wrote: "How dear how soothing to man arises the Idea of God peopling the lonely place, effacing the scars of our mistakes & disappointments. When we have lost our God of tradition & ceased from our God of rhetoric then may God fire the heart with his presence" (*JMN* 4:342; *CW* 2:173). Like the divine catastrophes that were believed to have founded the different epochs of the earth's history, Emersonian revelation makes new desert places before repeopling them. It levels in order to rebuild. The fragmenting effects of this process leave sharp edges in Emerson's crucial passages; and one can trace these edges not just in his statements of principle but also along the inner terrain of his writing style.

None of this changes the fact that the ultimate force of his insight drives toward the high vistas, toward Cole's version of the Notch. As opposed to all their critical rejections and discriminations, the decisive moments informing Emerson's work spark visions of unity. As such, they become his master technique for pursuing the enormous representative scope he demanded in his writing, a scope he identified with nature and with his own angel or individual genius.

But this was also a scope he identified with America; and behind Emerson's pursuit of the whole lies the historical drama of a nation that, as it emerged into literary power, was expanding, consolidating, and coming to pieces in spectacular ways. "It is a country of beginnings," he said in 1844, "of projects, of vast designs, and expectations. It has no past: all has an onward and prospective look" (*CW* 1:230). Under the pressure of converging internal and historical demands for unity, Emerson developed a writing practice uniquely suited both to the whole prospects of his insights and to the serial, revisionary nature of their production: "Neither by detachment, neither by aggregation, is the integrity of the intellect transmitted to its works, but by a vigilance which brings the intellect in its greatness and best state to operate every moment. It must have the same wholeness which nature has" (*CW* 2:201). Individual revelation, along with the manifold particular materials of reading and experience that provoked it, made up one side of this vigilant practice. His unique critical and compositional method, his "natural history of the intellect," made up the other.

In this book I aim to take account of Emerson's pursuit of the whole. Against whatever vagueness may otherwise attend the term, "the whole" for Emerson is best described not as an object of faith or philosophical inquiry but as a project, a pursuit, a work discipline that employs many local positions of belief and skepticism, of renunciation and fresh commitment. "Because the soul is progressive," begins his essay "Art," "it never quite repeats itself, but in every act attempts the production of a new and fairer whole" (209). As a literary ideal, the aim of representing the whole belongs characteristically to romanticism. Coleridge was by far the most powerful English exponent of such ambitions; and I will begin by considering the example his work presented to Emerson. My interest in Coleridge is not the usual one, however: I will be less concerned with tracing recurring concepts and terminology than with considering the fate of his own writing practice. Emerson learned more from Coleridge's concrete successes and failures than he did from any of Coleridge's famous theories.

Coleridge was to Emerson what romanticism itself was: a massive display of ends and means largely determining the boundaries of what he saw as possible in literature and criticism. Chief among these means—it was a prospect as much as an instrument—was the mode of intellectual activity Emerson conceived in terms of his immensely capable figure of "transparency." This figure opens a corridor leading out from Coleridge into the whole of Emerson's work; and I will make a brief excursion through it on the way to more specific questions about Emerson's development of his writing practice. These questions center on his appropriation of the aims and techniques of natural history, which he found displayed in spectacular form at the Muséum d'Histoire Naturelle during his visit to Paris in July 1833, exactly a year after his decision at the Notch.

Contemporary science was itself informed by romantic demands for wholeness of prospect, and its methods offered Emerson a way to address an American reality in which any demonstration of unity— literary, political, philosophical, psychological—had to be brought into line with an expanding and fragmenting field of dynamic elements. As in the discussion of Coleridge, my interest in natural history extends to more than the transmission of influential concepts. To see how Emerson put the model to use, one must see, from as far within it as possible, how contemporary natural history worked, and how it proved itself the one compositional discipline central to the age. This in turn involves recovering aspects of cultural and intellectual history as they pertain to Emerson's invention of his literary project—not superimposing theories or etiologies, but showing how history gets transformed, both idiosyncratically and in a representative manner, in the startling textures of the writing itself.

Chapter 2, the title chapter of this book, is synthetic in approach. It seeks to bring many subjects into convergence: literature, philosophy, science, economics, politics, and cultural and material history. So there is bound to be a strong shift of focus as I move, in the last two chapters, to closer analysis of the ways Emerson's project actually works within the experimental formats of his essays. This turn in the book aims to reconcile the impersonality and institutional nature of a museumlike practice with the stubborn uniqueness of individual experience, a uniqueness that Emerson, in one of his most difficult and enduring claims, insisted was essential for democratic representation. Hence I will proceed by changing the emphasis from biology to biography—call it "life's writing"—in which individual history becomes not just subject matter in a vast representational project but a method of experience and practical experimentation indistinguishable from the project itself—indistinguishable, in other words, from the new way of working that Emerson invented for himself and passed on, in one sense or another, to all of us who come after him.

1

ॐ ॐ ॐ

Ruins in the Eye

Coleridge and the Prospect of the Whole

The feeling for projects—which one might call fragments of
the future—is distinguishable from the feeling for fragments
of the past only by its direction: progressive in the former,
regressive in the latter. What is essential is to be able to idealize
and realize objects immediately and simultaneously: to complete them and in part carry them out within oneself. Since
transcendental is precisely whatever is related to the joining
or separating of the ideal and the real, one might very well
say that the feeling for fragments and projects is the transcendental element of the historical spirit.

—Friedrich Schlegel, *Athenaeum Fragments*

The idea of organic unity in literature has been attended by extremes
of faith and doubt ever since its broad dissemination in early romanticism. Both the doubt and the faith respond to the immense difficulty of the concept of wholeness itself. Organic unity (as opposed
to coherent disposition) has always entailed more than the interre-
lationships of formal and figural elements in a piece of writing: the
literary work, it seems, should express itself by virtue of a vital integrity akin to the integrity apparent in nature, and akin to that which
characterizes intuitions of one's own bodily or psychic identity.

This idea makes rather extreme claims about relations between
literary texts and their meanings. Its largest claim—that the essential

21

feature of the "whole" text is a sort of semantic self-reliance—has also proved the hardest for recent critics to accept. Critics are no longer willing to credit literary claims of wholeness, though many will passionately argue the existence of cultural or ideological totalities that can never appear directly to view. Of course, exactly what seems to obstruct textual wholeness will depend upon the interests of the observer. For the most part, contemporary rationales of obstruction divide into two major critical perspectives: the linguistic perspective, which uncovers fissures within texts at every stage of semantic organization, all the way down, if one prefers, to the elemental level of signs; and the historical perspective, which reads texts as fragments of the "cultures" within which they are written (this view holds regardless of whether the historicist sees the text as subverting or as affirming aspects of its culture). The linguistic perspective looks skeptically at the apparent coherence of semantic units and finds literary texts disjoined or even cracked into pieces from within; the historical approach, on the other hand, treats the same texts as telling fragments of larger contexts (which are themselves only partially determinable), thus denying the referential autonomy that an organically unified text must exhibit. Coherence of reference or autonomy of reference—one of these two factors in the ideal of textual wholeness will seem to be missing, depending on which of the two perspectives the critic adopts.

Of course, linguistic and historicist critics are alike in defining their programs in opposition to New Criticism's previous embrace of literary organicism. Whereas romanticism had applied the metaphor of organism to notions of poetic composition as well as to theories of the nature of poetic meaning, the New Critics set aside the issue of organic genesis and focused on organic unity as the chief factor in discussions of poetic meaning.

Cleanth Brooks spoke for the New Critical preoccupation with unity and autonomy when he shifted the metaphoric terms governing interpretation from "content and form" (where interpretation opens the formal package to retrieve the author's intended message) to the more architectonic, and ultimately mysterious, "parts and whole." Following Coleridge, Brooks identified the whole of a poem as both "more than" and "prior to" the aggregate of tropes and figures comprising its parts. The parts, which might well be incommensurable with one another *as parts,* were the "text"; the whole was the "context" transcending the text even as it qualified the meanings of each textual part: "The total meaning was a complex built up out of partial meanings. Not only that: that parts of the work, including the individual words that made it up, had their individual meanings, altered by the pressure of the whole context. Whether or not one called that alteration an *ironical* qualification, or, discovering that the term *irony* was likely to mislead, used some other term, the fact of alteration was there."[1]

Brooks's passage illustrates how, to the generation that followed them, the New Critics were vulnerable precisely where they were most compelling: they had made wholeness the spoken or unspoken telos of every poetic text. And yet wholeness was an essence irreducible to figure or paraphrase: it was something other than the literal text, and something other than any set of propositions that might supplement the text in interpretation. The New Critical idea of the poetic whole was paradoxical, for it held that the poem becomes whole (that is, it becomes a poem per se) only when the whole itself works back upon the poem's sum of tropes and figures. This necessarily involves a reader as well as a text. "Wholeness" is nothing less than a reading or reflection upon the text (in its *wholeness* as well as in its parts), a hermeneutical "context" that properly belongs neither to the text on the page nor to the reader bending over the page. Poetic wholeness—the animating "context" of the "text"—was for New Criticism more than the starting point for interpretation: it was a transcendental ligament of unnamable origin, joining the double corpus of poetic text and critical supervision.

Often forgotten in contemporary dismissals of the ideal of literary wholeness is the manner in which the vexed issue of textual integrity derives from the legacy of romanticism. With the concept of organic unity, romantic critical theory transformed a relatively unstressed branch of rhetoric—*dispositio,* the judicious arrangement of elements—into an ideal whose mandate overruled and redirected the claims of all other rhetorical interests. The ascendency of organic unity had a price, however, and this was the characteristic fragmentariness of romantic writing. Coleridge presents the most obvious example. Following German theorists, he hypothesized a textual whole that was both more than and prior to its parts; and yet his own writing, both poetry and prose, manifests a degree of literal brokenness proportionate to the severely difficult status of his ideal of wholeness.

The fragmentation of Coleridge's textual corpus is spectacular in light of the fact that he, more than any other poet or critic, is responsible for the establishment of wholeness and organic unity as standards of value for literary works.

While critics have observed the massive degree to which "fragmentation, incompleteness, and ruin" designate the general shape of romanticism, the all-important nexus between textual fragmentation and the contrary ideal of textual wholeness is less understood. Through fragments romanticism propounds its ideal of wholeness; yet fragments themselves are evidence of the ideal's capacity to restrict and even forbid perfection of textual wholes. This antithetical relation needs to be explored, for it offers a paradigm for the larger interdependence between creative and theoretical pursuits that is so pronounced in romanticism and that, since Coleridge, has become a regular feature of the modern literary dispensation.

❧ ❧ ❧

Many of Coleridge's poems introduce themselves as "remains" testifying to earlier promises of whole poems. The promises, like the poems, are broken. This way of framing a poem places special restrictions on its range of semantic applications. When, for example, "Kubla Khan" or "Christabel" presents itself under the provision that it is a fragment, the reader understands tacitly that the poem's meanings are to be sought largely in its relation to an unrealized textual whole. The result is a curiously non-Platonic version of transcendental signification: the reader understands that meaning will not exceed the boundaries of textuality, even though—and precisely because—the whole, vitally integrated text constituting the fragment's meaning is absent. The fragment is remarkable among poetic forms for the conspicuous way it establishes the meaning of its text as another text—and not just any other text, but the whole text of which it claims to be a part.

This understanding, established as a kind of contract between the fragment and its reader, also conditions the semiotic work of figures within the fragment. One might usefully recall Cleanth Brooks's dictum on textual wholeness: the whole is a "context" altering the meanings of every textual part. When the whole poem (the "context") is pointedly and dramatically absent, as is the case with poetic fragments, every figure actually found on the page will be of the same kind as that formed by the entire fragment: no matter how minutely

specified, all "remains" of the absent text are synecdoches, parts signifying a whole. Poetic form itself becomes a figure to be considered
alongside the rest of the fragment's figures. Indeed, if the fragment
may be said to constitute a poetic genre, one of its generic marks is
the particular semiotic mode Coleridge conceives of as "symbolic."

The symbol, in Coleridge's familiar definition from *The Statesman's
Manual,* "always partakes of the reality which it renders intelligible;
and while it enunciates the whole, abides itself as a living part of that
Unity."[2] Understanding of this definition has been impeded by ide-
alizing devotees, who take it on faith that the Coleridgean symbol
actually conducts an imaginative reader into the realm of whole
truths. In the opposite camp, debunkers of the Coleridgean symbol
see it as a lie against semiotic and epistemological discontinuity. Unfortunately, the debunking argument responds to the idealized version of the symbol rather than to the peculiarities of Coleridge's own
definition. Later I will pursue implications of the quoted passage in
some detail; for now it is enough to note that the poetic fragment,
considered in the light of its claim to a particular sort of poetic semiosis, does fit Coleridge's definition of the symbol insofar as the
unity it enunciates is the whole poem of which it is supposedly a part.
For the sake of emphasis, the lesson learned from the coincidence
of the theory of the symbol with the literal appearance of the poetic
fragment can be expressed as a theorem: *A textual object qualifies as
"symbolic" if the reality it signifies happens to be the textual matrix from which
it has been excerpted.*

To justify itself as an excerpt, and to manage its show of semiotic
continuity, the poetic fragment often introduces a story extrinsic to
both the fragment and the unwritten whole poem: it asks the reader
to believe that its fragmentariness is the result of some extratextual
deforming cause—interruption, lassitude, forgetfulness. The story
effectively substitutes historical accidents of composition or transmission for the unanswered question of how to complete an organically
unified text; it frames the text against a background of practical aims
and their fulfillments. This is how the poetic fragment manages to
"symbolize" a poem; but of course it must pay the price of renouncing its own claim to *being* a poem. In the preface to "Kubla Khan,"
for example, Coleridge claims to be publishing the fragment as
"rather a psychological curiosity, than on the ground of any supposed
poetic merits." The reader will never be able to say whether the sig-

nified texts—the real poems advocated by "Kubla Khan" and "Christabel"—would themselves qualify as "symbolic" writing; for the result of the fragment's semiotic continuity is the permanent postponement of any determination of the meaning of the whole text.[3]

Coleridge's exaltation of wholeness is so persistent throughout his work that critics have been tempted to blame it for the ruins and fragments of his poetic corpus, as though fragmentation were the predictable result of obsessively high standards. To call the fragments incomplete, however, is not to say that they fail to serve their aim. Fragments "fall short" because they aim at a paradoxical target: a wholeness that is also, in every way, a text.[4] Indeed, Coleridge's poetic fragments testify to the disintegration of textual economy before an ideal of wholeness whose practicality has become so doubtful that the ideal can be figured only negatively, by the genre of the broken or broken-off. By framing themselves as "parts," poetic fragments substitute the problem or challenge of wholeness for the proposition of a whole; thus wholeness becomes the topic rather than, as New Criticism had it, the automatic attribute of a literary text. Textual wholeness is not so much lost as it is deferred or displaced into the question of its possibility: no longer residing in the realm of literal or literary textuality, it finds its home in the realm of speculation.

Like all spectacular remains, poetic fragments imply a history of their ruin. As opposed to the factitious tales of interruption or neglect that often accompany fragments, the true story of the poem's lost affiliation with wholeness remains, at most, mutely indicated. Only the critical speculator ventures to retell it. Hence poetic fragments, whose meanings rely on the confrontation of literal textual parts with ideal textual wholes, place special demands on their readers. Coleridge offers a way of assessing these demands in his famous "final definition" of a poem in *Biographia Literaria*. The definition centers on the quality of wholeness: "A poem is that species of composition which is opposed to works of science, by proposing for its *immediate* object pleasure, not truth; and from all other species (having *this* object in common with it) it is discriminated by proposing to itself such delight from the *whole*, as is compatible with a distinct gratification from each component *part*."[5]

The complete poem, in Coleridge's formulation, proposes "to itself" the delight of the whole. This suggests that the poetic fragment, whose generic identity depends on the pointed absence of such a proposition, solicits a counterproposition from its reader, who "places" the fragment in relation to a more comprehensive ideal. This counterproposition is not an archaeological judgment as to the aboriginal whole poem (the whole "Kubla Khan," for example), but is the reader's speculative reply to the problem posed by the fragment—that is, the problem of how to realize wholeness in a practical way. By framing itself as one moment in a sequence of dialectical "propositions," the poetic fragment creates an interpretive occasion in which the theory of the poem (which Coleridge makes identical to the theory of wholeness or the possibility of wholeness) circumscribes the fragment at hand.

Unfortunately, the reader's counterproposition can never participate in the *meaning* of the fragment, for this meaning has been thoroughly consigned to the textual matrix (the whole poem) from which the fragment claims to have been excerpted. In the absence of the signified textual whole, this exchanging of propositions offers the prospect of an endless sequence of fragments and fragmentary interpretations. Since the absent whole represents the promise of a new order of legibility, it appears that the kind of reading occasioned by the fragment would best be termed "reading in lieu of reading." In other words, we "read" poetic fragments by speculating about a better, but unavailable, way of reading. The New Critics, who believed in reading wholes, never realized that, for Coleridge, the actual reading of an organically unified text was a promise often renewed but never fulfilled.

Coleridge himself plays the part of the theorizing reader of poetic fragments in *Biographia Literaria*, where his insistence on defining the nature of poems in terms of wholeness combines with a remarkable tendency to *fragment* Wordsworth's poems. This fragmentation goes beyond the exigencies of ordinary citation. Coleridge's discussion of Wordsworth proceeds not only by extracting pieces of text from the poems, but by isolating with italics even smaller textual parts within the citations.[6] *Biographia Literaria*'s presentation of Wordsworth stresses passages rather than poems, parts rather than wholes. Coleridge explains the necessity for this emphasis by saying that Wordsworth's poems, even though they may frame themselves as finished texts, actually read like bundles of fragments,

> because the pleasure received from Wordsworth's poems being less derived either from the excitement of curiosity or the rapid flow of narration, the *striking* passages form a larger proportion of their value. I do not adduce it as a fair criterion of comparative excel-

lence, nor do I even think it such; but merely as matter of fact. I
affirm, that from no other contemporary writer could so many lines
be quoted, without reference to the poem in which they are found,
for their own independent weight or beauty. (*Biographia* 2:106)

Wordsworth's striking passages bear quotation "without reference
to the poem in which they are found." Coleridge finds them as
though finding jewels among the rocks: they seem to have a detach-
able, merely adventitious relation to their poetic frameworks. Of
course it is hard to tell whether this is a feature of Wordsworth's
poetry or a consequence of Coleridge's own critical practice. In either case, the passages Coleridge isolates derive their "independent
weight or beauty" from being fragments. If they make "reference"
to a poem, it is to a whole poem as yet unwritten by Wordsworth but
that Coleridge senses to be there in the realm of real possibility. The
isolated passages, in this case, would be independent from their given
contexts not just because Coleridge has chosen to highlight them,
but because of their dependence on an ideal, prospective context.

Coleridge leaves little doubt as to what this context is. He reads
Wordsworth's passages as symbolic parts of the unprecedented whole
poem he deemed Wordsworth alone capable of writing: "What Mr.
Wordsworth *will* produce, it is not for me to prophesy: but I could
pronounce with the liveliest convictions what he is capable of producing. It is the FIRST GENUINE PHILOSOPHICAL POEM" (155–156).
This is, of course, the consummately grand poem that Wordsworth,
under Coleridge's guidance, contemplated as the textual whole
promised by the mere "ante-chapel" of the fragment now known as
The Prelude.

Reading Wordsworth in *Biographia Literaria,* Coleridge shows himself to be precisely the kind of reader already called for by his own
poetic fragments. He not only brings theories of wholeness to bear
in interpreting textual elements, but he also breaks up nominally
whole poems into fragments testifying to the authentic, but lamen-
tably absent, higher poem of which they are parts. His fragmenting
practice as both poet and reader comes full circle in *Biographia Literaria* when he suggests, with excessive humility, that his analysis of
Wordsworth provides a model for the way his own collection of poems, concurrently published in *Sibylline Leaves,* ought to be approached: "Were the collection of poems published with these biographical sketches, important enough, (which I am not vain enough

to believe) to deserve such a distinction: EVEN AS I HAVE DONE, SO WOULD I BE DONE UNTO" (159).[7] Coleridge strikes a pattern for future criticism when he demonstrates that reading with an eye to the whole means finding or even making fragments out of what authors present as literary integrities. Following Coleridge, criticism will suffer these fragments not as the decay of literature but as the best available testimony to literature's prospects.

It is hard to avoid Emerson at this point, since he also held that the striking passages in what we read are precisely those that beg to be struck forth from their initial contexts. He filled his journals with such independent fragments, excerpting them from across the entire range of his reading. Like Coleridge, Emerson justified this activity as a matter of critical respect for the whole. In "Nominalist and Realist" he declares:

> I am faithful again to the whole over the members in my use of books. I find the most pleasure in reading a book in a manner least flattering to the author. I read Proclus, and sometimes Plato, as I might read a dictionary, for a mechanical help to the fancy and the imagination. I read for the lustres, as if one should use a fine picture in a chromatic experiment, for its rich colors. 'Tis not Proclus, but a piece of nature and fate that I explore. It is a greater joy to see the author's author, than himself. (*CW* 3:137)

Despite the negligent timbre of this passage, there is nothing arbitrary about the practice Emerson describes. Being faithful to the whole involves dismembering authoritative texts; the reader breaks up their nominal integrities in order to identify the membership of their striking parts in a higher provisional whole. The sense of reflective gloss in Emerson's "lustres," however, argues something that Coleridge was less than willing to admit about his own critical practice: that wholeness dwells in the reader's prospects, and not in any text.

Coleridge always feared the unmooring of criticism from literary text, in which reading can degrade into narcissism or groundless free play. Though critics have mistakenly ascribed both qualities to Emerson, it should be noted that his "lustres" are too transitive and indistinct to reflect a personal reader, and too surprising to be put down to the caprices of fancy. Emerson's metaphor rather suggests that our glosses reflect a principle of constructive power, "the author's author," ultimately capable of joining all the "members" recognized by criticism. In reading, Emerson does gather "colors" for his private palette (this was the journal-resource he used for his own pronouncements in orations, essays, and poems), but the work of the palette serves "the author's author" more than any historical author, including Emerson himself. For Emerson no less than for Coleridge, making fragments means finding "members"; and he too has faith that these will turn out to be not just shards or ruins but parts furnished toward the whole.

∾ ∾ ∾

It is Coleridge's critical vision, then, and not just personal anxiety or lassitude, that drives so many of his poems into the realm of fragment. The splintering of his own work before the prospect of wholeness becomes even more dramatic when he turns from poetry to speculative prose. All Coleridge's prose texts, from his marginalia and notebook entries to long works such as *Biographia Literaria, The Friend,* and *Aids to Reflection,* are fragmentary in the sense I have been exploring here. This is not to say that extended and continuous arguments fail to appear (though the long texts also are internally discontinuous) but that Coleridge brackets all his prose works as fragments by announcing through them a superior, systematically unified text: the *Logosophia* or magnum opus, which may be the most famous book never to have been written.[8] Like the poetic fragments, the prose fragments ask to be read in light of their fractured relationship to an absent unified text: their own brokenness substitutes, apologetically, for the wholeness they signify.

Thomas McFarland captures the effect of this postponed textual ideal when he observes that "the reflexive pressure of the *magnum opus* made the whole of Coleridge's actual prose achievement provisional in its nature."[9] Coleridge turned away unhappily from poetry to devote himself to speculative prose; a reflection of this turn is the far greater distance separating his prose fragments from the wholeness they indicate. Whereas, on the one hand, the poetic fragment claimed to be a synecdoche for the mostly absent poem, the prose fragment advocates the entirely absent magnum opus typologically. Rather than framing itself as part of that systematic whole, the prose fragment claims, in every case, to serve as a rehearsal or preparation for it.[10] Each of Coleridge's prose texts plays the role of a John the Baptist in regard to the *Logosophia.* Were the divine text indeed to come, the proleptic ones would withdraw to the wings, having served to prophesy its entry into the world of merely human reading and writing.

While some critics have sought to reconstruct a unified system from the Coleridgean fragments as if they were the pieces of an aboriginal Humpty Dumpty, it remains that what one says of each of Coleridge's prose works one must also say of their aggregate: put together, they do not make a whole that is more than the sum of its parts. Coleridge's promised system, the magnum opus or *Logosophia,* is not an original text that gets diffracted or ruined through transmission; nor is it simply an unfinished structure. It is a prospect of textual wholeness maintaining itself through the fragmentation of the literal textual corpus; and as such it can no more be recovered by critical archaeology than the whole of "Kubla Khan."

When discussing the ruinous state of Coleridge's extant prose, one must decide whether to think of its fragmentariness only as a sort of symptom of frustrated intentions—that is, as meaningful biographical evidence—or as a purposeful kind of structure, a singular genre serving to regulate, in a unique way, the production of literary meaning. McFarland argues that Coleridge used the promise of the magnum opus as a way of beguiling himself into writing: by keeping alive the prospect of the complete magnum opus, Coleridge found relief from the pressure, debilitating to him, of expecting completeness in whatever text he was presently writing. The benefit of this psychic ruse, in McFarland's calculus, was a remarkable degree of productivity: "The provisional nature of his prose writing actually allowed him a certain achievement that the ultimate demands of his poetry did not."[11] Of course, the trick's inevitable cost was a life's work of "deformed" textual remnants. McFarland's account is indispensable, especially in its illumination of Coleridge's abandonment of poetry, but it does not address the way that the reference point of the magnum opus, looming in its absence over Coleridge's archipelago of fragmentary texts, establishes specific conditions for the meanings enacted in the fragments. Coleridge's fragments stand for the magnum opus in a peculiar manner: each fragment, like an apologizing debtor, repays interest rather than principal, renewing the promise of textual unity just as it postpones the advent of the unified text. This postponement recurs as each fragment reprojects the prospect, which is the trope or trick of the textual whole.[12]

Of course fragments do not accomplish such things by themselves:

their readers also contribute to this peculiar syndrome of reference. Coleridge's prose fragments engage readers to view the text at hand with an eye on the prospect of a wholeness that is also a text, but that is not present for reading. Part of what we, as readers, have inherited from romanticism is a willingness to trade our demand to comprehend a text for a certain latitude in the register of speculation: we look for something more and other than what we find on the page, something more and other than what we have found, so far, on any page. As Emerson points out, literature leads us to read in the way "least flattering to the author," which is only another way of saying that "in hours of high mental activity we sometimes do the book too much honor, reading out of it better things than the author wrote,— reading, as we say, between the lines" (*W* 8:196–197). Literary fragmentation is just as thoroughly a consequence of this romantic attitude toward reading as it is a contributing cause. The path may well descend into modern literary manners, where the original urgencies are forgotten and fragmentation becomes only another formalism. Yet if we continue to prefer fragments over smooth generic fulfillment, and if our criticism makes fragments even where it does not initially find them, it is because, one way or another, they answer more strikingly to what Coleridge and Emerson still teach us to demand from our reading.

❧ ❧ ❧

The major oppositions at the core of Coleridge's critical vocabulary—symbol and allegory; whole and aggregate; imagination and fancy; reason and understanding; genius and talent—all have to do with the creation and interpretation of parts in relation to wholes. Since Coleridge's prose texts—the fragmentary places of invention for these critical distinctions—consign their ultimate meanings to the prospect of the magnum opus, one might surmise that the sort of wholeness invoked by all these paired terms is, like the wholeness invoked by "Kubla Khan," that of a whole text. And yet the prose texts themselves prefer to reside in the special genre of the fragment, excused altogether from the realm of textual wholeness. This raises the question of whether, in the course of theorizing about literary wholes, Coleridge may have realized something about the nature of parts and wholes per se that crystallized his tendency to promise but never to deliver an ultimate whole of his own.

A closer look at the famous distinction in *The Statesman's Manual*

between allegory and symbol reveals some of the conceptual difficulties troubling Coleridge's "whole" intentions. Coleridge would
like to show that allegory and symbol, as particular semiotic determinations, are opposed in kind:

> Now an Allegory is but a translation of abstract notions into a pic-
> ture-language which is itself nothing but an abstraction from objects
> of the senses; the principle being more worthless than its phantom
> proxy, both alike unsubstantial, and the former shapeless to boot.
> On the other hand a Symbol . . . is characterized by a translucence
> of the Special in the Individual or of the General in the Especial
> or of the Universal in the General. Above all by the translucence
> of the Eternal through and in the Temporal. It always partakes of
> the Reality which it renders intelligible; and while it enunciates the
> whole, abides itself as a living part in that Unity, of which it is the
> Representative.[13]

Perhaps the best approach to the claims made in this passage is by
way of Paul de Man's influential objections to them. In "The Rhetoric
of Temporality," de Man attacks Coleridge's idea of the symbol for
the "ontological bad faith" of its claim that a transcendental reality
can be "enunciated" without radical discontinuity between the sign
and the object of the sign's reference: no textual sign can "partake"
of its meaning in a part-to-whole relation.[14] De Man focuses on the
crucial metaphor of "translucence" in order to demonstrate how
Coleridge's passage, in its anxiety to assert the possibility of semiotic
continuity, ironically encodes a representation of the very semiotic
discontinuities that threaten all textual integrity (de Man finds these
fundamental discontinuities more forthrightly reflected in allegory).
Whether "translucence" is read as entire or only partial transparency,
it implies that the meaning—"the Reality" shining like a light *through*
the medium of the still-present symbol—must of necessity inhabit a
realm distinct from that of present textuality. The meaning may be
"reflected" in the symbol, but it cannot coincide with it.

In his critique of Coleridge's definitions of symbol and allegory, de
Man seeks to do more than rehabilitate the reputation of allegory;
he also takes aim at New Criticism by attacking the notion that organic unity can ever characterize a literary text or indeed any linguistic product. As an attack on the ideal of the semiotic integrity of
texts, de Man's discussion has been seminal. In the service of this
polemic, however, de Man maintains an overly reductive notion of

the semiotic structure of Coleridge's terms, allegory and symbol.[15] De Man assumes, for example, that the "Reality" Coleridge mentions is a meaning existing beyond the boundaries of textuality. Yet as far as Coleridge's own poetic and prose fragments are concerned, their ultimate meanings must be consigned to the whole *texts* of which the fragments claim to be either broken-off pieces or jagged forerunners.

For Coleridge, the actual difference between allegory and symbol lies in the way each of them expresses, or fails to express, specific relationships between fragmentary signs and textual wholes. In the case of allegory, both the sign and its conceptual referent are "abstractions." As the word implies, abstraction (*ab-trahere,* to draw away from) always involves the departure of the abstracted object from a relative state of repleteness.[16] The allegorical sign consists of a "picture" (say, of a hill) generalized from individual objects of perception (the objects called hills); its "shapeless" referent (say, the idea of holiness) is the product of an even further degree of abstraction. And just as both the allegorical sign and its referent have been selected and juxtaposed arbitrarily, the *relation* between the two is limited to the relation between pieces juxtaposed in a semiotic aggregate, forced together by the free fancy of the author or handed down by the usages of the past.

It may clarify things to recall that allegorical meaning takes place entirely within the realm of what Coleridge calls the "mechanical understanding" of Lockean empiricism. Indeed, the concept of abstraction is central to Locke's theory of language development: "Words become general by being made the signs of general ideas: and ideas become general, by separating from them the circumstances of time and place . . . By this way of abstraction, they are made capable of representing more individuals than one; each of which having in it a conformity to that abstract idea, is (as we call it) of that sort."[17] Once abstracted from prior matrices, all signs and referents become equivalent in value, since there are no longer any contextual standards by which to gauge their differences. For this reason, Coleridge finds that the vectors of allegorical reference extend horizontally, across an aggregate of abstracted parts, instead of vertically, beyond the fragmented sign and into the realm of "whole" meanings. Unless a whole system is invoked, abstractions will only refer to other abstractions. Allegorical predication boils down to a qualitative tautology.

The difference between allegory and symbol turns out to be the measure of whether or not the sign is read in terms of its relation to a whole text. The whole itself—the extra quality that is something more than the sum of its parts—would be the "Reality" communicated in the translucence of symbolic meaning. Coleridge goes out of his way to highlight the symbol's vital placement or situation within a hierarchically organized textual whole. Indeed, the content of the moment of translucence seems to be the symbol's *classific* nature. A figure is symbolic when it appears as a member of a higher class—"a translucence of the Special in the Individual or of the General in the Especial or of the Universal in the General." From the Individual to the Universal, symbols refer to one another as classes within a systematic nesting of classes.

Coleridge conceives of the physical universe as just such a hierarchically organized, systematic whole: "by the eternal identity of Allness and Oneness, the whole Universe becomes an infinity of concentric circles—i.e. every thing has its own system, besides its relations to the Universe."[18] (This traditional image reappears, with different dynamics, in Emerson's "Circles.") Hierarchical classification is at the heart of the definition of symbol because it is the only "method" by which organic systems—biological as well as textual—can be created and interpreted. Coleridge's enduring interest in biological method centers on the fact that natural history, more than any other science, is self-conscious about its use of classification to organize aggregates into systematic wholes.

Coleridge also insists that interpretation of scripture (recall that *The Statesman's Manual,* like *Aids to Reflection,* largely concerns itself with the problem of how to read scripture) should be identical in kind with the interpretation of nature through natural classification. Nature and scripture share the quality of being truly "systematic" or whole texts because the multitudes of individual signs that comprise them refer to a vitality that is transcendental even as—or insofar as—it is the extra feature making the system as a whole something more than the sum of its parts. The magnum opus, which in some of Coleridge's forecasts was to begin with "a full commentary on the Gospel of St. John" (*Biographia* 1:136), would interpret the texts of scripture and nature in terms of their systematicity or textual wholeness: it would, in other words, determine relations between scriptural or natural figures by reference to the transcendent "reality" that provides the systematic continuity of the textual organism. To read such texts systematically (by the light of a realized wholeness), the magnum opus would itself have to be just such a textual whole.

It is true that the allegorical ciphers of the understanding are also products of a sort of classification. Lockean theory conceives of nouns as labels for classes of empirical data: simple ideas classify objects of the senses, while more complex ideas of "mixed modes" are in effect classifications of classifications. An infinite variety of aggregates can be put together from such abstracted classes; pseudo-wholes can be fashioned; but their coherence will be mechanical rather than organic—the relations between parts will be accidental and external. Coleridge's attack on allegory and the mechanical understanding carries precisely the same force as Blake's polemic against Locke and Newton:

> I turn my eyes to the Schools & Universities of Europe
> And there behold the Loom of Locke whose Woof rages dire
> Washed by the Water-wheels of Newton. black the cloth
> In heavy wreathes folds over every Nation; cruel Works
> Of many Wheels I view, wheel without wheel, with cogs tyrannic
> Moving by compulsion each other; not as those in Eden: which
> Wheel within Wheel in freedom revolve in harmony & peace.[19]

The Lockean/Newtonian wheels compel one another's motion in the way of interlocking gears. If they comprise a unit, it is only through contiguous mechanical association. The wheels of Eden, on the other hand, are concentric; they are parts of one system, classes nested within one hierarchy. Any of these truly systematic wheels, seen in its relation to the whole, qualifies as a Coleridgean symbol.

Coleridge turns to the idea of classification out of a desire to discover how a part can be related to a whole in such a way as to preserve their distinction *in kind* without forfeiting the sense of systematic continuity between them. But deep trouble lingers in the very notion of classification. Modern theories of classes have emphasized the fundamental discontinuity between a class and its elements, even if those elements are themselves classes or classes of classes. Carnap, for example, presents this discontinuity as a rule of logic: "*Classes cannot consist of their elements as a whole consists of its parts.* Classes are quasi objects in relation to their elements; they are complexes of their elements, and, since they do not consist of these elements, they are autonomous complexes of these elements."[20] Carnap is restating, in regard to classes, the Aristotelian/Coleridgean maxim that the whole is always something more and other than the sum of its parts. In the early twentieth century, this stubborn distinction presented the greatest single challenge to philosophical efforts to use concepts of class in establishing a logical ground for mathematics. Coleridge's deep reading in medieval logic made him just as conscious of the problem as Russell and Frege would later be.[21] Whether considered as "Special," "General," or "Universal," the class appears as an autonomous whole, and as such it is unthinkable in terms of its elements or "parts."

For Coleridge, this qualitative distinction is both intractable and central; and he suggests that it may be addressed by either allegorical or symbolic practice. We choose allegory if we decide that the difference between parts and whole (elements and class) results from abstraction. If this is the case, acts of classification will always bring new objects forward from prior objects, and the intellect will seem repeatedly to fall from a state of relative completeness. As it abstracts from its object, classification will work to analyze or break up wholes rather than to gain access to them. This is just how the "Loom of Locke" operates. Lockean epistemology pictures intellectual and linguistic development as a process of abstraction from sense-experience through a telescoping formation of classes. Such a procedure generates a lineage of "quasi objects" related to one another through a historical sequence of juxtapositions—the mechanical clock-time, in fact, that Blake associates with Locke and Newton.

Blake would have seen a similar mechanism in de Man's valorization of allegory over symbol. Since a concept of sequential and irreversible temporality underlies allegorical representation, de Man finds allegory to be the more authentic account of literary practice:

> It remains necessary, if there is to be allegory, that the allegorical sign refer to another sign that precedes it. The meaning constituted by the allegorical sign can then consist only in the *repetition* (in the Kierkegaardian sense of the term) of a previous sign with which it can never coincide, since it is of the essence of this previous sign to be pure anteriority . . .
>
> Whereas the symbol postulates the possiblity of an identity or identification, allegory designates primarily a distance in relation to its own origin, and, renouncing the nostalgia and the desire to coincide, it establishes its language in the void of this temporal difference.[22]

The terrible implication of empiricist epistemology is that in the geometrical progression of abstract thinking the observer falls more and more deeply into a solipsistic void, constructing ever more complex mechanisms of association and substitution, ever more thoroughly breaking up the fragmentary remains of the corpus of wholeness. Efforts to remedy this solipsistic fall will result in fictitious integrities drawn and redrawn, as contracts are, over history. The scene of this terror gets enacted repeatedly in Blake's mythos, as when Urizen's body divides and grows over the abstract void in *The Book of Urizen*. De Man, in the Heideggerian manner, embraces the unhappily discontinuous mode of allegory for precisely the reasons Blake and Coleridge recoil from it.

Locke, Urizen, and de Man have no place in the realm of Coleridge's symbol, where the differential relation between part and whole reveals itself by "translucence" rather than abstraction. De Man is inaccurate in his claim that symbol denies the constitutive factor of time in favor of an ideal of simultaneous identification. In fact, the symbol constructs temporality just as determinately as allegory does, but in the opposite direction. To use terms I have already developed to account for the semiotic structure of textual fragments, it might be said that allegory is "retrospective" while symbol is "prospective."

In allegory both the sign and its referent are abstractions, classifications whose elements have been selected and brought forward from prior wholes. The referent will always be prior (in time) to the signs that have been abstracted (and made into new classes) from it. Hence, as de Man shows, allegorical reference is always retrospective; it encodes the sense of "thrownness" (Heidegger's term, not de Man's) in temporal experience. The translucence of the symbol, on the other hand, implies that the referent has, in the event of symbolic meaning, been "put off" or "pushed ahead" to the far side of the sign. Instead of abstracting the sign from its present location, symbolic semiosis consigns all final meanings to a place (the *topos* of textual wholeness) lying beyond the conceptual horizon formed by the sign. Once this is accomplished, the "remaining" sign can be recognized as the fragmentary forerunner of its whole meaning.

When picturing allegorical and symbolic semiosis in terms of "bringing forward" and "pushing ahead," I am using spatial metaphors to map out the properties of what is actually a temporalizing process. Speaking in more strictly temporal terms, I should say that in symbolic semiosis the sign signals the postponement or deferment of the practical advent of its referent. Instead of representing the referent as prior to the sign (allegory), symbols stand in *prospective* relation to their referents. And just as allegory involves the reference of a present sign to a prior text, symbol promises a transition from the present sign to a future text.

If there is an irony in Coleridge's metaphor of translucence, it consists in the way that translucence projects the future or prospective text as a repetition of the *classific* nature of the sign at hand ("a translucence of the Special in the Individual or of the General in the Especial," etc.); so that, while it promises (once again) an ultimate *summum genus,* a text to end all texts, all that it can literally envision is an endless repetition of the process of classification and postponement now taking place in the translucence of the symbol. As Emerson writes in "Circles," "the extent to which this generation of circles, wheel without wheel will go, depends on the force or truth of the individual soul" (*CW* 2:180). Generating new symbols, and casting up revised prospects of the whole, becomes the pattern of literary life.

When Coleridge repudiates allegory in favor of the symbol, he does not, as de Man would have it, seek to substitute a semiological "mystification" for a representational mode that happens to reflect, in an uncomfortably authentic manner, the arbitrariness and discontinuity that darken human experience, at least in its linguistic dimensions. Emerson, who is no less preoccupied than Coleridge with problems of fragments and wholes, would later declare, "The reason why the world lacks unity, and lies broken and in heaps, is, because man is disunited with himself" (*CW* 1:43). For Coleridge, allegory and symbol are alternative ways of reading the significant products of this "disunited" condition. Both ways acknowledge the intersection of temporality and rhetoric by stressing the isolation of the sign, in time, from its meaning; and both ways invoke the concept of classification to explain the intertextuality, in time, of all representational processes.

Most important, both allegory and symbol, as Coleridge defines them, hypothesize a temporality not given but given off, either backward or forward, in a perpetually renewed moment of critical vision. Allegory forms abstracted "pictures" through selection of particulars from prior matrices that are themselves products of earlier efforts of abstraction. The symbol, on the other hand, frames itself not merely as the fragment of an unfinished text but as a literature that can only be fragmentary in light of the whole text, the truly systematic magnum opus, which has yet to be written or read.

❧ ❧ ❧

I have been reflecting on the ways that a severe emphasis on wholeness can generate new views of how meaning is produced in literary work. That this emphasis finds expression both in romanticism's grandiose synthetic projects and in its tendency toward fragmentation is a familiar story. Less familiar are the oddly practical implications of the fact that Coleridge, by far the major disseminator of romanticism in English, insisted on conceiving of his whole as a text. Unlike continental versions of wholeness, his *Logosophia* was neither an otherworldly ideal, nor a dialectical historical totality, nor a pantheistic union with nature. It was something to be *done,* an opus or work, the material realization of a capability rather than a fitting into some preexisting order. True, Coleridge foresaw its advent as a kind of cross between the miraculous incarnation and the Second Coming (one imagines it would mean the end of literature as we know it); nevertheless, he pictured wholeness as the practical perfection of human effort.

The consequences of Coleridge's reliance on this goal, so far as they concern all provisional critical efforts, have a no less practical cast to them. In place of the material realization of Coleridge's goal, we find ourselves involved in a practice in which "Reality" and literature coincide where they can, and where a criticism of prospects fills the massive gaps where they cannot. We so constantly and thoroughly revise our own deeds of insight that the work of critical revision becomes indistinguishable from insight itself. Such a criticism is sure to be more concerned with possibility than with describing literature as we find it; and when it does describe present literary objects, it will render them, at the cost of their seeming integrity, in terms of ends to which they only partially contribute. This is something criticism cannot do merely by giving us another map of the aims and obstacles of literary life. Instead, criticism itself must become their most vital performance. Hence for Coleridge criticism approaches both literature and life; it becomes a *biographia literaria* insofar as it works toward the whole, revising its own means every step of the way. There is bound to be a strong sacrificial aspect in this performance, since criticism pays for its superior aims with the ruinous condition of its own text. In this sense, too, it begins to converge with literature—

not with literature as initially found or previously conceived, though, but with literature as already rendered by criticism. And as criticism gets drawn into the condition of literature, it suffers literature's fate with the added burden that it continues to act (often against its own local interests) as the most aggressive agent of this fate. Criticism beholds itself in literary ruins as it maintains, but fails to realize, just what quickens all its endeavor—the prospect of the whole.

"Prospect" is, of course, a word that belongs to Emerson rather than to Coleridge. I have been using it all along—somewhat anomalously as the history of the word goes—to help account for Coleridge's devotion to the aim of a future whole text. Coleridge would have understood the word to mean merely an outlook, a vista, or an expectation. It took the wilder American experience in mining and commercial speculation, during the Jacksonian era, for the word to acquire the sense (especially in the plural, "prospects") of one's chances for material success. Emerson finds this commercial sense useful for describing our future goals because it suggests that they entail practical investments and deferrals to be made in the present. We realize our prospects through the materials and instrumentalities we find readily at hand; and looking forward to them cannot be separated from working toward them as inventively as we can. Like everything we do in pursuit of them, our prospects will be of our own making. "Step by step we scale this mysterious ladder," he says in "Circles," "the steps are actions; the new prospect is power" (*CW* 2:181).

Perhaps this sounds too resolutely American to describe Coleridge. Yet before Coleridge's melancholy ruins and inspired false starts, before even his unacknowledged borrowings from other authors, lies the vision of the whole work he aimed to realize. If the actual shape of his writing suffered because of its prospectiveness, it also enjoyed a combination of aphoristic intensity and visionary scope that would have been inconceivable in the service of any lesser, or less material, end. This is not to say that the literary means wind up justifying Coleridge's failure to realize his end, and that the projected end, like a donkey's carrot, is finally beside the point. On the contrary: it is to say that, insofar as Coleridge sets a standard for criticism to come, conceiving a transcendental end as a prospect—as criticism's own practical and material possibility—is the only real way to work at all.

No less than Coleridge, Emerson was receptive to the glamor of the one grand project; indeed the encyclopedic ambitions of his youth made him deeply sensitive to Coleridge's influence. In all its phases, Emerson's pursuit of the whole was part of what made him romantic. But it was also part of what made him American, for union and practical integration have always been central aims in the nation's life—just as much now as in the antebellum years. Emerson's ambition to found an originally American literature within the scope of his own writing project was no less responsive to this American urgency than the political efforts of Daniel Webster, and later Lincoln, to cement a whole national identity in the face of divisive interests and ruinous passions. For Americans in Emerson's time, the challenge of national wholeness accorded with romanticism's, and especially Coleridge's, legacy of a literature founded in the prospect of the whole. Thus one cannot account for Coleridge's influence by simply cataloging the conceptual vocabulary—reason and understanding, talent and genius, and so forth—that Emerson took over from him. One must see his import in the larger force of his critical practice, in his vast demonstration of the stress between whole aims and the fragmentary realizations and breakdowns that come in their pursuit.

Emerson's response to romanticism and his address to the challenge of American originality are to be found together in the systematic writing practice he developed during the 1830s. I will examine that practice in detail in following chapters. First, however, it might be useful to consider one particular thread, drawn from Coleridge, as it turns up in Emerson. This is less a concept than a metaphor, and less a metaphor, perhaps, than a certain prescription for activity. In *The Statesman's Manual* it appears in the image of translucence that centers the famous definition of the symbol. In many other places Coleridge uses the sheerer event of transparency to picture the way meanings come forth from behind their representations. Transparency proceeds from Coleridge to become perhaps the most crucial single term in Emerson. All prospects, it seems, break down into transparent episodes of one sort or another. Barbara Packer has shown that the figure of transparency appears at the heart of Emerson's concern with issues of epistemological unity and discontinuity.[23] My interest in the figure concerns the ways Emerson uses it in a criticism of prospects. As with the Coleridgean symbol, this involves negotiations among fragments and across intervals. It also begins to define the role that Emerson's critical vision plays in creating those same fragments and intervals.

Emersonian Transparency

> Were our bodies transparent to our souls, we should be angels.
> —Coleridge, "Notes on Hooker"

In his meditations on the nature of color and light, Leonardo surmised that angels could not possibly see in the way human beings see: "Nothing that is spiritual or transparent can see anything set over against it, for this requires that it have within itself a thick opaque instrument and being thus it is not termed a spirit."[24] It made sense to assume that angels, the perfect messengers, must be wholly transparent beings; otherwise they might color or distort God's descending light. At least since Plato, the natural constitution of the eye had been deemed an impediment to clear transmission of the light of truth. In the medieval tradition, Bartholomew of Bologna had asserted that, in moments of sublime vision, "the pupils of the saints are made transparent, and they can see the uncreated light directly and with a sight which reveals its essence."[25] Leonardo applied optical laws to this traditional premise and deduced that completely transparent eyes must be blind to natural or created light (as opposed to supernatural or "uncreated" light), for they lack a "thick opaque instrument"—the retinal surface that lies behind the pupil of the eye. Hence if angels are invisible to us, we are just as invisible to them.

Leonardo's argument also illustrates the fact that transparency as such cannot be hypostatized. Transparency manifests itself only as an attribute of the medium lying between two discontinuous realms: the opaque eyeball that beholds and the opaque surface that appears "behind" or "on the other side of" the transparent medium. Moreover, the phenomenon of transparency becomes impossible in the absence of either or both of these two discontinuous realms. In theory and in experience there can be no transparency without some contiguous opacity. Something in particular always appears beyond the medium, for the essence of the transparent medium is to be between two things. In the grammar of seeing, the eye sees *through* one thing *to* the next thing: the eye sees at once "by means of" and "despite" the intervening transparent medium. The two realms enclosing the open space of transparency are characterized by color and figure, which define opacity. We learn from Leonardo that a transparent being can never be a seeing being; we also learn that a thing is transparent only as it plays its part in the larger enterprise of vision.

If the perfect messenger of God's light is transparent, then by the law of transparency that angel must be blind. Should we take Emerson for such an angel? The well-known optical metaphor from *Nature* would seem to have it so: "Standing on the bare ground,—my head bathed by the blithe air, and uplifted into infinite space,—all mean egotism vanishes. I become a transparent eye-ball. I am nothing. I see all. The currents of the Universal Being circulate through me; I am part or particle of God" (*CW* 1:10). In contemplating Emerson's figure, we, his readers, are like Leonardo contemplating the angel: we can easily imagine a head or an eyeball uplifted into space; we can try to imagine its transparency and its participation in the currents of Universal Being (whatever those are)—but who can conceive that it *sees* while being so entirely transparent? The Emersonian eyeball, like Leonardo's angel, lacks the interior opacity requisite for vision. Its ability to see becomes even more inconceivable in light of the fact that what surrounds the eyeball, "infinite space," is identical in its transparency to the inner space the eyeball encloses. As Emerson admits in "Intellect," there is no sight without a definite object: "The ray of light passes invisible through space, and only when it falls on an object is it seen" (*CW* 2:199).

Leonardo's blind, transparent angel might plausibly have declared: "I *see* nothing. I am all." But if that angel were to make the Emersonian claim ("I *am* nothing. I see all."), then we could not believe it.[26] It might be, of course, that Emerson means "seeing" in the Platonic or Christian sense—that is, seeing intellectually, "getting it"—but this disregards his insistent reliance, in this passage, on figures of actual physical sight, as well as his anxious parenthesis in the statement that precedes the transparent eyeball passage: "I feel that nothing can befal me in life,—no disgrace, no calamity, (leaving me my eyes,) which nature cannot repair" (*CW* 1:10).

In prose as in poetry, complex metaphors make complex arguments. Anyone who reads Emerson must come to terms with the depth of his insistence on the paradigm of visual perception. And it is indeed an insistence, an aggressively asserted argument rather than an unsophisticated throwback to the problematics of British empiricism. The difficulty of the passage from *Nature* lies in the fact that it seems to disregard the physical laws of eyesight while at the same time holding itself responsible to the smallest particularities of the *figure* of eyesight. By itself, the transparent eyeball is blind; yet a voice does declare, "I see all." The voice belongs to an "I," a self—a self that cannot, according to the physiology of vision, be equated absolutely with the eye it claims to have become. Let me approach this difficulty by way of a statement from "Circles," where Emerson offers a less startling version of the transparent eyeball: "Our globe seen by God, is a transparent law, not a mass of facts. The law dissolves the fact and holds it fluid" (*CW* 2:179).

"Our globe" is the globe of the eyeball as well as the corresponding globe of the earth (recall the first sentence of "Circles": "The eye is the first circle; the horizon which it forms is the second" [179]). "Seen" by God's eye, it becomes transparent like the eyeball in *Nature*. The overseeing eye is not merely looking, however: it *reads* the meaning of "our globe." Emerson stays true to his Puritan ancestors in his characteristic assertion that seeing is always a sort of reading; and yet for Emerson it is just as true that reading or interpretation reduces to optical laws. The law that dissolves "our globe" represents, in a sense, the last circle: it is the transparent double of the final eye of God.

In the transparent eyeball passage from *Nature*, Emerson says that "mean egotism" has vanished; but an ego watches nevertheless. The eyeball in the text becomes transparent only when a higher eye sees something *through* it. In this case the higher eye is not the eyeball itself: it is the higher eye of the Emerson who, while writing, recollects the scene of uplift; it is also the eye of the reader looking like God down upon the transparent globe figured in the text and reading a law. Such a reader cannot help but be "egotistical" (though not meanly so), for the law that appears in the figure of the eyeball—the law dissolving it into transparency—has to do with the reader's own identity. An "I" that cannot appear in the text—but that is present nevertheless as the reading eye—sees itself seeing or reads itself reading. It oversees its own projection into the shifting figures that comprise the text of experience.

ↂ ↂ ↂ

Transparency, far from signifying a passive state of continuity or unity, testifies to the way the eye manufactures its own discontinuous intervals. It is a mode of awareness of the necessary distance between the self and its provisional objects. Emerson, who asserts that optical laws make up a common constitution for both the eye of vision and the "I" of identity, presents the dynamics of transparency as an allegory of mental life as a whole. Most important, the metaphor of transparency allows him to describe the way meanings replace one another through acts of mind that are best compared to efforts of visual focus. He applies the metaphor, as Coleridge often did, to the sense of illumination that sometimes comes in reading, when meanings appear to "shine through" the formerly opaque surface of a printed text. In such fortunate moments, one cognitive realm seems to give way to another; we forget the letter and catch sight of the spirit. "The one thing which we seek with insatiable desire," Emerson writes in "Circles," "is to forget ourselves, to be surprised out of our propriety, to lose our sempiternal memory" (190). But elsewhere he qualifies the point by noting that "we forget also according to beautiful laws" (*W* 12:107). One of transparency's "beautiful laws" is that, when the eye sees *through* something, it secretly insists on what it seems to have denied. The medium—the word or figure that the reader sees through—is no less present for being transparent; it is only transparent because it is in fact there.

Emersonian transparency occurs in the shift of intellectual focus, in the gesture of negation that enables the eye to pass from the previously visible sign to the previously hidden meaning of the sign. As such, transparency should not be pictured as an ideal ontological condition, nor as a "place" upon which the eye might dwell. It appears (or disappears) only in the context of the shifting relations created by the intellect in its transit from old to new objects of focus.

The fact that such shifts of focus entail seeing one thing *through* another attests to the compensatory structure of ocular experience. Emerson's doctrine of Compensation states that "for every thing you have missed, you have gained something else; and for every thing you gain, you lose something" (*CW* 2:58). According to the economics of transparency, we see one object only at the cost of another. By efforts of focus, the eye converts old objects into the transparent media necessary for seeing new objects: one thing becomes transparent in the exchange of its opacity for the commodious space of its use.

Emerson conceives of experience in terms of optics, and of optics in terms of economics. Mental life, when pictured according to the metaphor of transparency, works in an economic or compensatory manner: quantities are neither gained nor lost, but simply converted and exchanged. Thus experience is neither additive nor progressive, but substitutive. The intellect comes to "know" new objects (here knowledge implies a form of possession or propriety) when it substitutes their visibility for the prior visibility of old objects. By the same logic, the transparency of old objects is both the reward received and the price paid for new objects.

Transparency, which Emerson often equates with the death of old objects, is the one fatal condition of moving on intellectually; it is the way we pay for all worthwhile adjustments of attention. Paying this price, as we constantly do, we get what Emerson calls the "new prospect," which is at once the new object and the prospect of its future conversion into transparency. After we have had enough new prospects—after we have seen through enough of them—we must admit, as Emerson finds himself compelled to admit in "Circles" (and even more grimly in "Experience"), that there is a circular pattern to the process. Seeing this pattern as a universal description of the course of human action has its own unhappy consequences, for regardless of what we know (or see), the pattern cannot be broken but only repeated. In the lectures and essays following *Nature,* Emerson admits that something more must be "forgotten" or rendered transparent than whatever local opacities stand between the eye and its aims. Somehow we must relieve ourselves of the lesson of the "circular philosopher"—that the real prospect of any new prospect, any promising object, is that it will also yield to transparency.

Emerson would not have drawn so deeply on the idea of transparency if its implications were merely epistemological—that is, if they were not also practical and ethical. These emerge in some of the disturbing arguments he makes about friendship and death. In *Nature,* he closes the crucial chapter on "Discipline" with a passage that presents the death of a beloved friend (actually his brother Charles, who died while Emerson was writing *Nature*) as an allegory of the mechanics of eyesight. Locating the terms of his description wholly in the realm of visual perception, Emerson speaks not of human beings, but of human "forms": "the eye,—the mind,—is always accompanied by these forms, male and female." These forms are ocular commodities, visible functions of the mind's desire; but to the relatively immature mind (as all minds are, whether adolescent or adult) *of self below*

they seem to be essential parts of the self: "We are associated in adolescent and adult life with some friends, who, like skies and waters, are coextensive with our idea; who, answering each to a certain affection of the soul, satisfy our desire on that side; whom we lack power to put at such focal distance from us, that we can mend or analyze them. We cannot chuse but love them" (*CW* 1:28).

There is more protest than tenderness here, where Emerson suggests that friendship, whatever its pleasures, reflects an intermittent disorder of perception. Love itself is the automatic consequence of a lack of "focal" power. Growth involves refinements of focus; the passage shows us that new clarifications always generate distances or separations as newly transparent intervals open up. In "Experience," Emerson expresses the ruinous personal consequences of this law of growth in a grand formula: "The great and crescive self, rooted in absolute nature, supplants all relative existence, and ruins the kingdom of mortal friendship and love" (*CW* 3:44).

Emersonian growth is compensatory rather than additive; that is, growth takes place not in the teleological sense of "growing up" but in the substitutive sense of outgrowing one self-objectification and growing into another one. In the passage from "Discipline," where Emerson correlates his outgrowing of a friend with the friend's death, the basically organic notion of growth translates into purely optical terms. When Emerson speaks of friends as "coextensive with our idea" ("idea" is etymologically close to the meaning of "form"), he indicates a rather ambiguous sort of self-objectification: one in which "our idea" is both the reflection of the self and the disposable property of the self. The relationship between the absolute self and its "idea" is not so much like that of Narcissus and his image as it is like the relationship between an investor and a piece of real estate.

Property demands improvement. The "forms" of friends at first appear to be "coextensive" (as if sharing the same picture plane) with "our idea"; but a more powerful focus will analyze and detach these forms en route to a sharper, more ample self-objectification. As he turns to the event of the friend's death, Emerson raises disturbing questions of priority and causality: "When much intercourse with a friend has supplied us with a standard of excellence, and has increased our respect for the resources of God who thus sends a real person to outgo our ideal; when he has, moreover, become an object of thought, and, whilst his character retains all its unconscious effect, is converted in the mind into solid and sweet wisdom,—it is a sign to us that his office is closing, and he is commonly withdrawn from sight in a short time" (*CW* 1:28–29). Which is the fatal event? Does the friend first withdraw into death; or does our own perception, our recognition of the *use* of the friend (he supplies us "with a standard of excellence"), actually push the friend away toward death? Emerson will not say whether the death comes from the refocusing, or vice versa; yet it seems that the needs of the eye have a fatal influence on the objects seen by the eye.

The seeing eye detaches objects from its own "idea" and gets a clearer perspective on them by creating a new transparency. In a larger sense, this shift of focus signals a withdrawal of investment from an older self-objectification and reinvestment in a newer one. The price of the new perception is necessarily the old attachment. Emerson's play on the word "office"—"it is a sign to us that his office is closing"—indicates the profoundly economic nature of the psychic transaction that, in his account, prefigures the event of someone else's death. The friend's death is subsequent to and perhaps dependent upon a refocusing, an outgoing of the old ideal; indeed, the friend's entire role in this process is his "office," his *officium* or performed duty. As the eye converts this real person into his use or "office," the friend comes to serve as "an object of thought." The new objectification signals proleptically that the friend will die or be "withdrawn from sight" in a future act of optical adjustment. Precisely in the way the word "office," meaning ministration of duty, came over time to stand for the commodious space of such ministration, the ultimate use of the friend will occur when he converts from an opaque object to the transparent medium that enables clearer vision, an "office"-place through which the eye can invest in an even newer prospect.[27]

Death, as "Discipline" pictures it, is only another word for transparency, which is a function of the eye's relentless drive toward clearer focus. In "Nominalist and Realist," written eight years after *Nature,* Emerson applies the metaphor of transparency in an even more mysterious and unsettling way. Here the logic of transparency defines not only death but all psychic, and in a way all bodily, motion:

> Nature keeps herself whole, and her representation complete in the experience of each mind. She suffers no seat to be vacant in her college. It is the secret of the world that all things subsist, and do

not die, but only retire a little from sight, and afterwards return again. Whatever does not concern us, is concealed from us. As soon as a person is no longer related to our present well-being, he is concealed, or *dies,* as we say . . . All persons, all things which we have known, are here present, and many more than we see; the world is full. As the ancient said, the world is a *plenum* or solid; and if we saw all things that really surround us, we should be imprisoned and unable to move. (*CW* 3:142)

Emerson's source for the natural "plenum" is Parmenides, who refutes the reality of both void (not-being) and time with his concept of nature as a spherical solid.[28] The Parmenidean solid is one version—perhaps the most extreme version—of a universe governed by the laws of compensation or conservation: nothing is gained or lost through action; equivalent quantities are merely exchanged. The world, the sum of all natural or objective facts, is full and immobile. In his merely "natural" being, Emerson could no more move in such world than could a man imprisoned in stone. Nor is eyesight possible under these circumstances, for the natural plenum is solidly opaque: there are no transparent spaces. We do manage to "see" and to "move," however, by tricking or troping our way through the suffocating solidity of the natural sphere. Emerson finds that we move through the natural plenum not by displacement, as if shouldering our way through a crowd, but through the purely fictive, tropical gesture of transparency, in which an interval seems to open between the eye and its object. Our apparent motion takes place by virtue of the, again, only apparent disappearance or "death" of the obstacle that had blocked or blinded us by making us continuous with the natural solid.

The solid globe of Parmenidean nature is an opaque version of the transparent eyeball in *Nature.* By itself, the transparent eyeball is blind; in fact, it would be void rather than transparent if it were not for the oversight of a higher eye that focuses on an object (or meaning) beyond it. The solid plenum, on the other hand, being nothing *but* object, allows no interval between the eye and its point of focus; without the magical intervention of transparency, with its trick of "concealing" imprisoning presences, we could neither see nor move. In both metaphors—the transparent eyeball and the solid globe— Emerson has made an absolute state out of one pole of what is actually (or optically) a dynamic antithesis. Eyesight is impossible in a realm of either unconditioned transparency (which is not transparency at all, but only a blank or void) or unconditioned opacity. As Leonardo deduced, this is because vision depends upon a combination of supernatural transparency and natural opacity.

The passage from "Nominalist and Realist" continues to conflate terms of sight and locomotion: "For, though nothing is impassable to the soul, but all things are pervious to it, and like highways, yet this is only whilst the soul does not see them. As soon as the soul sees any object, it stops before that object" (*CW* 3:142–143). Emerson makes the analogy with mental life irresistible. If thinking works as seeing does, our thoughts "stop" almost as soon as they start in any direction. Of course what stops the eye is the "thing" or "object" attended to in the most recent act of focus or revision. Our ocular constitution demands that our aims direct us toward the focal point of some new figure; we go there and, confronted with the opacity of that figure (in Saint Paul's terms, the letter of the figure rather than its spirit), we have to repeat the turn or trick of transparency:

> Through solidest eternal things, the man finds his road, as if they did not subsist, and does not once suspect their being. As soon as he needs a new object, suddenly he beholds it, and no longer attempts to pass through it, but takes another way. When he has exhausted for the time the nourishment to be drawn from any one person or thing, that object is withdrawn from his observation, and though still in his immediate neighborhood, he does not suspect its presence." (143)

As in the passage from "Discipline," Emerson judges that we acquire our new objects when we need them. Such a need is purely constitutional, given automatically by the laws of ocular conception. The eye needs the new opacity, the new figure, in order to focus beyond, or through, the figure that more immediately blocks its observation.

All figures are opaque until we read meanings through or in spite of them. Of course transparency is also a figure for Emerson, but its negativity makes it different in kind from all other figures. Emerson says we find our road through things "as if they did not subsist," but by the logic of transparency they subsist nonetheless. The "as if" emphasizes that transparency is actually the refiguring of a figure. In an entirely practical version of what Freud would later call repression, Emerson's claustrophobic eye "sees" *as if* the old figure were not in the way; the eye "turns" it to use by projecting a new figure or prospect a little farther down the road. The eye's investment in that new figure is at the same time an unconscious *di*vestment of the old one.

But such divestment is far from simple erasure or annihilation. We might say that transparency clothes the blocking object in invisibility in much the same way as the emperor's new clothes conceal his nakedness with fictive garments—for Emersonian transparency requires that the eye keep up this kind of confidence or belief.

It is fruitless to ask whether this happens for the sake of our investment in the new object or whether the new opacity is the real price we pay for relieving ourselves of the imprisoning circumstance of the immediate object; the solution to this question is circular, for our aims are always double. In any case, nothing is got for nothing; investment and divestment are two sides of one act, two arcs that meet in the circle of any finished turn or trope. The world is full, as Emerson is fond of saying, and the dice of God are loaded. The transparent medium subsists though we "see" as if it did not; and the new figure promises another stop, a further turn, and a renewed transparency.

I noted that the special structure of Emersonian transparency bears a more than accidental similarity to Freud's concept of repression. The concept of transparency, like that of repression, purports to account for a psychic transaction that both Emerson and Freud see as operating at the generative core of all experience. It should not be forgotten that Emerson details this crucial psychic event as fully as Freud does. In the formulations of both writers, the mind cannot simply erase or disregard an object it would prefer not to "see": though conscious eyes may trick it out of sight, the former object nevertheless subsists, clothed in its transparency. The mind "represses" a threatening drive, which itself appears as a literalized figure or idea, by an act that is no less figurative; we "forget" it or render it transparent. But in the economy of the psyche, a prior figure is granted invisibility only when the eye manages new investment in a visible substitute; we forgo one focus only for another; and so a new figure always appears before the eye. Thus in the event of transparency or repression we do not delete an object from before our eyes (if we were able to do this, to forget so wholly, we would all be as blind as Leonardo's angel); instead we are driven to find a focal replacement. For Freud the definitive constellation of substitutive figures is created early, so that on the whole we are compelled to repeat the drama of repression using the same round of characters. For Emerson *all* figural characters are equivalent in light of the demands of the eye, so the range of players is infinite, even though the sum value of the event is fixed.

There is no need to rely on a Freudian vocabulary in making such claims for Emerson. It is enough that the ocular psychology I have been examining concurs in most respects with Freud's psychic economics. In fact, an indirect but nevertheless highly charged path of influence extends from Emerson to Freud. This path of influence goes through Nietzsche—and the intellectual tradition it delivers is the idea of the economically constituted psyche. Nietzsche's work after *The Gay Science* remains the most powerful and original revision of the Emersonian problematic yet offered. This holds particularly for *The Genealogy of Morals,* where Nietzsche explores the implications of the crucial Emersonian paradigm that represents the psyche as an economy in which nothing is lost or gained but only values are exchanged. The claim that Nietzsche is a link in a chain of influence gains strength from the fact that Emerson is one of the few philosophers Nietzsche spares as an object of nihilistic polemic—and that the trope of the economic is utterly indispensable to Freud, who for the modern reader is the most unavoidable of Nietzsche's revisionists.

If I seem to be claiming that Emerson is something of a grandfather to Freud, then so be it. The picture of an economic mental life loses neither force nor complexity in moving back from Freudian dreamwork through Nietzsche's transvaluation of values to the American event of transparency. Emerson's arguments are powerful enough to enable an Emersonian reading of Freud instead of what we are more conditioned to expect—a Freudian reading of Emerson. American criticism, not to mention American psychoanalysis, sleepily awaits such a reading

∾ ∾ ∾

In *Nature,* we are told that "the visible creation is the terminus or circumference of the invisible world" (*CW* 1:22). The metaphor of transparency offers a complex definition of the entire "invisible world" as well as an ideal genealogy of the "visible creation." Emerson's development of this figure illustrates the transcendentalist enterprise insofar as transcendentalism is preoccupied with ways of negotiating the interval between the mutually exclusive realms of natural signs and supernatural meanings. Transparency serves to interpret our experience as readers of both our natural and supernatural being. As I have noted, this happens in allegories depicting the eye's transactions with absolute extremes of void and solid.

Having isolated some key terms in the ocular allegory, let me turn to the "Orphic Poet's" difficult formula near the end of *Nature:* "The problem of restoring to the world original and eternal beauty, is solved by the redemption of the soul. The ruin or the blank, that we see when we look at nature, is in our own eye. The axis of vision is not coincident with the axis of things, and so they appear not transparent but opake" (43).

The way into this passage lies not so much through the figure of "coincidence" as through Emerson's pairing of the terms "ruin" and "blank." They are apposite, but are they in fact the same? Critics generally assume so, as if neither term were quite precise enough to stand for what the real problem in the eye might be. Emerson's phrase, however, is "the ruin *or* the blank." That particular conjunction, while it does not compel us to make a choice between the two figures, still indicates that the ruin and the blank are not the same thing, even if they are versions of the same annihilating prospect that the exchange process of "redemption" is to solve.

The idea of transparency teaches that, for Emerson, the ruin and the blank are the Janus faces of blindness. Either term, when conceived of as an absolute condition, becomes a metaphor of final and literal death (blindness for the eye) rather than the multiple figurative "deaths" brought about in the process of transparency. "The ruin" is opacity without interval, or figure without meaning (as in the solid globe of the natural plenum). "The blank," on the other hand, is transparency without focus, or meaning without figure (as in the blindness of both Leonardo's angel and the transparent eyeball from *Nature*). Of course if the Emersonian blank is transparency without a focal object, it is not real transparency—for nothing would be seen *through* it—but only an abyss of empty freedom. In the event of real transparency, the eye makes combinations of ruin and blank, reconciling the antithetical terminals into vision. The polar terms of ruin and blank can be reduced to more general dialectical pairings: all and nothing, presence and absence, one and zero. In any case, the eye is responsible for setting these terms against one another in productive interaction. The calculus of transparency constantly casts up new figures through a binary code of particular ruins and blanks. Thus the Emersonian eye writes the text of human history by its various recombinations of the same two antithetical terms.

The miracle of transparency saves us from the pseudochoice between the blinding options (ruin or blank) of spiritless figure or unfigured spirit. Our binary arrangements of these fixities give us the beauty of the world. We constantly "redeem" this world by deeds of seeing, reading, and moving. But the very fact that such redemption must be successively renewed, that its beauty obtains only in our transactions or transitions, shows that we must also bow to fate. *Both* the faces of blindness are "in our own eye." The price of refusing the deathly continuities of plenum and abyss is the discontinuity created by the transparent interval. I have pointed out how this discontinuity appears when the eye focuses "beyond" on new objects, "seeing through" old objects that have, in a sense, been converted into the clear space of their ultimate commodity. *Nature* says that "the reason why the world lacks unity, and lies broken and in heaps, is, because man is disunited with himself." Through the disunities it induces, transparency, which is the miracle of our redemption, is also the prescription for a ruined world. All objects of vision are "ruins" in the sense that they are fragments constantly being precipitated into the world by the eye. Out of the monolithic ruin that lies "in the eye," we cast up in heaps and fragments the ruins of nature.

The difficulties Emerson encounters in searching for "unity" stem from the fact that the ocular constitution, by its very nature, divides the self, detaching a higher, transcendental eye (or "I") from the eye of the self. Emerson laments in a famous passage from his journals: "A believer in Unity, a seer of Unity, I yet behold two . . . I yet find little access to this Me of Me" (*JMN* 5:337). The twin opacities of subject and object, mediated by the transparent interval, make up the fatal "two" that Emerson beholds. As in the transparent eyeball episode, we find no access to the higher, unifying eye that, Emerson supposes, sees *through* our own ocular constitution. The overseeing "I" never appears as an object of the eye, even though nature's cipher of ruin and blank signals back to the "seer" the history of that transcendent identity.

At this point in my argument, the distinction between ruin and blank needs to be treated more closely. To see something as a ruin, for Emerson, is to see it as pure figure, opaque in the sense that it resists efforts to discover what meaning it contains; its contents seem, in fact, to have deserted it. (The metaphoric convergence of optics and semiotics, extremely pronounced in Emerson, is a staple of Western epistemology.) The eye "sees" only when it focuses on a specific figure. The sum of these specific figures or ruins would be the *Ruin*, the solid plenum. On the other hand, it is also the case, in accordance with the Newtonian optics pervading Emerson's texts, that the sum of all colors is white or *Blank* (as in the French *blanc*). Thus the definitions of "the ruin" and "the blank" do overlap to a certain extent; however, the two concepts must not be conflated. Considering the blank in the Newtonian sense of white—that is, of white light as the simultaneous presence of all the spectral colors—again reveals the double nature of blindness as both vacuum and opaque solidity. Things in nature are colored; they are tropes or figures in God's book. If *all* such figures were at once present, we would find ourselves in an abyss of white, with nothing for the mind to grasp, no object on which the eye could focus. For the eye, the practical consequences of the whiteness of total figural presence and the blankness of complete figural absence are the same. Without some colored figure toward which we can direct our focus, and without a clear space through which to see, we would be as blind, once again, as Leonardo's angel.

The traditional identification of rhetorical figures with colors reflects the premise that the relation between figure and meaning is comparable to the relation between color and light. A visible color signifies the presence of light, the illuminating principle that by itself remains unfigured or white. Newtonian optics complicates this metaphor by redefining white light, which is "not so much a color as the visible absence of color, and at the same time the concrete of all colors." This last phrase comes from *Moby-Dick*, where Melville translates the Newtonian concept of whiteness into the darkest of allegories. For Melville, who loves to play on the etymological identity of "white" and "blank," whiteness is "the colorless, all-color of atheism." Some version of confidence or belief is necessary if the blankness of unmediated nature is to be tricked into colors. This blankness, remember, consists of both complete fullness and total emptiness. Even as he takes issue with Emerson in other regards, Melville agrees with his acknowledgment, in "Experience," that identity depends upon color: "We have learned that we do not see directly, but mediately, and that we have no means of correcting these colored and distorting lenses *which we are*" (*CW* 3:43; emphasis added).

For both Melville and Emerson, color saves us from a shroud of solid whiteness. In the event of transparency, the eye manufactures color by clothing a part of the (white) plenum in apparent invisibility. Surely Melville is thinking of the Emersonian lesson when he illustrates the fate of the "infidel" who refuses the confidence game of transparency and tries to behold the uncolored prospect of pure possibility: "Like wilfull travellers in Lapland, who refuse to wear colored or coloring glasses upon their eyes, so the wretched infidel gazes himself blind at the monumental white shroud that wraps all the prospect around him."[29]

If the sum of all colors is white, then perception of any particular color shows a part of the colorless. Any single text, color, or figure stands as a synecdoche for the white whole even as it serves to protect the eye. "There is no fact in nature," as Emerson says in "The Poet" and repeatedly throughout his work, "which does not carry the whole sense of nature" (*CW* 3:10). Every natural fragment would seem to answer Coleridge's definition of the "Symbol" in *The Statesman's Manual:* "While it enunciates the whole, [it] abides . . . as a living part in that Unity, of which it is the representative." Although the concept of synecdochic or "symbolic" reference raised intractable problems for Coleridge, who could neither embrace nor relinquish its totalizing possibilities, Emerson freely accepts such a mode of reference, as long as it is understood to operate in a purely natural realm:

> The Metamorphosis of nature shows itself in nothing more than this that there is no word in our language that cannot become typical to us of nature by giving it emphasis. The world is a Dancer; it is a Rosary; it is a Torrent; it is a Boat; a Mist; a Spider's Snare; it is what you will; and the metaphor will hold, & it will give the imagination keen pleasure. Swifter than light the World converts itself into that thing you name & all things find their right place under this new & capricious classification. (*JMN* 8:23)

A close understanding of Emersonian transparency has value for anyone interested in theories about how meaning is created. Words, according to Emerson, as signs of natural facts, present limited versions or fragments of the solid plenum. When we grant that each fragment can be read as a synecdoche for the sum of those fragments, we free ourselves for the more difficult question: How do these symbols or types stand in relation to the self, the reader, who *uses* synecdochic representation—substituting the colored part for the blank whole—as a defense against the blinding, imprisoning effect of the white plenum? The ruins of nature cannot be continuous, in Coleridge's sense, with a self whose ocular constitution requires that it detach itself entirely from its objects, each of which remains as the vestige of an earlier, inadequate act of focus or self-conception. These ruins cannot "abide as a living part in that Unity" of which they are representative—for then they would be, under the Emersonian laws, conceptually invisible. According to the semiotics implicit in the concept of transparency, a specific fact can stand in a continuous or synecdochic relation to the sum of all "natural facts" but must stand in a discontinuous relation to the reader of those facts. The reader can be truly represented only by detaching parts of the self *from* the self through a shifting of focus in which what was once a "part" of the eye, too close to be seen, is detached from it through the creation of a transparent field. Though bits of the self can therefore be focused on, the reading part of the self remains, for Emerson, outside the natural realm.

Certainly such a reader has access to a kind of power through the economics of transparency. "Power," Emerson states in "Self-Reliance," "resides in the moment of transition from a past to a new state; in the shooting of the gulf; in the darting to an aim" (*CW* 2:40). But of course the switch of focus, the darting across a conceptual threshold, is beyond visible or literal representation. We may infer that such an event occurs by our own measurement of differences, by comparisons between the ruins of the past and those being made in the present. To see ourselves, in other words, we must see historically, in terms of causality and generation. Out of such revision arises the endless metamorphosis or generation of the world, which appears as the story of a power that has always moved beyond it.

2

~ ~ ~

The Emerson Museum

In the Gardens of Natural History

See yonder leafless trees against the sky,
How they diffuse themselves into the air,
And ever subdividing separate
Limbs into branches, branches into twigs,
As if they loved the element, & hasted
To dissipate their being into it.

—Emerson, *Poetry Notebooks*

After Emerson's visit to the Jardin des Plantes in 1833, the first observation that appears in his journal is: "How much finer things are in composition than alone. 'Tis wise in man to make Cabinets." There was truly nothing out of place in the many "compositions" of the Muséum d'Histoire Naturelle, as the institution was formally named. The massive displays of mineral, plant, and animal specimens in the Cabinet of Natural History illustrated the classificatory models of individual naturalists.[1] Outside the monumental Cabinet building, Emerson found these classifications demonstrated again on a larger scale in the menagerie and the botanical gardens, where living representatives of species were laid out to illustrate the systematic ranks of genus, family, order, and class. The entire display literalized the commonplace of nature as God's book: it offered the viewer a synopsis of the original text whose characters Adam named and under-

59

stood, a text whose integrity had since fallen into the apparent babble of natural diversity. In contrast to the evanescence and partiality that Emerson often lamented in his experience of nature, the Muséum was a spectacle of reconstituted fullness—as Cuvier described it, "Le temple le plus grand et le plus beau qui ait été consacré à la nature."[2]

Clearly this was the sort of place where an American, whose country was just starting its own natural history institutions, would expect to be impressed. But what Emerson found there seemed no less than providential. The Muséum's spectacular effect consisted in its assignment of huge varieties of natural particulars, brought from all parts of the earth, to the unifying structures of a few ideational systems. Faced with this startling combination of multiplicity and "reduction to a few laws," Emerson found the occasion of his visit to be, in a strange way, sacramental.

He noted—strikingly for a bereaved husband (Ellen Tucker Emerson had died two years earlier)—that looking at the ornithological collection "makes the visitor as calm & genial as a bridegroom" (*JMN* 4:199). This association of natural history with the marriage ceremony persisted in Emerson's reflections on nature. It appeared in his first lyceum lecture, "The Uses of Natural History," when he told his audience at the Boston Natural History Society that the naturalist "marries the visible to the invisible by uniting thought to Animal Organization" (*EL* 1:24). And again, in 1837, Emerson spoke of the naturalist's encounter with facts as a sort of automatic conjugation: "He cannot see a star, but instantly this marriage begins of object and subject, of Nature and man, whose offspring is power" (*EL* 2:221).

Emerson was not alone in conceiving the naturalist to be the new minister of the nineteenth century; Cuvier had made much the same claim in his introduction to *The Animal Kingdom*. While social orders shifted and collapsed, the great pre-Darwinian naturalists united their audiences before prospects of a consolidated natural order. In Paris, Emerson found this "marriage" formalized in the systematic compositions of the gardens, the menagerie, and the various cabinets. The Muséum's arrangement of visible things revealed the higher forms—family, order, and class—that contained them; these forms were invisible but presumably just as real as the things themselves. In fact, natural history suggested that such forms might be presupposed by both nature and intellect; thus the exhibitions unveiled an "occult," or invisible, relation between the viewer and each element within the viewer's natural prospect:

> The Universe is a more amazing puzzle than ever as you glance along this bewildering series of animated forms,—the hazy butterflies, the carved shells, the birds, beasts, fishes, insects, snakes,—& the upheaving principle of life everywhere incipient in the very rock aping organized forms. Not a form so grotesque, so savage, nor so beautiful but is an expression of some property inherent in man the observer,—an occult relation between the very scorpions and man. I feel the centipede in me—cayman, carp, eagle, & fox. I am moved by strange sympathies, I say continually, "I will be a naturalist." (*JMN* 4: 199–200)

The ecstasy recorded in this passage foreshadows Thoreau's sudden urge, in *Walden*, to seize a woodchuck and devour it raw, as "the wildest scenes had become unaccountably familiar."[3] But the "strange sympathies" excited in Emerson by the Parisian displays were hardly signs of the rousing of his bestial nature; rather, they heralded new prospects for his "glance," his critical abilities of discernment and composition. (The same was ultimately true for Thoreau, who cooked his woodchuck before tasting it.) Series, form, organization, relation—these are the key terms of the visual experience Emerson describes. They pertain to the intellectual practices, actual and possible, of "man the observer." Confronted with the multiple cabinets and gardens, Emerson was amazed to find his eye caught up in a kind of universal reading. We begin to understand his "strange sympathies" when we see that what he was reading was a version of precisely the kind of writing to which he had long aspired.

In fact, a similarly diverse collection of specimens was already "in" him, or at least in the maturing corpus of his journals. Emerson had many terms for the entries that, by 1833, had been filling up journal volumes for eight years: he referred to them variously as facts, individuals, deposits, pictures, materials, or fractions. They represented the lumber of intellectual life: musings of all sorts, critical definitions, quotations, drafts of poems and sermons. And indeed, among these specimens were many with qualities not unlike those of scorpions, centipedes, or other animals in the Muséum: rhetorically at least, some had a backward sting, some soared, some fed on the words of the dead, some moved on a hundred legs. In the period of his visit to the Jardin des Plantes, however, Emerson was anxiously aware that he lacked the ability to present himself, as a writer, with the universal focus he had always longed for. Two months before departing for Europe, soon after resigning his pastorate for a wide open future, he noted his need for an effective compositional approach: "We have thoughts but we don't know what to do with them, materials, that we can't manage or dispose. We cannot get high enough above them to see their order in reason. We cannot get warm enough to have them exert their natural affinities & throw themselves into crystal" (*JMN* 4:49). Emerson wished for a way of seeing his work that would bring out its "natural affinities," which until then had lain buried in his miscellaneous journal materials. For this to be possible, he needed not only guiding principles but also efficient techniques. More precisely, he needed to master a working framework in which principle and technique were bound up one within the other.

Such was his revelation in Paris. In the cabinets and gardens of the Muséum, he had the uncanny experience of beholding his own writing—the Emersonian project of writing that he had not yet clearly envisioned—augustly prescribed for him. If he felt like a bridegroom, it was because, at that moment, he began to wed himself to a new model of identity and experience, as well as to a particular method of collection, preservation, and composition.

Emerson's revelation in the Jardin des Plantes was the crucial event in his European tour of 1833—more momentous even than his first meeting with Carlyle six weeks later. The vow he made to himself in the zoological cabinet signaled a decisive turn in the hard process of intellectual and emotional reorientation that had begun in 1831, with the death of his first wife, and that would come to issue the following October, with the public lectures he started giving after crossing back to America.[4] Already, one of the consequences of this long crisis had been his renunciation of the ministry. The final result would be his mature vocation as journalizer, lecturer, essayist, and poet. Emerson's experience in the Jardin des Plantes and his subsequent reflections on the topic of "natural history" would lead to a set of working ideas about the intellectual technology of writing, a technology that established a framework of possibility within which the characteristically Emersonian practice of writing "up" from journals and notebooks could take place. Soon after returning to America, he would publicly repeat his vow: "I will be a naturalist." At the end of his life, when his power of memory survived only within the technical apparatus of the journals, he would still, in his way, be holding to it.

The Eye Is Satisfied

> The eye is satisfied with seeing and strange thoughts are stirred as you see more surprising objects than were known to exist; transparent lumps of amber with gnats and flies within; radiant spars and marbles; huge blocks of quartz; native gold in all its forms of crystallization and combination, gold in threads, in plates, in crystals, in dust; and silver taken from the earth molten as from fire. You are impressed with the inexhaustible gigantic riches of nature. The limits of the possible are enlarged, and the real is stranger than the imaginary.

—Emerson, "The Uses of Natural History"

Wherever we focus, in examining the Jardin des Plantes' impact on Emerson, we will never find ourselves far from the ways it devised to strike the eye. The effect was always one of systematic integrity, beginning from the moment the visitor entered the grounds through the eastern gate by the Seine. Coming through the gateway, "one gathers in at a glance [*d'un coup d'œil*] the whole of the establishment," noted J.-P.-F. Deleuze, the Muséum's historian. Deleuze's plan of the Jardin des Plantes after its reorganization in 1821 (see figure) shows how its flat, rectangular grounds were geometrically divided and subdivided, with wide walkways separating the large squares (*carrés*) and smaller walkways defining the individual parterres. The building of the Cabinet of Natural History stretched along the entire western border of the formal gardens. To the north of the formal gardens was the *labyrinthe,* a hilly zone covered with a network of serpentine paths.

The *labyrinthe* was a romantic supplement to the neoclassical Jardin du Roi; it provided Parisians with a stylized version of the forest beside the gridwork of the gardens. As its name suggests, the *labyrinthe* was a place to play at getting lost in nature, though its uneven ground also offered the visitor a prospect of the entire layout of the Muséum's formal grounds.[5] From such a Pisgah-view, one beheld a more venerable paradigm (a paradigm that was the precondition for wandering through romantic mazes) in which nature regained its integrity in the architectonics of reason and commodity. It is instructive that,

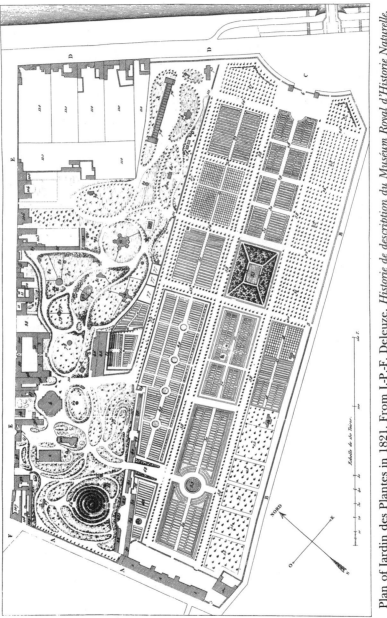

Plan of Jardin des Plantes in 1821. From J.-P.-F. Deleuze, *Historie de description du Muséum Royal d'Historie Naturelle*, vol. 2 (Paris, 1823).

in his journals and lectures, Emerson had nothing to say about the picturesque side of the Jardin des Plantes. His sensibility inclined toward a contrary aesthetic—in Emerson's terms, "the sublime of analysis"—a severe aesthetic fulfilled in the sequences of glass-doored armoires lining the Cabinet's galleries and, with correspondent power, in the subordinated, pagelike surfaces of the formal gardens.

All nature, in the Muséum, yielded itself to the conceptual graphics of outline, series, and hierarchy. Not only did the spectacular institution, with its emphasis on technologies of classification and information retrieval, dramatize what Emerson would later celebrate as "the radical correspondence between visible things and human thought" (*CW* 1:19); its entire structure demonstrated the way "visible things," once converted into ideational currency, became ingredients of ever larger forms. Deleuze's plan shows that, on the largest scale—the propaedic scale visible from the hill in the middle of the *labyrinthe*—the formal gardens resembled nothing so much as a library of books. Then again, the gardens evoked the outlines of a classified table of contents. Indeed, unmistakable resemblances to modes of textual organization abounded all through the Muséum. In just the way that a "cabinet cyclopedia" (such as Emerson's beloved *Encylopedia Americana*) sought to epitomize and classify the useful contents of all the world's books, the Muséum selected, abridged, and arranged the useful contents of nature's hieroglyphic plenitude.

The encyclopedic format of the Muséum, its careful division and subdivision, was not arbitrary—not merely alphabetical, for example—but mirrored both the latent anatomy of its subject and the patent techniques of the naturalists. As Cuvier's gifted and belated disciple Louis Agassiz later explained in his *Essay on Classification*, the naturalist's compositions sought to clarify the order "inherent in the objects themselves, so that the intelligent student of Natural History is led unconsciously, by the study of the animal kingdom itself, to these conclusions, the great divisions under which he arranges the animals being indeed but the headings to the chapters of the great book which he is reading."[6]

The *Essay on Classification* unfolds points that Agassiz, like Emerson, had seen presented with great force in the visual compositions of the Muséum. Chief among these was the notion that each layer in the hierarchy of organizational forms was equally real and necessary; thus each stage of classification combined the actual with the provisional.

The chapters, sections, and paragraphs in nature's book—even the book as a whole—repeated the same representational form found in seemingly elemental units such as sentences and words: this was the form of the classification.

The lesson of the Muséum was that all individual facts stood for the propositions of classifications. On the smallest scale—the micropaedic scale of the single living animal or plant, the mineral sample, the fossil, even the heart or skull shown in the comparative anatomy cabinet—the representative aspect of the thing superseded the thing itself. So instead of particular creatures the visitor beheld "specimens," the representatives of species; and just as "species" were the conceptual containers of specimens, a shift upward in the conceptual register resulted in species themselves being treated as "specimens" placed within the more abstract container of the genus; and so on to the family, the order, and the class. Whether it was stuffed, dried, cultivated, or caged, everything in the Muséum was haunted by its own referentiality: because the aim of natural history was to make the living individual point beyond its idiosyncrasies to its place in a system of classes nested within classes like wheels within wheels.[7]

With the hermeneutic traditions of New England Puritanism behind him, Emerson was well prepared for the Muséum's preoccupation with the hieroglyphic aspect of nature. The strong difference in the Muséum, however, was that nature's emblematic sense derived not from retrospective reference to the dicta of scripture or sacred history (as it had for Puritan readers of nature such as Cotton Mather and Jonathan Edwards) but from the efficiency with which visible things yielded themselves to the critical devices of natural history. The Muséum's classifications were not only vehicles for communicating nature's meanings; in a surprisingly literal sense, they made up the form and content of meaning itself. A kind of iconoclasm worked within such reference—opaque images were conceptually broken and dissolved—for natural history assumed that the meanings indicated by visible nature were more like practices than static essences. In the light of the practice of classification, all objects in the Muséum satisfied the fundamental principle Emerson identified in *Nature* as "the great doctrine of Use, namely, that a thing is good only so far as it serves" (*CW* 1:26).

This was a difference Emerson was ready to appreciate. While his largest reason for renouncing the ministry, one year earlier, had been

that the pulpit offered far too constricted and subservient a vehicle
to fit his ambitions, the issue over which he chose publicly to resign
was the old problem of the proper function of religious representation. Emerson could no longer countenance a venerable symbolic
form, the Eucharist, because it sought to produce meaning by ob-
serving the form of a historical precedent. "Forms are as essential as
bodies," he declared in his farewell sermon, "The Lord's Supper,"
"but to exalt particular forms, to adhere to one form a moment after
it is outgrown, is unreasonable, and it is alien to the spirit of Christ"
(*W* 11:20).

Emerson was always severe in his insistence that meaning could
only be found in present activity, not in repetition of authoritative *ritual*
moments in history. He brought this semiotic insistence to the Jardin
des Plantes. Seizing meanings from visible nature, like seizing them
from the canons of scripture and history, would have to involve fresh
moments of action, whether such action pertained to deeds of natural creation or deeds of writing. This meant overcoming the literal
textual surface of nature's book, which, in its initial opacity and in
its situation in an irreversible historical framework, appeared merely
as visual evidence of prior activity. The Muséum demonstrated that,
once objects were represented as "specimens" within a classification,
the process of overcoming had already begun to take place. Thus
Emerson, in "The American Scholar," identified classification as the
first and fundamental stage in the scholar's education: "The ambitious soul sits down before each refractory fact; one after another,
reduces all strange constitutions, all new powers, to their class and
their law, and goes on forever to animate the last fibre of organization, the outskirts of nature, by insight" (*CW* 1:54).

For the Muséum spectator, classification belonged to the contemporary realm of intellectual activity; it recovered a divine plan that
was immanent in nature rather than one dictated at the beginning
of history. It might be said that, in the Muséum, the significance of
natural facts shone forth in just that semiotic mode Coleridge had
called "symbol" as opposed to "allegory"; once displayed as specimens of their classes, natural facts introduced the eye into an otherwise invisible world of referential and compositional practice. That
invisible world was revealed as belonging equally to the latent reality
of nature and to the intellectual prospects of the spectator. It was by
virtue of this revelation that natural history offered Emerson the

means for a constructive answer to the question his ancestral religion had raised, but then only evaded. This was the question of originality posed at the opening of *Nature:* "Why should not we also enjoy an original relation to the universe?" (7). The Muséum demonstrated that nature's meanings could be reclaimed in no other sense than *as one's own*—or, more properly, as what one might intellectually and practically do.

∾ ∾ ∾

To Emerson in Paris, the domain of "one's own" comprised more than the scientific panorama immediately in view. It extended to his own special history, where the facts of what he had already been and done verged into the uncertain prospect of what remained for him to do. Remembering his European tour in "Self-Reliance," he wrote: "I pack my trunk, embrace my friends, embark on the sea, and at last wake up in Naples, and there beside me is the stern Fact, the sad self, unrelenting, identical, that I fled from . . . My giant goes with me wherever I go" (*CW* 2:46). The giant questions of what to do, and how to do it, guided Emerson away from America and then back, in foreign places, to the America of his own questionable future. It is impossible to read his experience in the Jardin des Plantes in terms other than those of his future, so one must keep looking to the ensuing work, and especially to *Nature,* where his "marriage" to natural history achieves its first published celebration.

Reclaiming an original relation to nature, for Emerson, meant seizing power in the unruly domain of his own work, getting "high enough" over his fragmentary writings to "see their order in reason." The Muséum recommended such elevation not only in its large-scale compositions, but also in the specimens themselves. Each specimen, merely by virtue of being in the Muséum, already reflected the focal distance of the heightened viewpoint from which it appeared as a member of its class. Natural history did not concoct these specimen forms; it claimed only to isolate and clarify the representational character lying already there in all natural facts. By the same logic, the higher orderings restored by natural history—family, order, class— were also "already there": they had abided from the beginning both in God's design and in the naturalist's godlike power to gain sight of that design. Accordingly, the naturalist's intellectual detachment, the perspective from which order became visible, was also built into the "history" of specimens. The history or meaning recovered from specimens by the naturalist was not a static essence, but a design for both natural and intellectual activity. Rather than finding an image of himself in natural objects, the naturalist found a prescription for his own means of looking into things.

When Emerson resigned his pastoral duties, he concluded with a promise to persevere privately in what he saw as the ministry's most important work: "I am consoled by the hope that no time and no change can deprive me of the satisfaction of pursuing and exercising its highest functions" (*W*11:25). He did not tell his congregation just what these functions would be. From the course of his work, however, it is certainly clear that one of them consisted in the endless project of interpreting sacred texts, including those of poetry, philosophy, and nature itself. In Paris Emerson found grand demonstration of an interpretive focus that, he realized, worked with aims and methods corresponding to those animating radical Protestant approaches to sacred writing. In the following passage from *Nature,* Emerson joins the rewards of heightened scientific perspective to one of the dicta of George Fox, founder of Quakerism: " 'Every scripture is to be interpreted by the same spirit which gave it forth,'—is the fundamental law of criticism. A life in harmony with nature, the love of truth and of virtue, will purge the eyes to understand her text. By degrees we may come to know the primitive sense of the permanent objects of nature, so that the world shall be to us an open book, and every form significant of its hidden life and final cause" (*CW* 1:23).

In *Nature,* Emerson defines and solemnizes his dedication to his new ministry. One may speak of this ministry, with its combination of diligent research and provisional publication, as "criticism" in the largest sense, though Emerson also insisted on referring to it as "natural history." In the passage just cited, Emerson calls not merely for original but for aboriginal criticism, a criticism whose quickening principle is somehow already in place prior to any text it would interpret, just as the creator is already in place prior to creation.

Even on such aboriginal ground, however, criticism is still a matter of technical capability; criticism relies on an arsenal of means rather than on fixed standards. Emerson's "life in harmony with nature" hence has little to do with tree hugging or with some nebulous fusion into organic oneness. Harmony, like criticism, depends on precise instrumentation. To purged eyes, nature's "permanent objects" deliver up the living technology behind the scrambled, opaque flow of phenomena. Emerson's play on "primitive sense"—it is both original meaning and original seeing—suggests that the sense found in natural objects is precisely the viewer's own original *means* for seeing them: objects are designs of new perception and prescriptions for newer perception. By virtue of these means, vision rises to a place of authority over objects, to a kind of perspectival remove sufficient to reveal relations within the whole scope of things.

As an "open book," then, nature calls for the highest acts of reading, ones in which elevated perceptions are made possible by practical work and all work serves the aim of still higher perception. *Nature* sets the reading soul on just this hermeneutic watchtower: "It is a watcher more than a doer, and it is a doer only that it may better watch" (36). This was the lesson taught in the Muséum and brought home by Emerson: that the promise of nature was the prospect of his own visionary remove.

Of course poetry since Milton has accustomed its readers to visionary removes. Imagination finds its métier in looking out from high vantage points, fixing on stars, tracing the horizon across wastes of sea or desert places. But Emerson's imagination, as deeply schooled in the poetics of science as in poetic tradition, located possibilities of remove not just on speculative promontories but also in the closest views of specific details and facts. Emersonian "natural history" manages intimacy with textual objects in exact ratio to the remoteness of its focal adjustments. This is fully in keeping with what he beheld in Paris; for one of the most striking aspects of the Muséum's exhibitions was the way they forced together the particularity of single specimens and the vast scope of distanced perspectives. The more closely spectators looked into a thing, the further, conceptually, they could see.

Emerson carried this scientific approach deliberately into literature in his treatment of his own journal specimens. In April 1834, as he was developing the new journalizing practice on which he would found his future work, he declared: "This it is to conceive of acts & works, to throw myself into the object so that its history shall naturally evolve itself before me" (*JMN* 4:285). It is characteristic of Emerson's critical and compositional procedure that writing, like any work, must have an "object" with which to deal. Whether that object is an incident of the day, a quotation from another writer, or a journal fragment from Emerson's own hand, producing its "history" will entail the closest possible relation between the revising eye and its material point of focus. Emerson will have to "throw" himself into the object, making it "conceive" in an almost procreative sense. At the same time, however, the critical eye will need to observe from a distance sufficient to comprehend the results, "so that its history shall naturally evolve itself before me." Contact with a specimen, even to the point of union, is offset by the necessity of remove.

As he was inventing the arguments of *Nature* in 1836, Emerson identified the power of critical remove as one of the key weapons in the scholar's arsenal. He described it in a journal as "the power to stand *beside* his thoughts, or, to hold off his thoughts at arm's length and give them perspective; to form *il piu nell' uno*" (*JMN* 5:116). Emerson had found the Italian term in Coleridge, who cited it as another affirmation of his famous concept of "multaeity in unity," which Coleridge developed in meditations on organic form in Shakespeare. In *Nature*, Emerson pointed to two correspondent ways of framing *il piu nell' uno;* and both of them reflected practices essential to natural history. The first way required standing back from the object, setting one fact "in composition" alongside others. Emerson found himself thrust into just such macroscopic removes in front of the Muséum's cabinets, gardens, and herbaria. Since these compositions were only more specific types of the total form of the Muséum, each of the particular perspectives they created was a précis of the ultimate perspective promised by the institution as a whole.

According to *Nature*, the prospect of whole form, of which any individual object will be a part, makes up the "standard" (an ensign or rallying point as well as a criterion for judgment) for both beauty and meaning: "Nature is a sea of forms radically alike and even unique. A leaf, a sun-beam, a landscape, the ocean, make an analogous impression on the mind. What is common to them all,—that perfectness and harmony, is beauty. Therefore the standard of beauty is the entire circuit of natural forms,—the totality of nature; which the Italians expressed by defining beauty 'il piu nell' uno.' Nothing is quite beautiful alone: nothing but is beautiful in the whole" (*CW* 1:17).

Behind this definition of beauty lies the perspectival mobility of Emerson's scientific eye, which can adjust its focus instantly from a single leaf to a whole landscape. Beauty, while it depends on the prospect of a whole circuit, also involves something more than the revelation of a wholeness already shared by things. Emerson treats wholeness as a relation achieved by the eye rather than as a quality discovered in things; hence organic unity gives way to practical unifications of one sort or another. In *Nature,* then, "what is common" to all individual forms consists not only in their actual or possible placement in a larger whole; it also consists in their instant readiness to the focal enterprise that can hold them off "at arm's length." By this logic, the beauty of things obtains technically rather than naturally, through practical adjustments of relation between the beholder and his object: "The eye is the best of artists. By the mutual action of its structure and of the laws of light, perspective is produced, which integrates every mass of objects, of what character soever, into a well colored and shaded globe, so that where the particular objects are mean and unaffecting, the landscape which they compose, is round and symmetrical" (12). This is no ordinary landscape. Emerson's perspective makes the landscape a convex "globe," which excludes the viewer, rather than the concave dome of familiar experience. Whether in ecstasy or in exile, the viewer moves back from the object like an astronaut lifting off from earth. The figure created expresses the technical constitution of the new optical relationship, doubling the orb of the eye, even while it measures the necessary distances involved.

The picture of this technical capability grows more complex when one considers the second way that *Nature* proposes for forming *il piu nell' uno.* Like Blake, Emerson finds prospects of the whole available within the strict frame of the particular. The scientist, no less than the prophet, can see a world in a grain of sand. Normal perspective is reversed in this microscopic way of looking: the horizon that includes the object as a part within the whole is no longer an expression of the viewer's remove *from* the object but instead expresses conceptual distances already there within the texture of what is seen. In a way once again reminiscent of the Coleridgean symbol, Emerson finds that a fragmentary object can serve as an aperture for a view of conceptual removes comprising the real interior of a natural fact. Thus he discovers a new world lying inside each of nature's old things: "Every particular in nature, a leaf, a drop, a crystal, a moment of time is related to the whole, and partakes of the perfection of the whole. Each particular is a microcosm, and faithfully renders the likeness of the world" (27).

Later, in "Compensation," Emerson invoked this same principle as "the doctrine of omnipresence": "God re-appears with all his parts in every moss and cobweb. The value of the universe contrives to throw itself into every point" (*CW* 2:60). Such statements have been cited by readers who attack or applaud Emerson as a cheerful mystic who vaguely sees everything in everything. Considering Emerson in light of the model of natural history, however, ought to warn his critics away from that sort of reduction. A major lesson of the Muséum was that any "point" in nature, set in proper perspective, might become an instance of *il piu nell' uno,* a specimen indexing a history of contrivance on the part of the universe and, at least potentially, in the view of the critical beholder.

It was the technical, "scientific" nature of such vision that came into view in the Muséum. Seeing the whole in the part required the same focal instrumentation as seeing the part in the whole, only in the former case it was the object, rather than the beholder, that seemed to "move." And this was the point: the ordinary veneer of natural objects concealed a world of intellectual animation. The way to behold this animation was not just to stand back from the object but to inspect it in such a way as to reveal the object already "standing back" within itself in multiple removes of meaning and possibility.

With this in mind, it becomes hard to ignore the deeply practical sense in Emerson's famous definition of nature, in "The Method of Nature," as "a work of *ecstasy*" (*CW* 1:125). Emerson asserts that the poet, like the naturalist, "must look at nature with a supernatural eye. By piety alone, by conversing with the cause of nature, is he safe and commands it. And because all knowledge is assimilation to the object of knowledge, as the power or genius of nature is ecstatic, so must its science or the description of it be" (131–132). The Muséum offered a grand demonstration of the idea that perspectival remove had to be discovered *in the specimen*—indeed, as the essential nature of the specimen itself. And the branch of natural history that exposed the microcosmic structure of specimens was the all-important discipline of comparative anatomy, a discipline pioneered by Cuvier and seized by Emerson as a model for his own work.

The Muséum taught Emerson to treat his journal fragments as if they were specimens of natural history. This had extreme implications for his writing practice, which like Coleridge's came to rely on the most jagged fragmentariness in passionate pursuit of the whole. If Emerson wrote by collecting and composing "specimens," he could not see writing simply as the direct expression of ideas and the recording of information. Nor could he envision a sequence of sentences or paragraphs in the ordinary sense of one point adding to another in a steady accumulation of argument. Rather, natural science gave Emerson the key to treating his prose poetically, which is to say "ecstatically"—not embellishing or sentimentalizing it, but fixing on the invisible *verses,* as it were, within and between each prose statement: the beautiful turns, aversions, transitions, and removes that made up the implicit "history" of any textual specimen, however large or small its ostensible scale.

Looking for the innate turns or removes within prose specimens and then composing larger prose units by virtue of the standard of such turns was a practice as scientific as it was poetic; indeed, in Emerson's view science and poetry were products of the same imaginative discipline, that of "conversing with the cause of nature." Emerson began to arrive at his special form of prose poetry, his own "metre-making argument," when he began to see his writing quite self-consciously in terms of practices recognized as belonging to both natural history and criticism: practices in which fresh insight derived from relentless work of detachment, analysis, and classification.

Comparative Anatomy

> So the great word Comparative Anatomy has now leaped out of the womb of the Unconscious. I feel a cabinet in my mind unlocked by each of these new interests. Wherever I go, the related objects crowd on my Sense & I explore backward & wonder how the same things looked to be before my attention had been aroused.
>
> —Emerson, *Journals* (1837)

Natural history taught Emerson to treat the fragments of his own writing as natural objects and to see them constituted by the same sort of "history" as that exposed in natural subject matter. The same insight extended to his treatment of the impressive productions of others. Soon after returning to America, Emerson crystallized a thought that would inform his later calls for a self-reliant criticism. In a journal entry quoted in part earlier, he declares that appreciating the technical means behind all composition (material as well as textual) destroys the aura of authority possessed by even the most brilliantly rounded-off objects:

A ship, a locomotive, a cotton factory is a wonder until we see how these Romes were built not in a day but part suggested part & complexity became simplicity. The poem, the oration, the book are superhuman, but the wonder is out when you see the manuscript. Homer how wonderful until the German erudition discovered a cyclus of homeric poems. It is all one; a trick of cards, a juggler's sleight, an astronomical result, an algebraic formula, amazing when we see only the result, cheap when we are shown the means. This it is to conceive of acts & works, to throw myself into the object so that its history shall naturally evolve itself before me. Well so does the Universe, Time, History, evolve itself, so simply, so unmiraculously from the All Perceiving Mind. (*JMN* 4:285)

In England and on his return voyage, Emerson had recently been impressed by the industrial products his passage names. Here he considers a means of undoing that impression, as well as the even stronger impression made by "superhuman" literary objects. The functional unity of such objects, it seems, condenses and conceals the outlines of their technical development over time.[8] What is striking about this point is not that Emerson treats powerful contemporary objects as products of a developmental history, but that history turns out to be the effect of a concealed but nevertheless contemporary process of composition. History is a matter of means rather than background; it comprises the working anatomy of the object. Similarly, the historical determinations of literary texts—genre, influence, tradition—appear as working features of compositional mechanisms, "parts" concealed or cast into dark background by the tricky veneer of the finished object. Emerson's critical eye takes over the "All Perceiving" ability of the Christian God, penetrating the specious integrity of surfaces to mark the numerous, perhaps contradictory devices that make up objects of powerful integrity. The outlines of device discernible in any such object suggest not miracles or irreversible tradition but our own practical possibilities.

As opposed to devised objects, however, device itself is invisible; and special techniques are needed to illustrate it to the reading eye. Emerson found these demonstrated everywhere in the Muséum. Its zeal for visual presentation, for *exposing* the natural order, stood in proportion to the degree of invisibility involved in the whole structure of nature. As opposed to the splendid multitude of colors, textures, shapes, and sizes presented in the Muséum, the classifications themselves, from the species all the way to the order, were imaginable only as outlines or conceptual boxes. This created a practical challenge for the naturalist, whose job entailed "showing" as well as "finding" the truth about nature. Herbaria, natural history catalogs (with or without engravings), botanical gardens, zoological cabinets, and menageries were all technical solutions to this double problem of finding and showing. The Muséum itself was such a solution, as a whole and in every part. Through the techniques of its various exhibition media, invisible forms of classifications attained democratic visibility. Wall cases, display tables, plant beds, groups of zoo cages, the very books in the library—these devices framed particular collocations of specimens, and so worked like transparent windows through which a visitor such as Emerson could "see" families, orders, and classes.[9]

Cuvier and Jussieu, the two naturalists most responsible for the overall look of the Muséum exhibitions in 1833, had been primarily interested in higher classifications, rather than in genera, species, and varieties. Though these higher classes were present and, to the naturalist, legible in single natural organisms, they could most clearly be shown by juxtaposing a number of representative members. The right arrangements could make ordinary specimens into means for extraordinary insight.

Let me take an example. In *The Animal Kingdom,* a textbook whose classificatory sequences were repeated and illustrated in the Muséum's zoological cabinets, Cuvier presents three families of living and fossil genera comprising the rather small, sketchily defined order of Edentata (Order VI of the class Mammalia). On first glance these three families seem quite different: Tardigrada (sloths); Edentata Ordinaria (armadillos, anteaters, pangolins); and Monotremata (echidnas and platypuses). Cuvier outlines the affinities that unite these families into the common order: "The Edentata, or quadrupeds without front teeth, will form our last order of unguiculated [having claws or nails] animals. Although united by a character purely negative, they have, nevertheless, some positive mutual relations, and particularly large nails, which embrace the extremities of the toes, approaching more or less to the nature of hoofs: a slowness, a want of agility, obviously arising from the peculiar organization of their limbs."[10]

It is difficult, if not impossible, to imagine directly the obscure type Cuvier describes, particularly since the chief "character" marking the order is the lack of an anatomical feature present in other orders; but the Muséum's methods of exhibition solved the problem of invisibility in two ways. Preserved specimens from the order were juxtaposed, in families, in the glass-doored armoires that lined the walls of the Cabinet; thus the visitor could see the obvious affinities between, say, an armadillo and a pangolin. But the Cabinet also brought the invisible natural order into conceptual visibility by another, higher juxtaposition. This consisted in the arrangement of the labeled armoires themselves. A proper arrangement of armoires served as a vivid emblem, a kind of scriptive enactment, of the higher classification.

Emerson was speaking as a reader of such composite emblems when he testified to the sublime effect "as you glance along this bewildering series of animated forms" (*JMN* 4:199). Glancing from one armoire to another meant passing through the genera and families; entire orders could be gathered up in a coup d'œil. In successive heightenings of perspective, the spectator's eye traced a passage analogous to the intellectual procedure by which the higher categories had been discovered. What bewildered Emerson's glance was not a lack of order, but rather its serial profusion; not opacity, but rather an excess of clarity.

The Muséum did not stop with the exterior forms of animals in demonstrating its techniques of analysis and comparison. In Cuvier's Cabinet of Comparative Anatomy, on the ground floor of the main building, the spectator could visually "find" (or be shown) classific characters even in the normally hidden interiors of animals. Arrangements of skeletons and of preserved organs let the visitor follow the process of abstraction, the leap from the visible to the invisible, by which Cuvier had composed his natural classes. The skeletons, Emerson reported to a lyceum audience, made "a perfect series from the skeleton of the *balaena* which reminds every one of the frame of a schooner, to the upright form and highly developed skull of the Caucasian race of man" (*EL* 1:9). Comparing the gap-toothed skulls of animals as superficially dissimilar as a sloth and a platypus, visitors could see how the characteristic features of an order such as Edentata had been derived: how the naturalist had begun by methodically choosing and abstracting such invariable affinities to form a higher classification; then how the naturalist had repeated the operation of selection and abstraction to form even higher classifications.

A crucial lesson lies in the way these means of exhibition, especially the armoires, made people "see." The primary aim of juxtaposing specimens behind the glass was to clarify their classification to the viewer; the mere curiousness of the exotic specimens was tangential to this aim. The spectator managed to "see" the classification not simply by looking at the specimens themselves but by looking, as it were, *through* them to the higher idea that contained them. There was always, in other words, an element of conceptual depth to the pagelike exhibition arrangements. The classification was the point: it lay on an invisible plane "behind" or "before" examples of its elements.

The clearest visual analogue to the classification consisted not in the contents on display but in the vehicle of display—the glass-covered casket of the armoire. Thus the armoire's presentation of the zoological family was in fact a complex image of the way classification produces the invisible out of the visible: the container displayed its elements; but then the elements "showed" the visitor what held them together—the classification that the (now rehollowed) rectangular box represented. The visitor was required, in a sense, to imagine the box empty in order to grasp the reality of its perceptible fullness. Cuvier's armoires revealed transparent orders nesting between the human eye and the animal body; they were materializations not just of natural history catalogs but of the recursive, depth-making compositional principle of natural history itself. They charted a natural world whose apparent surfaces were only an index to what could be "seen."

The Muséum showed how visible things could be put together; just as important, it showed how they could be taken apart with precisely the same results. As Emerson frequently noted, the relationship of composition and analysis was one principle that itself could not be dissected: "To separate & to knit up are two inseparable acts of life; it is forbidden to go out of the All into the particular, or out of the particular into the All & the more strictly these functions of the Spirit like inspiring & expiring breath, unite, the better for science & its lovers" (*JMN* 12:118).

Emerson's inspection of internal animal features in the Cabinet of Comparative Anatomy was no less a revelation of classificatory depth than his tour of the zoological and mineralogical cabinets. Indeed, the Cabinet of Comparative Anatomy was the nucleus of Cuvier's exposition of the animal kingdom. As Deleuze's guidebook pointed out, "the exterior forms are but a development of interior organization"; hence "it is in anatomy that one must search for principles."[11]

The catalog of anatomical preparations at the time of Cuvier's death in 1832 gives a sense of the prodigious range of the spectacle: 2,625 entire skeletons; 2,150 skulls; 249 myological preparations; 1,867 sets of viscera; 1,437 sense organs; 479 genital organs; 878 fetuses; 197 monsters.[12] An array of wax models of organs supplemented the preserved specimens. Display of these interior forms showed that yet another realm had been mined by the intellectual technologies of natural history. The deeper into the organism one ventured to see, the more evident became the specimen's membership in larger classifications.

ↂ ↂ ↂ

A crucial question arises in regard to the place of organic "life" in the Muséum. After all, the organism itself (unless it was fortunate enough to be selected for the menagerie or botanical gardens) had to be dissected, preserved, and encased for display. Scientific focus excavated not only the space between the eye and its objects, but also the dark, visceral reality of its objects. In "Intellect," Emerson suggested that any intellectual object, insofar as it served the practice of writing, had to undergo a similar process of purification and memorialization:

> [A] truth, separated by the intellect, is no longer a subject of destiny. We behold it as a god upraised above care and fear. And so any fact in our life, or any record of our fancies or reflections, disentangled from the web of our unconscious, becomes an object impersonal and immortal. It is the past restored, but embalmed. A better art than that of Egypt has taken fear and corruption out of it. It is eviscerated of care. It is offered for science. (*CW* 2:194)

Here Emerson gives us a view of the natural history of his journal specimens, whose fate is to be denatured and classified within a museumlike institution of writing. Composition, like natural history, aims to keep what it transforms; and in curing its materials of mortal idiosyncrasy it must turn to techniques comparable to those of taxidermy and herbarium preparation. The "fact" or "record" sheds the pathos of mortality as Emerson presses it into his journal; he offers this sacrifice for the sake of a model of wholeness more truly answerable to the demands of life at large. Whereas the specimen's former life issued from a dark, visceral nucleus, its "restored" life obtains wholly in relation to the outlines of other things—all subject to the vital regard of the scientific eye. Life, or the sense in which life matters, is clarified by Emerson's scientific sacrament rather than lost to it.

Even so, the costs of clarification prove to be somewhat as dear as its benefits. The passage from "Intellect" points back to Emerson's chilling explanation, in *Nature,* of the death of his brother Charles, who began by seeming a part of Emerson, but then, "when he has . . . become an object of thought, and, whilst his character retains all its unconscious effect, is converted in the mind into solid and sweet wisdom,—it is a sign to us that his office is closing." Objectifying Charles and converting him into wisdom were stages in a process of disentanglement or intellectual digestion, a process automatically working to undo everything in love's bond that was visceral and un-chosen. The final stage of disentanglement took place when the loved object was "withdrawn" from sight into the enabling space of his transparency. In this case, the transparent "office" of the dead turns out to be a kind of negative monument, a commemorative that nev-ertheless declines any obeisance to the unique image that had com-pelled love. In *Nature,* we learn again what Emerson learned in the Muséum about nature: that death is only another term for an object's having been turned thoroughly to use in the fatal project of illus-trating higher life. This hardly suggests that death is trivial or cheaply fictitious for Emerson; rather it affirms that death, like every fact in nature, "is good only in so far as it serves."

Like all the disciplines at the Muséum, comparative anatomy worked both analytically and genetically, breaking open individuals in order to build up classifications higher than individuals. It mur-dered to dissect, but then it restored the prospect of a larger life that "grew" by classification. The imperatives of intellectual growth, dic-tated by absolute life, crossed out the relative claims of individual attachment. Emerson is, of course, notorious for the detachment he attributes to himself in regard to the deaths of his dearest objects. His critics revert inevitably to the passage at the beginning of "Ex-perience" where he assesses the death of his firstborn in impersonal terms of investment and bankruptcy: "I seem to have lost a beautiful estate,—no more. I cannot get it nearer to me" (*CW* 3:29). Rarely noted, however, is the way Emerson also accounts for his son's death in biological terms of his own growth or, more exactly, of his own production and abandonment of leaves: "It does not touch me: some thing which I fancied was a part of me, which could not be torn away without tearing me, nor enlarged without enriching me, falls off from me, and leaves no scar. It was caducous."

"Caducous" (from Latin for falling) describes those early leaves that fall away in a plant's growth; by the same figure, it can describe early organs, such as a tadpole's gills, cast off in metamorphosis. Recapitulationist embryology held that organisms grow caducously into life as the embryo mounts through more primitive stages en route to its own specific form, shedding the marks of earlier classific identities at each developmental crossover. In the passage from "Experience," Emerson depicts biological growth and critical elevation as versions of the same process. The effect of this combination is not that life is rendered hollow and abstract so much as that elevation itself, with all its hollowings and removals, comes to seem a process of life. The scientific or critical logic of transparency Emerson expounds in *Nature* obtains relentlessly in "Experience": the "thing" that seemed a part of him was by nature already aimed, like every other thing, to fulfill or open up the office of the specimen. Even the dearest thing departs from him as another of his leaves, another page out of life— a leave-taking as well as a leaf remade, pressed and dried on another page in the museum of writing.

Placing death wholly within the terms of critical enterprise was a major corollary of Emerson's decision to rewrite the texture of experience through the poetics of natural history. The scientific conversion of a given thing into a specimen, cured into a representative of its class, became a paradigm for reading all useful crises as special instances of the same pattern of critical removal—of caducous "leaving" as a consequence of abandoning old objects while at the same time generating new subject matter. This was the pattern by which Emerson defined experience as experiment, a pattern repeating itself in conversions of unconscious acts into conscious thoughts, of thoughts into textual specimens, of specimens into higher textual wholes. This was also the pattern of deeds by which parts of given life were placed in a museum, where as specimens they acquired "life" of a new kind. By virtue of this paradigm, even the most ordinary conversion appeared to retrace the sacramental passage from life to death—or, in the Pauline sense Emerson liked to invoke, from corruption to incorruption:

> It is curious to observe how strangely experience becomes thought or life, truth. The conversion is hourly going on. Will & Necessity, or, if you please character & condition beget an act. It is a part of life & remains for a time immersed in our unconscious life being more or less a source of pleasure & pain. In some intellectual hour it detaches itself like a ripe fruit from the life to become a treasure of the mind. Instantly it is raised & transfigured. The corruptible has put on incorruption. Always now it is an object of beauty however base its origin & neighborhood. (*JMN* 5:320–321)

We cannot tell, in the "intellectual hour," whether the object rises and departs from the critical observer or whether the observer rises and departs from the object. In any case, the object instantly becomes something both old and new. Life transpires, and on one side *expires*, in the achievement of new focus. The spontaneous, generative spark of life resides in the crossover between speculative removes, in a crisis of aspiration itself unavailable to observation yet also ungraspable in terms of anything beyond a series of specialized observations. Hence the quick of life passes insensibly into science, while out of scientific abandon come new objects for one's own renewing life. Emerson's passage continues:

> So there is no fact, no event, how intimate, how great soever in our history, which shall not sooner or later lose its adhesive inert form, & astonish & rejoice us by soaring from our body into the Empyrean. Cradle & infancy, school & playground, the fear of boys & dogs, the love of little maids & berries, & many another once absorbing fact are gone already; friend & relative, party & profession, Boston & Concord, country, wife, child, & world must also soar & sing.

It is endlessly surprising, when contemplating this or any of Emerson's stories of death, how Emerson insists on accounting for fatal events—events we think of as blindly "befalling" us—as parts of a pattern of his own experimental activity. It suggests that we find useful meaning in things, even the most extreme things, only when we somehow affirm responsibility for them. The egotism of total responsibility would seem the province of the saint or the paranoid. For

Emerson, limitless responsibility falls also on the scientific eye—and not in spite of observational detachment but precisely because of it.

In the above journal entry of 1837, the fatal conversion of loved objects becomes a critical deed, perhaps a master technique, that sustains an ongoing process of composition. Emerson's museum, it seems, subsumes all life and experience. As with any project of natural history, it must preserve the organic material it transforms if it hopes to make a display of its insights. Thus Emerson describes a fatal "soaring" that strangely forces together forgetfulness and memorialization: those "facts" in his list of biographical leavings, ranging from the mundane to the calamitous, are preserved to just the extent they are abandoned. Finding their place in the empyrean, in the blindness of pure light, they abide in transparency, which is the technology of keeping them as means while letting them go as objects.

Even more strangely (and in a manner recalling Shelley and anticipating Whitman), these very human facts blow off like dead leaves from Emerson's "body." For all Emerson's focal detachment from his body—in *Nature* he consigns it to the specimen world of the "Not Me"—it is only in fresh embodiments that self can grow. Once again this brings to mind "The Lord's Supper," where in the autumn of 1832 Emerson repudiated the Eucharist by declaring, "The form out of which life and suitableness have departed should be as worthless in its eyes as the dead leaves that are falling around us" (*W* 11:21). He later made the same point even more magisterially in "Experience": "The great and crescive self, rooted in absolute nature, supplants all relative existence and ruins the kingdom of mortal friendship and love." In a growing body, the ineffable principle of life performs the transubstantiations of experience and keeps filling its museum.

∾ ∾ ∾

Emerson's startling readiness to treat biological growth and critical elevation as features of the same process carries into literature a strain of thought central to the displays he beheld at the Jardin des Plantes. The thought was that life formations, whether in ontogenetic development or in the hierarchical relations between lower and higher taxa, relied on technical patterns with which a true "natural classification" might coincide isomorphically. Biological life was not reducible to its ideal formations, but it was nevertheless conceivable only as something happening instrumentally in regard to those formations.

The same would hold for a criticism coincident with life, whether that criticism were scientific or literary: its efforts would transpire, as Emerson says power does, "in the transition from an old to a new state," in the leap to a new classification, in the encirclement of a new prospect. Whether in the abstract mappings of taxonomy or in the minute dissections of comparative anatomy, the vital principle performs its crossovers through enactments of design. For both natural history and literature, this complicates any easy dualism between life and its forms, between nature and artifice, or between meaning and its vessels. It is crucial to see, as Emerson did, that compositional technique, with all its boundaries and inhibitions, abides with life in the endlessly receding vital point on which the critical or scientific eye focuses. This same insight helps to show how the Muséum offered him an especially powerful revision of the romantic ideal of the organic text. Far from being the sort of textual organism whose literal formations were "expressed" continuously from a transcendental vital core, the Muséum (which looked aptly like a book rather than a plant) was an institution where organic "facts" were identified, cured, and recomposed. Like the very world it epitomized, it was a scene, wholly inclusive but open to new realization at every point, where natural history, as a science and as a criticism, might endlessly take place.

When we think about natural history before Darwin—or, for that matter, about romantic organicism—it is hard to dispel the dualistic opposition between life and form (or meaning and sign) by which "expressive" models for natural production or for literary representation have most often been propounded. This is largely because we tend to fabricate rather simple backgrounds to help leverage the task of getting hold of complex new theories. Paul de Man resorted to a flattened simplification of Coleridge's idea of organic semiosis in order to draw, more efficiently if not more persuasively, a new picture of the terms governing literary representation. In a similar way, the task of understanding Darwin's truly revolutionary theory (a task not fully accomplished, even in professional biology, until the middle of the twentieth century) has prompted facile reductions of the complex capability of pre-evolutionist natural history.

Michel Foucault, who does not claim to expound Darwin, has argued that Cuvier's anatomical method led natural history to confront a central organic reality, a core of undifferentiated vitality that was the basis for all classifications but that was itself unclassifiable. This is Foucault expounding Cuvier:

> Animal species differ at their peripheries, and resemble each other at their centers; they are connected by the inaccessible, and separated by the apparent. Their generality lies in that which is essential to their life; their singularity is that which is most accessory to it. The more extensive the groups one wishes to find, the deeper one must penetrate into the organism's inner darkness, towards the less and less visible, into that dimension that eludes perception; the more one wishes to isolate the individuality of the organism, the further one must go towards its surface, and allow the perceptible forms to shine in all their visibility; for multiplicity is apparent and unity is hidden.[13]

Foucault's idea that comparative anatomy established "life" as a central principle in contrast to all exterior classifications links Cuvier with familiar currents in romanticism and ultimately, Foucault suggests, with Darwin. But Foucault's emanative scheme overlooks something important about the displays at the Muséum, and about pre-Darwinian biology in general. The classificatory "depths" revealed by looking inside the animal *duplicated* the classifications that could also be shown by grouping the animal with other animals, and then by grouping the higher group with other higher groups. (Agassiz would argue that a like recapitulation of the animal's classificatory identity was evident in the successive stages of its embryonic development.) The surface of the animal body was not, as Foucault would have it, simply a degree on the scale of unity and individuation (with the transcendent zero degree hidden in the body's vital core); rather the body's surface was the starting point from which classification could take its departure in two directions with identical results.

One of these correspondent lines of departure was illustrated by the arrangements of armoires in the zoological cabinet; it proceeded outward, disclosing a hierarchy of classes by juxtaposing one animal body with others. The other way was made plain in the Cabinet of Comparative Anatomy; it proceeded into the animal's interior, uncovering organic characteristics that signified increasingly general functions and hence the animal's membership in increasingly general classes. In either direction, expanding outward or penetrating inward, the naturalist scaled the classificatory hierarchy. The ultimate landing place in the hierarchy was indeed that of biological or biotextual unity, the "book of nature" itself. Far from being an unresolvable essence, however, "unity" was nothing other than the highest classification. Later, in "Circles," Emerson pushed such realism into a skeptical nominalism by suggesting that the highest classification is, after all, only the most recent.

Once again classification leads into the realm of immediate practice. Instead of displacing or offering an alternative to the authority of classification in natural history, *l'anatomie comparée* extended the frontiers of the classifiable into what had seemed alien and exotic regions. The Muséum showed its public that the outlines of intellectual technologies could be traced beneath the body's visible surface, as if they had always been hidden there.[14] This extension of compositional forms and devices into the recesses of nature had the effect not of reducing the mystery of organic life to a static map, nor of subordinating classification to a principle of organic vitality, but of exhibiting the terrific power that lay within the technologies belonging to the naturalist. This was a power that in its most extreme demonstrations, challenged the priority of organic life itself.

We can understand, then, how Emerson managed to be overwhelmed by a sense of "the upheaving principle of life everywhere" in spite of the fact that most of what was "natural" in the Muséum was desiccated, stuffed, entombed behind glass, suspended in vinegar, or pressed onto a page. Life had not departed but had been magnified by translation into its "principle," into the wheels of classes illustrated everywhere. Emerson realized in the Muséum that nature *was* natural history. It was fitting, then, that he should come upon the "upheaving principle of life" not in the woods or at Walden Pond, but in a foreign metropolis, in the sophisticated devices of an international discipline.

The Opening of Method

> Memory is a presumption of a possession of the future. Now we are halves, we see the past but not the future, but in that day will the hemisphere complete itself and foresight be as perfect as aftersight.
>
> —Emerson, "Natural History of Intellect"

Emerson began a far-ranging inquiry into the subject of classification immediately on his return to America, in October 1833. His reading covered a multitude of books on natural history, including works by Cuvier, DeCandolle, Haüy, Humboldt, Playfair, Geoffroy Saint-Hilaire, and at least one account of Goethe's biological speculations. Emerson also returned to a text he had known since 1826: Coleridge's "Essays on the Principles of Method" at the end of *The Friend*. Coleridge was particularly influential in guiding Emerson's new determination to build a bridge between scientific and literary composition.

In the "Essays on the Principles of Method," Coleridge explored a question of first importance for his own project of universal representation, the magnum opus. The question was this: How is the vital principle that organizes and directs a representational system itself to be found manifested within that system? The question pertained to both the origin and fate of any systematic text. In regard to the magnum opus, Coleridge's "Essays" were, of course, entirely provisional: they were the theory of an adequate theory, the proposition rather than the employment of true method. But their extravagant proposals suggested a link between the infinite desires of poetic imagination and the practical methods of natural science.

In a spirit corresponding to the ambitions of the Muséum, Coleridge asked his readers to assume that "the productive power . . . in nature, as nature, is essentially one (i.e. of one kind) with the intelligence which is in the human mind above nature."[15] This daring assumption anticipated the claims Agassiz would later make for his project of natural classification: that when the intellect attains knowledge by systematic study of the natural world, it doubles—or doubles back over—the work of the supernatural creator of that world. True criticism, for Coleridge, had to catch up and unite with active creation.

Activity, transit, progression—these were key criteria for Coleridge's methodical path. Abiding in divine practices, showing itself in deeds rather than in static being, the same creative power was at work both in the natural world and, above it, in the domain of critical recovery. Consequently, mere knowledge *of* something was pointless. Knowledge had to participate or join forces with the active presence of its natural subject matter, precisely in Emerson's sense of "assimilation" to the "ecstasy" of the object. In natural history terms, it might be said that, in Coleridge's theory, real knowledge recovered the "history" immanent in its object, a dynamic history that was the real reflection of the project of knowing. Instead of a system of merely correspondential knowledge, then, the prescription emerging from Coleridge's "Essays" was for an ongoing process of interpretation and recomposition, an ecstatic method of knowing rather than a mapping of static objective contents.

In line with the dynamic stress of the "Essays," Coleridge insisted on the "progressive" nature of knowledge—the way the mind rises through a hierarchy of ideas rather than simply increasing the quantity of recorded data—and hence paid attention to methods of classifying objects, of crystallizing networks of relations under elevated perspectives. "Method," he wrote, "implies a *progressive transition* . . . literally *a way,* or *path of Transit*"; method is "the power in the mind to classify or appropriate" events and images.[16] One of the many places where Emerson echoes Coleridge's point is found in "Spiritual Laws": "A man is a method, a progressive arrangement; a selecting principle, gathering his like to him, wherever he goes. He takes only his own, out of the multiplicity that sweeps and circles round him" (*CW* 2:84).

Coleridge's stress on vertical transit, on rising from inferior to superior classifications, points to precisely the sort of hierarchical bridgings invoked in his definition of the symbol in *The Stateman's Manual.* As I have noted, the "translucence" of the Coleridgean symbol—the shining-through "of the Special in the Individual or of the General in the Especial"—makes the symbol a call to classification. In the moment of translucence, the leap to a new classification, the symbol exchanges its opacity for the light of a higher idea. The Coleridgean symbol, which is a "specimen" lambent with the promise of enlightenment, shows how natural objects can be assimilated to the classifying eye. Classification disposes of the world systematically, analyzing and enumerating relations between things, and relations between relations. Such an act does combine knowledge with creation, for it offers to bring together knowing and naming; it offers to unite critical insight with new, more comprehensive exposition.

Emerson's revelation at the Jardin des Plantes, as he quickly came to understand it, was percolated through Coleridge's influence. But the full importance of natural history to Emerson's literary self-invention emerges only when we also understand that the reverse was just as much the case. While Emerson had read deeply in Coleridge before his European tour, it was only after dedicating himself to the ministry of science that he managed to take possession of Coleridge in the clearest and most useful sense.

Emerson's takeover of Coleridge's metaphor of transparency, commencing after his return to America, is a particularly decisive example of his rediscovery or reinvention of Coleridge's romantic legacy. As was true in the zoological cabinet (and as I shall point out in regard to the botanical gardens), the Muséum's displays demonstrated how transparency, which for Coleridge signaled a sheerly hermeneutical event, might also serve as a principle of practical composition. Emersonian transparency was born in the Jardin des Plantes as an image of the *production* of nature's text as well as an image of the terms for reading it.

In a larger and correspondent sense, natural history made it possible for Emerson to foresee a way of practically negotiating, if not reconciling, the massive contrariety in Coleridge between whole ambition and literal fragmentation. For a literary latecomer such as Emerson, this same contrariety ran like a crack through the entire monument of the romantic dispensation. If Emerson could see the fragments of his own literary corpus as corresponding to the facts of nature, and if he could conceive of subjecting those literary fragments to the dissolving, diffusing, and reuniting practices belonging to the naturalist, then indeed it would be possible to imagine a work of writing that would "compose" all fragments in clear regard to the whole, yet do so without blurring over the pointed outlines of their individual natures. Given Coleridge's role in consolidating and disseminating European romanticism, and given Emerson's unrivaled role as founder within the American tradition, I would submit that natural history, as Emerson seized upon it, was one of the major means by which romanticism, already run to seed in England and Europe, was not merely imported but naturalized, scientifically "restored," on American grounds.

∾ ∾ ∾

This question of Coleridge's influence and Emerson's American foundation brings me to a place where clear boundaries are hard to maintain. Emerson touches on it in *English Traits* when he rather dryly concedes that "the American is only the continuation of the English genius into new conditions, more or less propitious" (*CW*

5:19). Here the word "propitious" seems to substitute for a more defining word, like "proper," keeping the decisive effect of America's new conditions up in the air. Emerson's remark leaves the frontier tentatively open between Old and New World genius, though replete with better and worse prospects for closure. For a while at least, we must be willing to get lost on this open frontier before we can overlook it from a useful perspective. It is the frontier defining America; and our ultimate view of it, like Emerson's, will necessarily partake of the perspective of natural history.

Considering the high degree to which Emerson's project was shaped by European romantic principles, the issue of his founding an original American literature is bound to be vexed with ironies. Similar ironies will attend any historical account of what is newly or natively American in Emerson's legacy. The recently renewed interest in Emerson's work has followed on the heels of a critical movement that discovered powerful and surprising things to say about European romanticism. Indeed, the chief figure of the latter movement, Harold Bloom, has been largely responsible for reestablishing Emerson, for American critics, as a writer who stands capably, even centrally, in the high ground occupied by the men he visited in Britain: Wordsworth, Coleridge, and Carlyle. The transatlantic pathways opened up (though not necessarily explored) by recent criticism make it more readily possible to find, at least in outline, most of Emerson's mature stances of self-reliance and orphic originality already prescribed in the work of his romantic forebears. All this makes the issue of Emerson's foundational role in American literary life a more complex one, as the boundaries between what Emerson founded and what he imported become harder to see.

Ironically, these boundaries seem all the more porous when Emerson sounds the most nationalistic. In Coleridge, especially, Emerson discovered arguments that would inform the heart of his famous summons to the sleeping American imagination. Eulogizing Coleridge in 1836, Emerson acknowledged that "the piercing sight which made the world transparent to him" (*EL* 1:380) also forced Coleridge, against his crustier opinions, toward a more general, "republican" stress on the self-relying disclosures of individuals: "His eye was fixed upon Man's Reason as the faculty in which the very Godhead manifested itself or the Word was anew made flesh. His reverence for the Divine Reason was truly philosophical and made him regard every man as the most sacred object in the Universe, the Temple of Deity. An aristocrat in his politics, this most republican of all principles secured his unaffected interest in lowly and despised men the moment a religious sentiment or a philosophical principle appeared" (378).

Emerson's point is finely accurate as a description of both Coleridge's and his own central arguments; it also testifies to the English writer's "continuation" in Emerson's prophetic vision even in moments when that vision seems most directly focused on America. With the same Coleridgean insight, for example, "The American Scholar" urges its audience toward a self-reliance in which political and literary identity might coincide: "Every thing that tends to insulate the individual,—to surround him with barriers of natural respect, so that each man shall feel the world is his, and man shall treat with man as a sovereign state with a sovereign state;—tends to true union as well as greatness" (*CW* 1:68). Just as European epistemology and political theory had backed up America's arguments for independence, so European romanticism, with Coleridge as its major exponent, laid the ground for Emerson's calls for American literary originality.

Beyond Coleridge, the urgent need articulated to Americans by Emerson—the need to recover an authentically native literary voice, yet a voice ultimately capable of enacting meanings transcendent of all fixed locality—was itself a principle emblazoned in romantic tradition by Wordsworth. Wordsworth's devotion to native place worked to cultivate an indigenous English muse; yet the genius of insular places led him to the brinks of sublime prospects in which all particularity of place either vanished entirely or threatened to do so in the revelation of a wholly unlocalizable imaginative power. Emerson ultimately saw a democratic tendency informing this pattern, as devotion to native place leads to impersonal, supranational vision: "See distinctly, that it is not insulation of place, but independence of spirit that is essential, and it is only as the garden, the cottage, the forest, and the rock are a sort of mechanical aids to this, that they are of value. Think alone, and all places are friendly and sacred" (109).

Wordsworth, of course, would have shuddered at such detachment, insisting that the universal sense was "deeply interfused" with native or natural place; still, the excursions in which he found larger sense showed that his vision was essentially portable. One might say that Coleridge, in his prose, elaborated the unlocalizable imaginative outlooks in Wordsworth into the more universal and encyclopedic project of "method." In doing so, Coleridge established a procedure that was European (it was as much German as English) only in the geographical traces of its discovery, but not in its prospects.

The fact that Wordsworth's and Coleridge's visionary outlooks were also matters of individual, "egotistical" realization shows these poets to be the prophets of a new kind of heroism or nobility. For Emerson, who advocated democracy on the basis of the common but Olympian nobility of every individual, this was precisely where romanticism spoke to the heart of both democracy and America. The sixty-year lapse between the founding of American political independence and Emerson's first calls for literary independence reflects a constitutional distinction between the founding arguments available for import. Romantic vision offered a new alternative to the Lockean contractualism that lay behind the famous rationale for American political independence. For Thomas Jefferson and the signers of the Declaration, the issue had rested on the putative violation of a contract based on natural law. America's struggle against England, as they justified it, aimed not so much at founding something new as it did at restoring obedience to a social contract that had always obtained, even if it had not been always respected. Independence was a means to this end, not an end in itself.

The natural basis for a restored social contract was the premise of equality, a premise self-evident to reason and to common sense. Coleridge and Emerson, however, celebrated reason as a new event, an eye-opening revelation akin to religious influx and conferring on the receiver the certainties of prophecy rather than of deduction. Emerson staked his vision of democratic equality on the authority of such prophetic moments, which were in themselves "superior" or noble. These were moments of self-creation, when independence constituted its own ends, and only as such were they moments of being fully equal to the work of national creation. For Emerson, both America and *being an American* were freshly born out of such moments, which promised to return again and again without foreseeable end:

> But every insight from this realm of thought is felt as initial, and promises a sequel. I do not make it; I arrive there, and behold what was there already. I make! O no! I clap my hands in infantine joy and amazement, before the first opening to me of this august magnificence, old with the love and homage of innumerable ages, young

with the life of life, the sunbright Mecca of the desert. And what a future it opens! I feel a new heart beating with the love of the new beauty. I am ready to die out of nature, and be born again into this new yet unapproachable America I have found in the West. (*CW* 3:41)

In this passage from "Experience," it is hard not to hear (and hard to hear) the ominous prediction of another great literary moment two decades later—Lincoln's vision, in the ripe ruin of Gettysburg, of "a new birth of freedom." Following Emerson, romantic rebirth in America meant being born again into literature, or into essentially literary self-creations, whether of individuals or of political regions, that may well have taken forms irreconcilable with one another. This suggests a dynamic politics based not on common sense so much as on the power, which all have in common, for superior sense.

It is disappointing to see the second birth Lincoln hoped for in Reconstruction or in the Gilded Age. I would rather think that Lincoln's hope was already founded for Americans in the literary urgencies of romantic rebirth, where union could hold by force of insight or necessity rather than by the suasions of common sense. I would rather think of it in regard to the West than in terms of North or South. In any case, during the antebellum time before the nation's hopes had to be raised on literal ruins, Emerson saw the West not as Kansas and Nebraska but as the open prospect of creation demanding a self equal to its work. Being equal to nature, this self would be equal as well to other selves; it would be the first stake in a system of political equality enforced by independence and respect rather than deduced from the hypothesis of automatic human sameness.

∾ ∾ ∾

We cannot easily wrap Emerson in the epic mantle of Cadmus or Aeneas. If his aims for genuine foundation were complicated by the question of what he imported into America from Europe, it is also unclear that America, in the 1830s, was a place so "bare and bald" (*CW* 1:243) as to cry out for a new literary foundation. Emerson returned from Europe not to an empty or alien place but to an intellectual ground cultivated by two hundred years of the most restless speculation and self-redefinition. His own place within this culture, however humble in its beginnings, had been nevertheless at the center of things. After all, the pastorate he renounced was at the Second Church of Boston, the church of Cotton and Increase Mather. Emerson's step-grandfather, the minister Ezra Ripley—in whose Concord home Emerson began inventing the arguments of *Nature*—was an embodiment of his deep family background in New England religious traditions. And long into Emerson's career, his aunt Mary Moody Emerson was there to remind him of the intellectual vitality of his radical Protestant heritage. While one might well take exception to parts of Henry James's picture of Emerson as seamlessly of a piece with his New England context, James was right in saying, "It is impossible to imagine a spirit better prepared in advance to be exactly what it was—better educated for its office in its far-away unconscious beginnings."[17]

Early American cultural history, as opened by Perry Miller, assures us that America's imagination was quite firmly "founded" by 1833, even if its most sublime contemporary discipline, the discipline of political eloquence, was already struggling for its soul against the fragmenting forces that would soon render differing speakers deaf to one another's voices. Only a reader captured by nineteenth-century European judgments, or blinded by the originality of Emerson's later achievement, could deny that American literary life was complexly and, in its own terms, capably developed before Emerson's intervention. Indeed, Emerson's formative ambitions, the very ambitions that primed him for his conversion in the Jardin des Plantes, testify to the prior demand of his American context.

The busy fullness of the American scene cuts against Emerson's picture of his own emergence taking place in a context of emptiness. In a corresponding sense, his self-designation as a naturalist calls into question his famous attack on the vacuity of American art: "The mark of American merit in painting, in sculpture, in poetry, in fiction, in eloquence, seems to be a certain grace without grandeur, and itself not new but derivative; a vase of fair outline, but empty" (*CW* 1:100).

The commonplace notion that Jacksonian America, to cite Tocqueville, had "properly speaking, no literature," must be seen as the product of a dubious but instructive background.[18] Of course Emerson was the most famous advocate of this notion. Yet his professed contempt for "the empty American Parnassus" (*JMN* 9:51) was less the genuine property of Americans than of European commentators such as Tocqueville, Harriet Martineau, and Carlyle, who all measured American letters not just against the strengths of their own traditions but also against the romantic fantasy, deduced from Europe's own idealisms, that political democracy would quickly set free a brood of poetic giants.[19] Emerson's rousing call for native originality in the peroration of "The American Scholar"—"We have listened too long to the courtly muses of Europe" (*CW* 1:69)—echoed the critical courts of Europe, from which he had recently returned, just as much as it surged from the bare common of New England. And Emerson himself, on occasion, was quite capable of bristling at just the sort of European judgments that he, in other moods, would echo: "An honest man may, perhaps, wonder how, with so much to call forth congratulation, our lively visitors should be so merry and critical. Perhaps they have great need of a little holiday and diversion from their domestic cares, like other house-keepers who have a heavy time of it at home, and need all the refreshment they can get from kicking up their feet a little now that they have got away on a frolic" (242).

One lesson taught by the history of originality is that the outer limits of a writer's capacity to reinvent a tradition are set by the degree to which the writer is created by it; and one of the means by which Emerson broached his American limits, and founded his own originality, was in imagining himself stranded at the foot of an empty Parnassus. His aspersions of native poverty were themselves the products of an anxiously mature literary self-consciousness; they were, as Emerson said American literature was, thoroughly "in the optative mood" (207). Europe's naive disappointment in American letters gave Emerson a device for staging his own advent into native ground. This was the advent of American imagination into the home it already inhabited. Whereas Wordsworth and Coleridge had inaugurated *Lyrical Ballads* with the verdict that native imagination had died in England, Americans (Emerson was not the only one) owned the privilege of claiming that a truly American literature had yet to be born.

Of course, pointing to the kinship between these two enabling claims is hardly to suggest that European views cannot also be American views. It is the peculiar virtue of America, and of romanticism, that such can be precisely the case. The European echoes in Emerson's calls for a genuine national literature paradoxically make those calls more, not less, American. They emphasize, once again, the curious openness of the frontiers where American genius found the clearest images of itself.

Whatever Emerson hoped to found, he was in the difficult position of having to come home to do it. As the last paragraphs of *Nature*

attest, the new work he envisioned would all take place within re-
storative terms. His momentous return to America in 1833 hence
partook more of romance than of martial epic; like Odysseus, he
came home to set his house in proper or propitious order—his own
household of writing and, at least prospectively, the larger household
of American imagination. Emerson realized in Paris that this special
task of founding, of coming to see the New World through new eyes,
called for a "naturalist." Only natural history, a method incubated in
the Old World, could adequately restore the ground for a literary
discipline original to America.

Emerson recognized in natural history a supreme method for
working from the indefinite, propitious basis of American openness.
If American literature hoped to live up to the abstract and universal
ideals by which Americans had always insisted on conceiving their
republic, then it would have to take its subject matter—indeed, its
literary form—from realities that transcended merely native, or literally "American," conditions. In order to be American, literature
would have to be more than American. Emerson addressed this antithetical imperative when he proposed, in "The Naturalist," that the
best cure for the American disease of unoriginality, of sheepishly imitating European literary models, was the practice of natural history,
a science imported into America from Europe:

> Imitation is the vice eminently of our times, of our literature, of our
> manners and social action. All American manners, language, and
> writing are derivative ... Time will certainly cure us, probably
> through the prevalence of a bad party ignorant of all literature and
> of all but selfish, gross pursuits. But a better cure would be in the
> study of Natural History. Imitation is a servile copying of what is
> capricious as if it were permanent forms of Nature. The study of
> things leads us back to Truth, to the great Network of organized
> beings made of our own flesh and blood with kindred functions and
> related organs and one Cause. (*EL* 1:74–75)

Descent into ignorance and willful nearsightedness was certainly
one way to cure imitation. Emerson saw this happening under the
leadership of Andrew Jackson's "bad party," but he could hardly look
forward to the literary consequences of such a cure. False sophistication would be better cured by impersonal, scientific sophistication.
Natural history, wherever it originated, claimed to transcend the native limits of both the Old World and the New; it was a critical disci-

pline drained of whatever natively English qualities were left in Cole-ridge's romantic method. At the same time, it demanded that its practitioners hold hard to the most idiosyncratic native details. If to be American meant being more than American, and if this "more" was only to be found in regard to the stubborn details of native ground, natural history was the perfect model for a genuinely American literary practice.

Emerson recognized the opportunity presented by this model; and he made sure that followers such as Thoreau recognized it as well. Thoreau's dedication to a literary practice based on natural history derived from the Emersonian conviction that the common things in American nature could be realized *as American* only when turned to use as representative instances in a universal prospect. This involved more than eulogizing American nature as a special or privileged in-stance of the universal order; it involved converting nature as a whole into his own workshop, a democratic workshop where representation of universal significance was to be made by virtue of deliberately sci-entific focus.

∾ ∾ ∾

Emerson saw his way home from Europe in the Jardin des Plantes. It lay in the project of reconceiving, clarifying, the romantic pursuits that had taken him away from home in the first place. Surely it is curious, though, to suggest that natural science might have recom-mended taking a path to one place rather than to another. How could anywhere on earth be the native home to a practice that enlarged itself only in removal from visible nature, and that did so by selecting, eviscerating, hollowing things into intellectual horizons? Yet if the monumental project of natural history pointed back to any aboriginal grounds, these were not in Paris but in Emerson's New World.

Once again, it was a matter of origins mixing with destinations. Natural history, as Emerson found it, had been brought forth in the confrontation of the Old World with the New; in fact, it was one of the Old World's most complex and capable means of coming to ad-equate terms with the outlandishness of the New. From its beginnings in the early sixteenth century, systematic natural history grew along a course parallel to that of European exploration and colonial ex-pansion. The same enterprises bringing new raw materials from the New World to European economies also generated the import of masses of exotic plant specimens. (Extensive imports of animal specimens came much later, only after new taxidermical methods made storage for sea passage possible; this was a large reason for zoology's notable lag in development behind botany.) Their impact was staggering. In the century following their entry into America, Europeans found themselves having to account for more than twenty times as many plant species as they had known in their entire previous history.[20]

Whereas medieval botany had centered on finding and systematizing the medicinal uses of plants, this urgent press of New World species provoked new strains of focus that emphasized botanical classification as a subject in itself. Increasingly the primary meanings of a plant no longer derived from its effects on the human body; they derived instead from the plant's capacity for subordination to more abstract integrities. By virtue of the wildness of its subject matter, classification had become a discipline in its own right. So botanists devised ways of displaying classifications as well as plants: botanical gardens, or "Gardens of Eden," were created at Padua, Pisa, Bologna, and somewhat later in Paris. The rectangular perimeters of these classifying gardens emblemized not only the book of nature, but the four corners of an expanded and now at least prospectively encircled world.[21]

Empires have always opened themselves to surprise through what they bring home. When we look at history, it is sometimes exhilarating, sometimes dismaying, to see how far out of their way the home disciplines have often gone in order to tame the exotic backflow of imperial triumph. Certainly aspects of both defense and transformation informed the scientific shift of focus with which Europe responded to the New World. The point might be made, all too knowingly, that early natural science mainly offered to domesticate New World import according to Old World models, ensuring a degree of immunity against outlandish infection while encouraging further adventure. But if such domestication was defensive, it was a defense that also transformed the Old World *domus* in line with the outgoing pattern of its larger adventure: not only its exterior walls, but the citadel as a whole was rebuilt in anticipation of further surprise.

Classification, which addresses lateral increase of subject matter with unifying removes of perspective, emerged within the framework of natural science as an epitome of the aggressive-defensive activity being considered here. Classification became a concern that absorbed many of the practices, but few of the steady reassurances, that belonged to older disciplines of meaning and order; these included medicine, logic, scriptural hermeneutics, and, as it would turn out, political theory. Ultimately there could be no exemptions from classification's subject matter (least of all the newly arresting *problem* of classification): old forms as well as new materials fell under the purview of the scientific eye. One need not leap to Marx's example to see how the ideal of humanity's own native home, of the local order of things where people expected to find themselves, would soon become bound up in scientific theories of classes. After the opening of the New World adventure, all ideas of home would start taking experimental outlines from urgent and endless enterprises of reclassification.

Natural science, as Emerson found it, had started in surprise over the New World; it proceeded to generate stances of guarded openness before the expectation of more surprise. In this sense the history of science introduces the prospectiveness identified with America. When great quantities of unaccountable facts are introduced at a growing rate into a system of understanding, one can imagine several things happening. First, the amount of fragmentariness will increase against the coherence remaining from the former order; second, as a response to this, the vectors of order will shift their referential field and develop a complex *prospect* of universal coherence. Everything, the old as well as the new, will become fragmentary and propitious in light of a future whole. This prospect itself will rely on a technology for making exotic items identifiable in terms of the whole; by the same token, the press of exotic import will become a permanent resource for new efforts to clarify the whole picture lying ahead of all incoming facts.

Thus scientific prospects, which are shaped and affirmed by surprising experience, are not just visions of the future but are also methods of welcoming new surprises. The prospect shades into the utopian when it depicts the future as a recovery of what is presently felt to be lost or obscured, and when it claims for its end the reconstitution of a primal order. On the other hand, this forward-looking stance will picture the recoverable, primal whole not literally as its own retrospective order (though the picture may take on some "classical" trappings of that earlier time), but as a crystallization of the method it has devised for incorporating into itself the newness that keeps confronting it. The method is "scientific" in that it seeks not merely to demolish the new; for, after all, the new is not an invader but an import, a surprising by-product of excursion. Nor in any way does the scientific method succumb uncritically to the "influence" of the new reality, as if it had no stake in traditional order. Instead it commences a process of transforming its views of both the new reality and its own present reality in regard to a whole that can only find completion in the future.

Contemplating the displays at the Jardin des Plantes, Emerson was impressed by the fact that the encyclopedic text of natural history also signaled a history of discovery and importation, the same history that founded the prospect of America. He put it this way to his first lyceum audience in Boston:

> I lately had an opportunity of visiting that celebrated repository of natural curiosities the Garden of Plants in Paris; and except perhaps to naturalists only I ought [not] to speak of the feelings it excited in me. There is the richest collection in the world of natural curiosities arranged for the most imposing effect. The mountain and morass and prairie and jungle, the ocean, and rivers, the mines and the atmosphere have been ransacked to furnish whatever was rich and rare; the types of each class of beings—Nature's proof impressions;—to render account of her three kingdoms to the keen insatiable eye of French science. (*EL* 1:7)

Besides acknowledging the "imposing effect" of arrangement, Emerson's strong terms of conquest and tribute—"ransacked," "render account," "keen insatiable eye"—ascribe to the Muséum an intellectual rapacity corresponding to the rapacity of economic and military empire. The Muséum's treasures, its classific "types" or specimens, could only be "rich and rare" by virtue of their places in a larger scheme of valuation.

The commercial market also nourished a steadily expanding complex of domestic demand by transforming exotic imports into the specimen forms of commodities. It managed its transformations less self-consciously (at least until the development of the science of political economy) but no less insatiably than natural history. Whether the subject is commercial or scientific demand, however, it remains that new specimens "furnished" open places that awaited them just as these same specimens filled the hollow chambers of armoires or the blank leaves of herbaria. The open place, the form of the classification, abided already in the scientific prospect, which was also the promise of fulfillment.

In regard to this underlying openness—an openness bounded and founded by the circumference of provisional closure—every last thing in nature had its place in the concentrated displays of the Muséum. One way to understand the prospectiveness of natural history is to see how this was so even for those things that were *not*—or not yet—there. In the encyclopedic gardens of the Ecole de Botanique, for example, placards were set up within the arrangement to denote the places of classific groups that could not be cultivated, such as those including mushrooms, mosses, and lichens. Like offices awaiting business, open places were also laid out among the subdivisions of the plant beds for exotic taxa that were anticipated but not yet discovered, much less represented in the gardens by living specimens. By including these prospective places within its larger composition, the Muséum established a difference in kind between openness and emptiness: for only to the superficial gaze did its open places look empty, in reality they worked toward the whole just as efficiently as those places colorfully occupied by specimens. Thus the Muséum's representation of nature was whole in spite of the fact that it was not completely furnished. Its tranquil open offices of expectation were as much part of the prospect as those busily negotiating the exchange of visible things into invisible realities. In fact, the places holding nothing but the future may well have been the whole prospect's most faithful images.

But what does it mean for a place to be open rather than empty? After all, I have been speaking of classifications as containers of a sort, and containers are empty, full, or somewhere in between. One must recall, however, what was observed in considering Coleridge's theory of the symbol. The relation between a class and its members, in early natural history as in scholastic logic, was never that of an ordinary container and its contents. One cannot simply say that specimens "filled" their specific classifications; instead they came forward as members representing them. Representation, which is a practice rather than a static content, accomplished the peculiar "filling" of classifications. Deeds of representation were affirmed—and, in the Muséum, memorialized—by the vital distance or remove that lay between the specimen and its classification, whether the specimen in question happened to be a preserved organism or a subordinate classification.

This distance, again, was not empty space but was made up in an activity that combined interpretation with composition; it was made up in a deed of science that promised to recover the vital "history" of its subject matter. Intellectual actions made distances in crossing them; and if science found such distances already there in nature's design, it found them both as the traces of divine actions and as the methodical prescriptions for future human actions.

Only with this rather difficult point in mind is it possible to appreciate the dazzling promise of fullness Emerson found in the Muséum: for if fullness was demonstrated there, it was in the quality of constructive action bridging classifications, not just in the classifications' myriad representatives. Pressing further, the ground of such fulfilling activity should be identified not as emptiness but as openness, a quality Emerson sometimes called "reception."

Scientific openness cleared the ground for fulfilling composition. In a time when European armies and economies were still extending their grasp into strange lands, the Muséum's faculty was confident that nothing could be discovered that did not have an open place waiting for it. As Deleuze explained, "since the exposition of the natural families has coordinated the facts, the prodigious number of plants discovered every day no longer present themselves as isolated; rather they come forth to fill in the open places [*lacunes*] still found in the general series."[22]

In the largest sense, specimens did not so much fill these *lacunes* as they disappeared into them. The Ecole de Botanique's confidence that, given the available fragments, an outline of the botanical whole could be methodically prescribed had an exact zoological counterpart: Cuvier's famous claim—which impressed Emerson enormously—that comparative anatomy made it possible to reconstruct the whole body of an extinct animal from a single fossil bone. Emerson stretched Cuvier's claim even further by saying that "one skeleton or a fragment of animal fibre intimately known is a zoological cabinet" (*EL* 2:26). In the *Essay on Classification*, Agassiz similarly extended this feature of Cuvier's method when he demonstrated, in a rational fantasy worthy of Descartes, how a naturalist entirely innocent of the arthropod phylum, if suddenly confronted with a single lobster, should be able to reconstruct the whole classificatory hierarchy to which the specimen belongs, from its genus all the way to its class.

Whether we see natural history opening its whole forms to exotic newcomers or whether we see it starting from fragments to build up open wholes, the romantic principle—that the whole precedes its parts—obtains with equal force. The Muséum could afford to welcome all new facts precisely because it was sure that every new fact would disappear into one *lacune* or another, and bring its encyclopedic representation of the world a step closer to perfection.

❧ ❧ ❧

All the revisionary stances I have been decribing—method, prospectiveness, foundational openness—were built into the pragmatic imperative "I will be a naturalist," which Emerson took home from the Muséum's manifold representations of ideal forms. Yet this imperative also addressed what for Emerson was the immediate problem of writing: once again, how to get "high enough above" his own material to see its "order in reason," how to rouse his journal fragments to "throw themselves into crystal." Getting the right view of the whole meant getting a grip on the technical means by which whole representation might be achieved.

As I have indicated, Coleridge's "Essays on the Principles of Method" were also preoccupied with the problem of finding means to just this end. Coleridge's speculations carried special force for Emerson because they derived from an ambition common to both writers: this was the ambition—final in Coleridge, initial in Emerson—to produce a grandly comprehensive, systematically unified whole text, a magnum opus. While critics have observed how Coleridge's textual corpus was in its very brokenness hammered out in devotion to this ideal, few have given much thought to the fact that Emerson, in the early years of his journal keeping, entertained an ideal of textual wholeness as grand, and in some ways as literal in its aims, as Coleridge's. One must look past Emerson's fierce deployments of fragmentary and experimental positions, in his mature writing, to regain a sense of the urgency of this early ambition.

Emerson began writing in the light of the prospect of the whole. The titles of his early journals and quotation books—"Wide World" (thirteen books), "Universe," "Collectanea," "Encyclopedia"—expressed his hope that the journals would lead to a final higher text comprehending the grand scale of nature itself.[23] In 1839, reflecting on the vicissitudes of twenty years of journalizing, he recalled his original ambition: "When I was quite young I fancied by keeping a manuscript journal by me, over whose pages I wrote a list of the great topics of human study, as, *Religion, Poetry, Politics, &c* in the course of a few years I should be able to complete a sort of Encyclopaedia containing the net value of all the definitions at which the world had yet arrived" (*JMN* 7:302).

Emerson smiles at his youthful grandiosity, yet desire for the whole drove the discontinuous bursts of his mature essay style just as surely as pursuit of the whole inspired the systematic dream out of which he first began to write. Romanticism, already well chronicled in its ripeness, predicted to Emerson his own pattern of encyclopedic aims and fragmentary results. There was the example of Novalis, whose grand "encyclopedic work" was cut off by early death. Carlyle described it for Emerson:

> The aim of Novalis' whole Philosophy, we might say, is to preach and establish the Majesty of Reason, in that stricter sense; to conquer for it all the provinces of human thought, and everywhere reduce its vassal, Understanding, into fealty, the right and only useful relation for it. Mighty tasks in this sort lay before himself; of which, in these writings of his, we trace only scattered indications. In fact, all that he has left is in the shape of Fragment; detached expositions and combinations, deep, brief glimpses: but such seems to be their general tendency.[24]

I have already shown how the ideal of wholeness acted to break up Coleridge's writing even while urging it infinitely forward. The drive toward wholeness—the irresistible work of what Emerson called "the great and crescive self"—forced Coleridge's textual corpus into the pattern of a ruined life, of a body in pain. Emerson, on the other hand, found means to celebrate the consequences of this same supplanting, ruinous drive; he treasured fragments and particulars because of the prospects they showed him—indeed, because they testified to the power that had cast them down like caducous leaves. Throughout his writing, the uneasy union of whole ambitions and stubbornly particular results marks Emerson as both American and romantic. As Emerson is, to a major extent, an American founder, this may further imply that to be American is to be subject perpetually to the interlocking pattern of hope and breakup first played out by romanticism.

Like Novalis and the young Emerson, Coleridge had experimented with the notion that an encyclopedia, "methodically" composed, might embody at least in miniature the aims of his magnum opus. But Coleridge's encyclopedia shared the fate of his magnum opus: it never came to whole form. Coleridge's more practical collaborators did finish their own version of the project he had begun: this was the *Encyclopaedia Metropolitana,* in which Emerson found once again (this time as an introduction rather than as a coda) the "Essays on the Principles of Method" he had originally read in *The Friend.* By then, however, Emerson had beheld a far more successful and confident example of universal representation in the Jardin des Plantes.

Emerson still nursed his unacted desire for encyclopedic wholeness during the period, before his trip to Europe, when he was casting about for a professional vehicle worthy of his ambitions. It was this original encyclopedic ideal, kept in view far more by frustration than by achievement, that ran into the stunning accomplishments of the Jardin des Plantes. The Muséum showed Emerson a vision of universal scope, a vision claiming to transcend the limits of any particular nation, ideology, or profession. What distinguished the natural history displays from an encyclopedia, however, was the dramatic confrontation of compositional technology with a subject matter comprising the immediately visible, fully present aspect of the world.

In regard to the present world, the Muséum most assuredly realized its goal of total representation; yet it was the dissolving, diffusing, and reuniting activity of composition that provided the center of focus in the Muséum's encyclopedic text. This pointed to another kind of presence, an ongoing critical activity as powerfully at work in the spectator as it was at work in the Muséum. As an activity, or at least a technical capacity, it could consume any text present to the eye, even the Muséum itself, with all its claims of total inclusion. In a sense that was defining for Emerson's career, the workshop would overcome all its products.

The effects of this critical principle on Emerson were both powerful and paradoxical. Chief among them was the fact that his assumption of critical practices such as those demonstrated in the Muséum coincided with his abandonment of the aim of literal encyclopedic representation. A year after returning to America, he acknowledged that his journal project would never be an encyclopedia, because by nature it could never fill up; it could only keep filling *out:* "Young men struck with particular observations begin to make collections of related truths & please themselves as Burton did with thinking the wheel, an arc of whose curve they discern, will, by their careful addition of arc to arc as they descry them, by & by come full circle, & be contained in the field of their vision. By & by they learn that the addition of particular facts brings them no nearer to the completion of an infinite orbit" (*JMN* 4:322).

Emerson's recognition turns on the curious term "infinite orbit," a term that forecasts in a nutshell the argument of "Circles." The ultimate aim of writing, if it is an "orbit," must be a whole, finished text. Yet Emerson's own experiments taught him that he would describe this orbit infinitely, with no literal possibility of completing the circle and closing on the point of origination. Perhaps this is because the origin, the place each act of writing begins, is not to be found anywhere in the circumference, that it lies instead in the unnamed center toward which all lines of description gravitate. Such a center is aboriginal in regard to all its circumferences; its "transcendental" remoteness, however, reflects not an unmediated essence so much as it betrays the immediateness of action, action bound to stand off somewhat distantly, yet centrally, ahead of its products. When those products are a series of journal entries, the orbit of production continues—Emerson's journals keep filling outward—by the addition of new "arcs," whose fragmentary curves represent the center. Each new arc both extends and turns away from the orbital line already described, while still offering accurate and novel evidence of the center's pull.

Emerson found the fate of his encyclopedic hopes prescribed by the fact that the active center plays a disruptive as well as an instigating role in the project of completing an "infinite orbit," since each new arc is an effort *of* the center as well as an effort to describe the center. This transcendental center determines the structure of the "history" traced out by the fragmentary arcs of writing. In terms developed in "Circles," each arc "generalizes" the center even while the center "generates" the new arc. Yet the fragmentary arcs, each one both newly extending and turning away from the old, also "generalize" in regard to foregoing bits of circumference. Every generalization, Emerson says in "Circles," admits of a new generalization. Efforts of truth or of grasping the whole cannot hope to consist in completing the orbit; rather they consist in acts of doing something, turning away, in regard to the descriptions already there.

A kind of antagonism, then, is built into the process of whole representation. New propositions represent the center by turning away from old ones. By the same token, every new generalization, each new arc, will seem to be only another fragment when viewed in retrospect. All fragments thus have telescoped histories, internal spaces that are both temporal and relational. And so by virtue of its appearance as a broken fragment, each "fact" of writing will also be a microcosm of the whole. Like specimens of natural history, each of these arcs will be seen to have "terrific interiors."[25] Whereas for Coleridge the ideal of textual wholeness had worked to render all actual texts fragmentary and prospective, Emerson turned from the spectacle of the Muséum—the spectacle of an ostensively realized textual wholeness—to see each of his own literary fragments as instances or enactments of whole meanings even if they remained, for him and for his readers, only prospects of the whole.

∿ ∿ ∿

Let me now take stock of the contrariety I have identified, for its strain reaches through the agonistic heart of all Emerson's further work. With some ceremony, Emerson took on the mantle of a science offering fabulous prospects for encyclopedic representation; yet this same act of devotion inaugurated a practice whereby he gave up his goal of an encyclopedia, abandoning himself to writing in the most fragmentary journal entries and, soon, in essays massively scored by stylistic and argumentative discontinuity. Paradoxically, Emerson's becoming a naturalist meant coming free from the totalizing demands natural history was uniquely poised to satisfy. For Emerson and for readers following him, the rugged edges where thought breaks off turned out to be at least as compelling as the strains of elegant relation holding thoughts together.

By 1834 Emerson was energetically at work in the vein he described to Carlyle four years later: "Here I sit & read & write with very little system & as far as regards composition with the most fragmentary result: paragraphs incompressible each sentence an infinitely repellant particle" (*CEC* 185). These two tendencies I am tracing—methodical pursuit of the whole versus extravagant piling up of new parts—would seem to stand at opposite extremes from each other, yet one must acknowledge that natural history invited them both. The monumental prospect of the Jardin des Plantes beckoned toward the former. Natural history's critical techniques, with their ability to open vast reaches of conceptualization in the smallest specimens, engendered the latter.

These competing yet somehow coinciding tendencies in Emerson's work, toward whole representation and toward fragmentary production, reflect the fact that natural history offered him a new initiation as a reader as well as a writer. For even though Emerson entered the gates of the Jardin des Plantes as a would-be encyclopedic writer, it was in his capacity as a critical reader that the displays turned him on his head. The intellectual removes enforced in the Muséum exercised Emerson in a way of reading that proved more than equal to the ever opening scale of nature's import. This interpretive power was reflected in natural history's ability to dispose of tremendous quantities of subject matter. More important, it was reflected in the intellectual stance that justified such fresh dispositions.

Natural history, for all its minute focus on material details, ultimately transported readers to an intellectual vantage point that claimed to be *prior* to material creation. But, unlike the divine substance to which religious faith traditionally offered access, this new vantage point, poised as it was over all possibilities of creation, extended to nothing more than the technical avenues for creation. This vision of "history" put enormous stress on the present moment, for God's work was not a text merely to be analyzed and cataloged ex post facto; rather, natural history claimed insight into compositional processes by which nature was constantly being built, as it were, from the ground up. The same means God put to use in making nature were those the naturalist recovered in intellectual form and in the outlines of public compositions. Hence the present interpretive moment appeared ultimately as a stance toward an open future, even though it had reached its position by criticism of a world already created. As a "naturalist," Emerson found himself guided through critical readings whose insights corresponded to the creative power that had spread nature's text before his eyes in the first place. In "History," he declared this same lesson to be affirmed inadvertently in all acts of reading: "It is remarkable that involuntarily we always read as superior beings" (*CW* 2:4).

To see what is remarkable in Emerson's point, it is necessary to pause over it for a moment. Obviously we cannot help being physically "superior" to the pages we read, yet for Emerson the reader's optical detachment from the text also marks an involuntary stance

of priority, a godlike superiority most readers tend to overlook. It is
not merely facile writing that teaches this lesson of superiority, either;
on the contrary, Emerson insists that the reader's critical advantage
is heightened in ratio to the magnitude of the writing at hand. In
"The Over-Soul," an essay devoted to the subject of critical superiority, he makes the same claim not only about reading "the frantic
passion and violent coloring of inferior, but popular writers," but also
about reading Shakespeare, whose works Coleridge and other romantics celebrated as partaking of the scale and vitality of nature
itself:

> The soul is superior to its knowledge; wiser than any of its works.
> The great poet makes us feel our own wealth, and then we think
> less of his compositions. His best communication to our mind, is,
> to teach us to despise all he has done. Shakspeare carries us to such
> a lofty strain of intelligent activity, as to suggest a wealth which beg-
> gars his own; and we then feel that the splendid works which he has
> created, and which in other hours, we extol as a sort of self-existent
> poetry, take no stronger hold of real nature than the shadow of a
> passing traveller on the rock. (171)

While Emerson always recommends informed despite over timid
adulation of great writing, the haughty color of his passage also betrays what he owes Shakespeare: precisely the critical superiority that
makes it possible to imagine overlooking Shakespeare. After all, to
despise something *(de-specere)* is to look down upon it, though from a
learned rather than from a naively involuntary perspective. Similarly,
"we think less of his compositions" when we think more of what our
own act of reading them actually reveals. "Our own wealth" is suggested not by Shakespeare's text but by our supercilious reaction to
it as readers, a reaction deriving from what Emerson, at the end of
"The Over-Soul," calls "the negligency of that trust which carries God
with it" (175). So we "overlook" Shakespeare, in a negligent or non-
chalant way, when we read him from just the heightened point of
view his work demands.

Emerson insists that such negligence is compensation for only the
most exacting critical responsibility. And he suggests that we can earn
an even greater negligence in regard to the highest text of all, nature:
"I am somehow receptive of the great soul, and thereby I do overlook
the sun and the stars, and feel them to be the fair accidents and
effects which change and pass" (175). To despise or overlook nature

in this manner requires all the painstaking discipline of natural science; by the same logic, to "despise" Shakespeare requires a critical eye that exercises an equally disciplined, scientific power. Such despite is the privilege of what Emerson calls "the Supreme Critic," the soul in its capacity to overlook, both piercingly and negligently, all the works it reads. If it seems that this attitude sets the reader alone in noble isolation, we must remember that Emerson describes the lesson of reading Shakespeare—that is, of being superior to Shakespeare—as a "communication." Critical superiority is equally available to everyone, and its enactment realizes something importantly *in common* between all readers, including Shakespeare.

Critical oversight puts us where natural history puts us: squarely before the prospect of an open future. It turns out that what Shakespeare best communicates is the preliminary stance from which he began composing poems and plays—in other words, his own stance as a reader, a reader momentarily done with reading. All readers share this stance as the repose or repoising of pure possibility always there before anything in particular gets written. For Emerson, criticism becomes original and democratic when readerly supervision reverses the background authority of history and returns imagination to a point in time when it is potentially equal to any task. Criticism lets us get over what we read insofar as it brings us back to a point before what we read. So reading restores to us a superior sense of exactly where we are: nowhere but at the brink of doing something new. We resurrect this prospect of new doing, Emerson argues, every time we bend over a page.

∾ ∾ ∾

I am speaking of a reading lesson whose iconoclastic force had been in many ways implicit in radical Protestant traditions of reading, yet it appeared in the Muséum as an impersonal, secular mandate for criticism. It had the effect not so much of devaluing natural or textual subject matter as of opening up the expectations that defined what a viable text must be. Any point in nature, read by a superior being, might disclose a view sufficiently vast so as to encompass the outline of all creation.

To say that this microcosmic power of focus only freed the reader to make capricious and arbitrary claims of whole vision would be to miss the point entirely, since whole claims, if methodically established, were founded in the possibility for coincidence between divine modes of creation and scientific techniques of recovery. The vastness available in specimens and fragments was always a technical vastness, an as yet unfulfilled and largely untried plan for methodical recovery. Its telescoping distances mirrored (if one can speak of mirroring where invisibles are concerned) the open marginal space surrounding the specimen, a space no longer empty but like a white page replete with possibilities for newer and greater work.

Once it gets into the system, the insight that the largest ideas are legible in and around fractional things seems a point from which literary return is no longer an option. All works will look fractional, for none will be big enough to hold the full prospects anticipated in the reader's supervision of them. Since *The Interpretation of Dreams*, Freud has complemented Emerson in extending a point already dominant in literature at least since the time of the Schlegels in Jena: that the fugitive image or fragment speaks more compellingly to our interpretive superiority than the finished contours of a generic set piece. This is inevitably the case when we identify the end of our efforts, the full meaning of the text, with the whole source or self responsible for creating texts. (I can speak indifferently of source or self here because my point holds equally true for readers who pursue psychological meanings and for readers who pursue cultural or sociohistorical meanings.) The material form of thought seems to break off just where it opens up, and for our own reasons we are mainly interested in the openness. Rather than reflecting on the polish of perfected form, we cannot help plunging into conceptual removes, which seem strangely to have more authority than the most beautiful things we see or hear. And even when criticism confronts finished forms, it will regard their finish as factitious and break them up into fragments in favor of the open places where criticism sees, or fails to see, the technical vistas of its own image.

Emerson is a major disseminator of this critical bias for Americans. But before conceding that all modern literary thought declines toward metapsychology, historicism, or theoretical speculation, it is worth remembering that Emerson indicates a further circumference. It may well be that one end of his interpretation is the self or source that creates texts; but as I have noted, Emerson also tells his audience that the character of an individual aims to be a sovereign state whose very sovereignty "tends to true union" (*CW* 1:68). Earlier in 1837, in his lecture "Politics," Emerson had declared that the critical force of

"Reason," the same isolating force that compels us to prefer open places over finished forms, "with its whole power . . . demands a Democracy" (*EL* 2:71).

Emerson's demand for democracy was just as practical as it was idealistic. Democracy requires a common ground of technical capability, even if the communications that cross it must come between superior individuals. Emerson sought to found a literature of this common ground, a literature that was national not in the old way but in a way answering a national nature that was both growing and already palpably there, vast and profuse in every sense. America's vastness was more than a mere matter of geographical magnitude; it was always a vastness tied up with intellectual technologies. The grandeur and loneliness of America's open places corresponded to the conceptual removes traversed in the private study, the lecture hall, and the natural history museum. Emerson's writing project, which he conceived as a scientific discipline, made up his own sovereign version of the nation's efforts to bring together a common ground in the place of what looked like an open continent. The western expeditions, the natural history collections, the geological and coastal surveys, the networkings of canals, railroads, telegraph lines, postal routes—all these consolidating enterprises had their analog in Emerson's methodical project of simultaneously expanding and working over the body of his writing.

Of course the open-ended research program in Emerson's journals drew its material from private experience, but this took nothing away from its national significance. Since representative democracy found its canon in the sovereign, superior individual, the technical devices operating in one were bound to be seen at large in the other. The individual was himself a kind of natural history institution, undertaking experiments and expeditions, evaluating specimens, essaying the public with new propositions of the whole. One thinks immediately of Thoreau's careful elaboration of the Emersonian enterprise both in his journals and in *Walden,* where Thoreau's methodical experiments also sheltered a blueprint of union: "I sometimes dream of a larger and more populous house, standing in a golden age, of enduring materials, and without ginger-bread work, which shall still consist of only one room."[26]

Emerson's and Thoreau's projects, with their dreams of an undivided household, differed in material scale but not in intellectual or political scope from Agassiz's grand institutional project, launched in the decade before the Civil War, of gathering and classifying specimens for a complete natural history of the United States. Nor did they differ essentially from Bronson Alcott's experiments in primary education, in which children's development as selves and as democratic citizens was fostered in the discipline of daily journal-writing.[27]

Before claiming, then, that Emerson's critical focus abandons literature to a realm of abstract distances and fragmented particulars, one must see that his lines of insight ultimately aim for union. "Bear with these distractions, this coetaneous growth of the parts," he writes in "Experience," "they will one day be *members,* and obey one will. On that one will, on that secret cause, they nail our attention and hope" (*CW* 3:41). Within, and at least prospectively *against,* all the hollowings and eviscerations of American progress, the very insights that pull things to pieces measure out the invisible plan of the "metres" Emerson calls for near the end of "The Poet": "Our logrolling, our stumps and their politics, our fisheries, our Negroes, and Indians, our boasts, and our repudiations, the wrath of rogues, and the pusillanimity of honest men, the northern trade, the southern planting, the western clearing, Oregon, and Texas, are yet unsung. Yet America is a poem in our eyes; its ample geography dazzles the imagination, and it will not wait long for metres" (22).

Whitman, who proved first among the poets Emerson looked for, would show how the critical principle of the self, "the Me myself," could distract, fragment, and dissipate not only the dazzling spectacle of American nature but also any coherent image of itself. But Whitman's catalogs, much like natural history catalogs, took the measure of the self's insights in order to gather together a new poetic body, re-creating a picture of the whole with open places for all of its contributing parts.

With these points in mind (points bearing precisely on the issue of what Emerson founded in America), we must recognize that Emerson did not really give up his hope for encyclopedic completeness on returning home from Europe. Certainly the experimental nature of his new project, which came to public issue in the provisional formats of lectures and essays, preserved his devotion to the original openness. On the other hand, the central revelation tied up with that openness always had as its most distant circumference the outline of a common domain. In his late lectures on "The Natural History of the Intellect," Emerson paid tribute to both the openness and its ultimate end:

> I cannot myself use that systematic form which is reckoned essential in treating the science of the mind. But if one can say so without arrogance, I might suggest that he who contents himself with dotting a fragmentary curve, recording only what facts he has observed, without attempting to arrange them within one outline, follows a system also,—a system as grand as any other, though he does not interfere with its vast curves by prematurely forcing them into a circle or ellipse, but only draws that arc which he clearly sees, or perhaps at a later observation a remote curve of the same orbit, and waits for a new opportunity, well assured that these arcs will consist with each other. (*W* 12:11–12)

The dream of an encyclopedia, of a house of representation whose divisions all "consist" in one circumference, animated Emerson's writing project in each of its fragmentary, contradictory turns. Time and attention are needed for being faithful to observed facts—particularly the facts of words, which show up in pieces—and Emerson's faith in the whole end of his work opened up for him the time he needed. There was no reason that the end of his own life should wrap up the conclusion he worked toward. Think again of Lincoln, who did not have the superior privilege, which he would have preferred, of holding off from forcing America into a premature outline. But Lincoln occasionally had the privilege of doing so in speech, as when at Gettysburg he briefly put off force to share the expectation of a union whose full accomplishment he could prophesy but could not by himself complete.

History in Return

> What is Nature? An encyclopedical systematic Index or Plan of our spirit. Why will we content us with the mere Catalogue of our Treasures? Let us contemplate them ourselves & in all ways elaborate them & use them.
>
> —Emerson quoting Carlyle quoting Novalis

Before considering the practical aspects of Emerson's reassessment of the ideal of encyclopedic representation, one needs a clearer sense of the possibilities an encyclopedia manages to suggest; for if Emerson abandoned his early project of representing the "net value" of everything, he did so, oddly enough, by laying hold of just the sort of work an encyclopedia performs. Emerson was able to put off literal comprehensiveness because he found himself, at every stage of composition, enacting crucial features of encyclopedic practice.

Let me begin with an exercise in visualization. We must bring before our eyes not just a table of contents, but the systematic table of contents of an encyclopedia, which is itself a kind of index to all other texts. Encyclopedias traditionally separate knowledge into basic classes (in Diderot and d'Alembert's prospectus to the grand *Encyclopédie*, for example, these were history, philosophy, and poetry), each of which comprises numerous subclasses, which themselves divide into sub-subclasses, and so forth. The table of contents shows us the whole systematic tree, which ideally should fit on a single page or a foldout chart.

In a discussion of the "emblematic" nature of such diagrams, Jeremy Bentham praised the way they manage to keep a "whole assemblage" of diverse topics "under the eye at once, . . . the articles being capable of being run over for all purposes, in all directions, and in all imaginable orders of succession, without interruption, and with that *rapidity* which is proverbial as being among the characters of *thought*."[28] Encyclopedic diagrams, with their nested hierarchies and parallel subdivisions, "emblemize" precisely what they offer to render available—the intellectual work of analysis, comparison, and classification. As Bentham shows, however, it is difficult to consign the effect of the diagram exclusively to either the encyclopedia proper or the present moment of thinking, since the diagram manages to unite the total framework of both the subject matter and the thinking "under the eye at once." As a piece of writing, the diagram seems to reside somewhere between the eye and its ultimate objects, which stand in either prospective or retrospective relation to the diagram itself.

Seeing becomes thinking, and thinking looks forward to further seeing, as Bentham's eye scans the outlines of subordinated and juxtaposed topics. Traversing the diagram's surface, passing along paths of relation from term to term, the eye's lateral dartings reflect the "opening" of categories and the disclosure of their members, which are also categories for further opening. But the synoptic arrangement of topics across a flat page, convenient as it is, also asks the reader to overcome the diagram's graphic two-dimensionality. It invites the mind's eye to make transitions from relative wholes to multiple parts as a matter of cognitive *focusing,* as if a certain mode of concentration could bring a general idea forward before its parts or make a general idea recede or go transparent in front of the elements that comprise it.

So the eye shoots across the page and, in spite of the page, ideas come closer or move farther away as the work requires. One realizes that the path from an idea to its elements is an event rather than a static relation: the path traces the transpiring of an intellectual deed. Since this deed involves leaping from one conceptual plane to another, it "interrupts" a train of thought even while joining separate parts to make another train; it abandons one object of focus and adopts new but related objects. In this way, the flat page of the diagram "stands for" the encyclopedic book we have read or are about to read, a book historically thickened by all the interruptions the page claims to surmount.

Much in the way of an encyclopedia—or rather in the way of multiple encyclopedic tables of contents—the Jardin des Plantes offered Emerson a spectacular view of how "unconscious nature" could be taken up into the register of conceptual transit and set forth legibly on public surfaces. The fact that compositional method was advertised even more emphatically than its results was nowhere more apparent than in the landscaping of the famous botanical gardens at the Ecole de Botanique. Emerson's description of this part of the Muséum emphasizes its booklike structure:

> Moving along these pleasant walks, you come to the botanical cabinet, an inclosed garden plot, where grows a grammar of botany— where the plants rise, each in its class, its order, and its genus, (as nearly as their habits in reference to soils will permit,) arranged by the hand of Jussieu himself. If you have read Decandolle with engravings, or with a *hortus siccus,* conceive how much more exciting and intelligible is this natural alphabet, this green and yellow and crimson dictionary on which the sun shines, and the winds blow. (*EL* 1:8)

While making an obvious point about the greater vividness of living specimens to those preserved in herbaria or outlined in engravings, Emerson nevertheless insists on the botanical garden's resemblance to devices (grammar, alphabet, dictionary) that classify elements of speech and prescribe rules for writing. The botanical garden, in other words, reorganized nature more effectively than an ordinary book, but the difference between the garden and the book was a matter of degree rather than of structure or intention.

Faced with the complex lines of organization, the multiple axes of abstract affinity, displayed in the botanical garden, Emerson perceived that the garden's sublimity was in no way a matter of *nature's* transcendence of intellect; on the contrary, it consisted in the completeness with which the device of the book—or, more precisely, those devices of organization and information retrieval that help people to use books—managed to subordinate (and hence transcend by classifying) the gorgeous diversity and magnitude of nature as it met the eye.

The botanical garden read like a protobook, a book of scriptive elements and rules, analyzed and classified for the uses of original writing. It was the prospect of such a book that ultimately provoked Emerson's own prospectus of the reorganized textual garden, *Nature*. "Natural history by itself has no value; it is like a single sex," he wrote in 1834, "but marry it to human history, & it is poetry" (*JMN* 4:311).

A closer examination of the botanical gardens shows how thoroughly the Muséum combined the aims of analytic display and information retrieval. The visitor paced through walkways (*allées*) that divided the area into sixteen *compartiments;* within the *compartiments,* narrower allées established a grid of 154 plant beds (*parterres*). Following a prescribed route through the allées, visitors were impressed, Deleuze writes, "by seeing each plant placed beside the one most resembling it, so that, save for a few interruptions and lacunae, one may pass by degrees from the Liliaceae, such as the tulip and the hyacinth, to the conifers, such as the fir tree and the Lebanon cedar."[29] A uniform system of color-coded placards gave classificatory breakdowns, along with details about habitat, cultivation, and uses, for each plant. All the information displayed in the botanical gardens could be carried away in René Desfontaines's pocket-size *Tableau de l'Ecole de Botanique,* which reproduced the details of the classificatory sequence in both Latin and French.[30] Desfontaines, who had laid out the botanical gardens under Jussieu's supervision, was careful to manage not only the proper sequence of plants but also the total volume of visible vegetation, in order to present the spectator's eye with a ratio corresponding to that existing in nature between the largest plant classes.[31]

As can be seen by looking back at Deleuze's ground plan (p. 64), the *allées de jardin* were technical devices of particular importance, for they provided both physical access to the plant groupings and conceptual access (through the map of the plant kingdom they established in the mind's eye) to the system of classification and information retrieval at work in the Ecole de Botanique. The serial parterres, which held cultivated specimens, had the same expository function as the interior spaces of the zoological armoires in the Cabinet. Just as important as the parterres, however, were the *allées de jardin.* These were media for both physical and intellectual transit: they themselves were clear, empty of visible forms; by means of them one walked through the plant kingdom just as one would "think through the steps" of a classific arrangement of information. The entire process of "thinking through" was modeled after the reading of a catalog or encyclopedia. Strolling through the allées along the margins of the plant beds, passing from one parterre to the next, was like turning the pages of Desfontaines's *Tableau;* the spectator read from family to family, order to order, class to class. The colored placards—quite literally blocks of information from Desfontaines—reminded the spectator that a multileveled conceptual edifice was being erected in the mind as he or she took note of each of the fifteen natural classes.[32]

So the whole tour dramatized a process of hierarchical conceptualizing. Even the clarity of the allées, like the transparency of the glass-doored armoires, was significant in its own right: it figured the transitive act of mind that "saw through" one form of conceptual organization to a lower form contained by it or to a higher form containing it. As with other aspects of the Muséum, the pedestrian function of the allées as media for exhibition converged with the way the whole network of the gardens managed to represent, in pictographic language, the skeleton of natural history practice itself. Hence the spectator's direct experience as a reader of nature's text was always complemented, even intensified, by depiction of the means by which that reading experience became possible. The total event was both visionary and critical: it was a process that Emerson, in *Nature,* began expounding in terms of his most famous, most complex metaphor—transparency: "If the Reason be stimulated to more earnest vision, outlines and surfaces become transparent, and are no longer seen; causes and spirits are seen through them" (*CW* 1:30).

I have already considered in some detail the dynamic structure of

Emersonian transparency, a concept as fundamental to Emerson as the concept of repression was to Freud. But the differences suggested by these two metaphors for mental life are as important as the similarities. Freud's figure draws comparisons between mental life and political or institutional domination. Transparency, on the other hand, refers events to the activities of reading and interpretation, in which the mind manages to see "through" (both by means of and in spite of) figured surfaces in order to clarify initially invisible meanings.

Coleridge had used the metaphor in this way; but the Muséum, which trained spectators to identify classification with efforts of visual focus, went beyond Coleridge in dramatizing the peculiar virtues of transparency. In cabinets and botanical gardens, the spectator's practice of critical focus saw "through" natural surfaces to meanings (classifications) that were themselves nothing other than means to higher meanings. So transparency mainly revealed more transparent conceptual space, with each circumscribed outline or allée either inviting or memorializing a critical deed of seeing-through. The real subject matter of the Muséum was not raw nature but rather was the specimen form of the classification, a form at once practical and ideal, and most clearly communicated through transparent media of display. Classification, as it appeared in the Muséum, was a technical form that converted everything, not only biological individuals but also the displays representing them, into new instances of itself.

Emerson beheld the figure of transparency nested within the compositional paradigm at the Jardin des Plantes. Reviewing the fragmentary corpus of his journals, he saw that transparency could be nested there as well. Alfred Ferguson observes "a new pattern of order" in the journals Emerson began on his return to America: "He began to letter them in alphabetical order, to buy rather than make them, to choose books of relatively uniform size for his records, and to increase his somewhat sporadic indexing into a major activity" (*JMN* 4:249).[33] The old hand-stitched, miscellaneously labeled fascicles of Emerson's youthful journals had been personal artifacts; they made an unruly row on the shelf just as they offered confused prospects for further work. But the new journal books looked almost interchangeable. These were impersonal parts—"members"—prefitted for the discipline of a much larger project. A similar change may be seen in the journal entries themselves. The journals before this time had been more fully devoted to extended meditations on specific issues; but after October 1833 the journals show a decided turn to the aphorism, a less limited range of subjects, a far greater willingness to experiment with radical statements and thoughts that could not be completed. Emerson could abandon the demands of closure in particular entries because he felt the whole enterprise to be fully methodical.

On the first page of the journal started upon his return (journal "A"), he characterized his stance toward the new undertaking: "This Book is my Savings Bank. I grow richer because I have somewhere to deposit my earnings; and fractions are worth more to me because corresponding fractions are waiting here that shall be made integers by their addition" (250–251). It is important to note that this passage is purely prescriptive: it comes not as a conclusion but as Emerson embarks upon a project. Only by the prior light of the vision of the whole, a light shining back, as it were, from the prospect of the future, could the fractional nature of his new entries appear in their quantitative aspect.

Emerson's discovery of classification provided this light. "A thought comes single like a foreign traveller," he wrote in 1835, "but if you can find out its name you shall find it related to a powerful & numerous family" (*JMN* 5:81). The 167 manuscript pages of journal "A" (December 1833–December 1834) are classified into eighty-two index topics, with headings such as "Analogy of Mind & Matter," "Being & Seeming," "Goethe," "Naturalist," and "Progress." A few other topics of enduring interest, such as "Compensation," he carried over from the relatively negligible indexes of his earlier journals.[34] Emerson's indexing activity increased in later journals; and soon he was composing grand indexes (these were actually indexes of indexes) classifying material deposited over years of journal writing.

Given the massive quantity of literary specimens preserved in the journals (which served Emerson much as herbaria had served Linnaeus and Jussieu), some means of information retrieval would of course be needed. From the start, however, Emerson developed his indexes as a vital staging ground within his writing project rather than as an adjunct apparatus. Like the armoires and parterres in the Muséum, index topics gave him access to material collected from throughout the journals; yet each index topic also repeated, in more general cipher, deeds of writing just as concrete as those in the individual entries. In his numerous book-length indexes, such as the 1847 "Index Major," Emerson not only classified entries under topics, but cataloged each entry by means of a generalizing tag or epigrammatic rule; and the most striking of these often reappeared as statements in lectures and essays. Thus the index topics themselves served as places of spontaneous invention, even though they were places built up by conscious, methodical discipline.

Natural history teaches us to understand that this happened precisely *by virtue* of the indexes' utility in the museum of Emerson's writing project. Their practical success in naming, organizing, and giving access to a vast range of specimens coincided with new acts of writing, new deeds of critical circumscription. The indexes, then, perhaps even more than the journal entries themselves, give insight into the genesis of a finished style remarkable for its fusion of generality and trenchancy.

Classifying and writing, discipline and spontaneity, means and meaning—all these converged to the point of identity in Emerson's work after 1833. The true material of his compositional practice was not just previously written texts—his own journal entries and extracts from other authors—but the natural history of writing itself. If this was so, then each fragmentary element of that material contained the prescription or genetic code for the whole of Emerson's project. Trying out his new practice in journal "A," Emerson could assure himself that "there is no need to fear that the immense accumulation of scientific facts should ever encumber us since as fast as they multiply they resolve themselves into a formula which carries the world in a phial. Every common place we utter is a formula in which is packed up an uncounted list of particular observations" (*JMN* 4:287).

Even before being indexed, it seems, the journal entries were commonplaces or topics, specimens recording past classifications and promising future ones. Emerson expanded the scope of this insight without changing its structure when he ascended to the diagrammatic format of the index, which, like Desfontaines's *allées de jardin,* defined classes of specimens, opening transparent pathways from one to another. There was, of course, no reason to stop with the journals and indexes. By this same compositional logic, the Emersonian essay, which first existed as a major index topic, was itself a higher circle or classification; and each volume of essays was yet a higher one: "The extent to which this generation of circles, wheel without wheel will go, depends on the force or truth of the individual soul" (*CW* 2:180).

It was this new way of working toward the whole that liberated Emerson from the literal demands of romantic encyclopedic form. He found he could perform the scheme of the encyclopedia, the diagrammatic statement articulating the whole, in individual instances of vision and writing, which took place both once and for all and again and again. After the Jardin des Plantes, the natural history of Emerson's writing can be traced only in its transitions.

❧ ❧ ❧

Natural history leads us into the enormous institution of Emerson's writing. And Emerson teaches his readers, just as thoroughly as the Muséum taught him, that deeds of classification (or "generalization") inform writing as both content and instrument, *logos* and *technē*. Classes themselves are quite literally the meanings, the transparent frames of relation the naturalist recovers from a dispersed, fragmented nature; but they also comprise the intellectual technology that made, and keeps making, access to new meanings a possibility for the naturalist. Cuvier explained this pragmatic convergence of meaning and technique in the introduction to *The Animal Kingdom:* "If the subdivisions have not been established arbitrarily, but are based on the true fundamental relations [*véritables rapports fondamentaux*], on the essential resemblances of beings, the method is the surest means of reducing the properties of beings to general rules, of expressing them in the fewest words, and of stamping them on the memory."[35]

In order to achieve this relation of identity between the essential constitution of nature and the technical requirements of systems (nomenclature, memory storage, and information retrieval), Cuvier understood that the hierarchical classification of natural history had to be more than just a static format. It had to be a method, a technique participating in the vital constitution of his subject matter. For these reasons, the validity of the Muséum's exhibitions depended on the "naturalness" of the classifying procedures themselves. The naturalist had to find and expose, as it were, the transcendental ligament that joined the a priori integrity of intellectual method with the a priori integrity of the world. Emerson called for this same project in *Nature:* "I cannot greatly honor minuteness in details, so long as there is no hint to explain the relation between things and thoughts; no ray upon the *metaphysics* of conchology, of botany, of the arts, to show the relation of the forms of flowers, shells, animals, architecture, to the mind, and build science upon ideas" (*CW* 1:40).

While "artificial" classifications, such as those of Linnaeus and Buffon, had made limited claims beyond their capacity to serve as efficient systems for identification and information retrieval, the "natural" methods of Jussieu and Cuvier sought to map the true structure of nature by initially finding affinities in as many different organic features as possible.[36] In spite of disputes as to which particular characters were in fact "essential," scientists seeking a natural classification shared a common goal: the discovery of an intellectual technology that not only described the hidden order of nature but whose methodical structure was homologous with that order, just as the root systems of trees are homologous with river systems and respiratory systems.

If the order latent in nature were fundamentally a compositional order, and if all natural facts, as part of being themselves, were also diagrammatic signs that "naturally" signified higher-level realities (this significance would inhere in the fact regardless of whether it was interpreted), then, indeed, it would be conceivable that such devices as catalogs, herbaria, cabinets, and botanical gardens could both represent the natural order and be structurally continuous with that order in their own right. This accounts for the peculiar luster of natural history media in the period before Darwin. Cuvier and Jussieu searched through nature as if a ruined book lay buried in it—its sentences, paragraphs, and chapters broken up, the very characters of its alphabet now opaque and dispersed.

The Muséum d'Histoire Naturelle, itself the great composite text of preevolutionary natural history, never let its visitors lose sight of the fact that even the smallest distinctions found in nature—things visible only under a microscope or through dissection—served the ultimate purpose of recovering the order of nature's book. And yet, however thoroughly the techniques of the Muséum managed to assimilate nature to the model of the book and its technologies, it was inevitable that *the model itself* had also to change under the pressure of nature's diversity and magnitude. The old *topos*—the tradition of the "book of nature" as outlined for us by Curtius and that Emerson found in Milton, Cotton Mather, and Jonathan Edwards—became something different in the Muséum.[37] Natural history showed Emerson the prospect of a new, more commodious kind of book, a book that would have to be written and read by unprecedented means.

Since the victory of the evolutionary paradigm in biology, it has become difficult to grasp the complex image of textual representation generated by pre-Darwinian natural history. This difficulty must be met, however, if one hopes to understand the influence of natural history on romanticism's project of reinventing or at least refreshing presumptions about the way literature gets written and read. Central to that project of reinvention was the semiotic and compositional model of the organic, a model that late-coming American romantics—especially Emerson, Thoreau, Melville, and Whitman—managed to warp into peculiar shapes.

Romantic organicism and the gardens of natural history shared a foreground in the commonplace of the book of nature. Dante's and Milton's use of the leaf as a metaphor for the written page derived from the same topical tradition as the discovery, by medieval and Renaissance botanists, of "signatures" (innate hieroglyphics) in plants.[38] As one could see in leafing through herbaria and botanical catalogs, or in walking through a botanical garden, plants had always been fitted to the model of the book.

With this in mind, it becomes clear that romantic organicism was not simply a matter of turning natural organisms into new metaphors for writing. When Schelling and Coleridge described a poem (or a poet) as being like a plant—whether this meant the poem was written as a plant grows, or that the various figures of the poem participated in a common wholeness—the force of the metaphor derived from the notions of textuality already associated with the plant. Rather than inventing a new metaphor for writing, romantic organicism resurrected an old metaphor, basing its idea of what a poem should be not on the plant itself, but on the model of textuality, the special "book," to which plants had always been fitted. In a real sense, then, the sources of romantic organicism could be approached more closely by looking into the Muséum, as Emerson did, than by going into the woods.

And yet, again, the book itself was constantly changing under the vast pressure of what was being fitted into it. Faced with the massive quantities of strange specimens flowing into Europe from the New World, the book of natural history became, or at least promised to become, as transcendental as nature itself.

Certainly there is a deep transcendental strain in the project I am describing, but it is peculiar and not easily assimilated to versions of transcendence handed down by the philosophical tradition. The peculiarity of natural history consists in the intimate degree to which technique inhered in the final nature of the reality sought after. Nature's "history" consisted in the recovery of a reality already being maintained as what might be called, for lack of a better term, a technical instance. The ultimate subject matter of Cuvier's discipline was not raw nature but the unrealized technical possibilities of the natural. It was precisely what Emerson designated the "NOT ME," the grand topic of *Nature*. In "The American Scholar" he called it, more frankly, "this shadow of the soul, or *other me*" (*CW* 1:59). For the natural historian no less than for Emerson, ordinary nature was a mask that concealed and encrypted agencies and techniques that were intimately one's own, and yet were recoverable only through scientific discipline.

History, conceived as description of such technical instance, was itself a dynamic technical activity, an activity immanent in the text of nature and at least prospectively immanent in the texts of natural history "books." Here it will be useful to return to Foucault, who entirely misses this point in his discussion of Cuvier's comparative anatomy. Foucault argues that Cuvier's science subordinated the classifiable patterns of animal organization to a core of undifferentiated "life" within all organisms. Biology, in Foucault's reading, becomes a kind of emanational dualism, a model of transcendent vitality not unlike the Neoplatonic model that informs Dante's *Paradiso*.

But this was not the transcendental prospect Emerson beheld in the Muséum. It is crucial to see that the transcendental element exposed in the Muséum was the element of technique itself, the a priori "device" through which nature was identified as both patent fact and latent power. The naturalist sought not merely to understand this transitive element, but, as far as possible, to reassume its capability. This is not to say that life was ignored as transcendent reality, but that life was conceived as identical with a kind of divine technology. Agassiz, who trained in the Muséum, caught the sense of this technological transcendentalism when he proposed that classificatory systems were "in truth but translations into human language of the thoughts of the Creator. And if this is indeed so, do we not find in this adaptability of the human intellect to the facts of creation, by which we become instinctively, and as I have said, unconsciously, the translators of the thoughts of God, the most conclusive proof of our affinity with the Divine Mind?"[39]

"Affinities" (as opposed to mere "analogies") were those relations between beings on which the scientist built a natural rather than an artificial classification. For Agassiz, the affinity that placed the human intellect in the same class as the divine mind was its "adaptability . . . to the facts of creation"—that is, its ability to classify. In spite of the apparent modesty of the term "translation," then, Agassiz's suggestion is no less daring than Emerson's in *Nature*. If "God's thoughts" are also his creation and his maintenance of the natural whole, and if classification (with all the techniques serving it) recovers those thoughts, then the ideal naturalist doubles God, reassuming a lost "affinity" and reproducing nature not just through techniques, but, quite literally, as technique itself. The Muséum was the grand example of the kind of book that prospected for such recovery. Following this model, natural history books might not only aim to write the history of nature; they might, in a strangely literal sense, essay to *be* its history, which is to say, their own.

Of course Darwin wrote a new book of nature, and now the old book is hard to read. Following evolutionary criteria, we have become accustomed to classifying relations between species by reference to their descent from common ancestors; thus we can schematize the living members of a phylum as the most recent ramifications of a single family tree. If there is a book to be recovered from Darwin's analysis of nature, it is a history in the ordinary sense of the word: a chronicle of births, deaths, and changes. The plot of Darwinian natural history, like the plots of classic nineteenth-century novels, follows the development of "characters" over time. But unlike the novel— unlike even the serially published novel—the chronicle of Darwinian natural history is unfinishable: given the endlessness of organic development, an infinitely greater number of this chronicle's pages will always remain to be written than have already been inscribed. An evolving natural world cannot be fitted to the model of the finished book.

Viewed from the perspective of evolutionism, natural history before Darwin is usually seen as nontemporal, as the reduction of nature to a legible, but finally only two-dimensional, format. Such, at any rate, is Foucault's judgment, though Foucault would exempt Cuvier as something of a protoevolutionist.[40] This conventional view ignores the striking fact, evident in the Muséum's exhibitions, that the compositional units of nature's book were not particular creatures but were nestings of classifications. Though the Muséum's models were indeed topographic, it would be a mistake to say they simply crushed nature into the cognitive equivalent of a flat page. They were mappings of technical rather than spatial relations. The whole point of the exhibition spaces in the Muséum was to encourage spectators to look "through" visible surfaces into telescoping depths of reference. Even though species were presumed immutable, even though organic nature was never more than the perpetual florescence of the same, the reality mapped out by preevolutionary natural history did not lie on one conceptual plane. Its topography consisted of multiple levels and to the mind's eye looked less like a flat map than like the transparent, "stacked" game boards in three-dimensional chess.

This book of nature, then, implied a kind of history that has become almost unrecoverable for the modern imagination.[41] Though it was entirely descriptive of the present instance, such history was replete with its own version of temporality: a version of temporality— if one can imagine it—freed from the irreversible sequences that lend themselves to narrative. *L'histoire naturelle,* as Emerson encountered it in the Muséum and in his subsequent reading, was an architectonics based on transition and transparency, with classes everywhere opening up a prospect of higher classes or breaking down into lower ones. The fundamental unit of structure and significance was the classification; and yet the classification was always "beside itself" in a curious way, since it contained inferior classifications while being itself contained and delivered by a higher classification. The preevolutionary classification had an ecstatic structure: it achieved meaning through both retrospective and prospective relations to other classes, which technically were other versions of itself.

This was vividly apparent in the Muséum. Deleuze's reticulated ground plan shows the way natural classifications worked as both mortar and bricks, marking differences within the structure and also joining different structural units with paths of conceptual access. Classifications were the history of the ruined edifice of nature in that they outlined the way it was first constructed and could perhaps be constructed again. The Muséum enabled the spectator actually to perform the history of nature by following the *series ordinum naturalium* from parterre to parterre (or from page to page in Desfontaines's *Tableau*). The colored placards over the plants and the classificatory trees in the guidebooks reminded the spectator that a three-dimensional hierarchy was being framed, in spite of the fact that the limits of perception made it necessary to follow the series along a two-dimensional plane.

The compositional processes demonstrated in the Muséum—processes reenacted by the spectator—were historical because they were at once analytic and genetic; they involved breaking units down and building units up. As such, these processes were identical, or at least homologous, to the history of nature in its double aspect of decomposition and restoration; they illustrated the mysterious equation by which Emerson defined history in "Circles": "The energy of the mind is commensurate with the work to be done, without time" (*CW* 2:188).

Time in the Muséum was not the irreversible time of Darwinian evolution; instead, it was a by-product of the conceptual process, something thrown off in splittings and bridgings of differences. The "history" in natural history described nature as it presently was—and in doing so, measured nature's fall and recovery (or, more precisely, nature's disintegration and reintegration) by reference to the prospect of a whole structure, a prospect that found initial representation in catalogs, cabinets, and gardens. Thus the temporal element in preevolutionary natural history had nothing to do with genealogy and irreversible succession; rather, it consisted in reversible operations that happened in both nature and intellect: processes of analysis or synthesis, breaking down wholes or building them up, scattering the contents of nature's book or else restoring them.

Paris and the Scientific Eye

Seven weeks after leaving Paris, Emerson boarded a ship in Liverpool for his return trip to America. By that time, he had settled on the idea of his inaugural lectures on natural history and was already contemplating the larger project of *Nature*.[42] His vision in the Jardin des Plantes had startled him with a grand paradigm for his own project of systematic composition, giving definitive focus to ambitions that had found no proper outlet in his earlier life at home. I have suggested that this consisted in the reconciliation of Emerson's aims for whole representation with a set of technical or critical means that made it possible to realize wholeness in matters of ongoing practice rather than in a final literary result.

The infinite desires of romanticism, in other words, were transformed into issues of practical power. Thus in the menagerie, the cabinets, and the botanical gardens, Emerson beheld techniques of collection, analysis, and display that inspired him to transform his longstanding practice of journalizing into a peculiarly "scientific" method of invention and disposition. Emerson's journals after 1833—with their expanded range of subject matter, their more compressed "fractional" entries, and their elaborate indexes—demonstrate most vividly the way that techniques of analysis and classification, working upon the specimens of individual entries, projected the texture of original writing. The new journals were not merely storage places for ideas: like the Muséum's Cabinet of Comparative Anatomy, they became workshops for collection, minute anatomizing, classification, preservation, and eventual display.

The path from such private research techniques to public delivery was a direct one, fitting nicely with the scientific orientation of the lyceums where Emerson tested his products. Whatever topics they addressed, Emerson's lectures and essays emerged as hypothetical, optative exhibitions of his arrangements of his own classified facts. In this sense, his lyceum lectures were less like other major models for eloquence in America—sermons and political orations—than like the public lectures he had attended in Paris, given by the naturalists at the Jardin des Plantes. Emerson's essays cast themselves in the provisional mode of "contributions" or "experiments" within a larger enterprise, an enterprise that promised to revise and reform all its initial positions. Hence he would describe himself in "Circles" as "only an experimenter . . . No facts are to me sacred; none are profane; I simply experiment, an endless seeker, with no Past at my back" (*CW* 2:188). What stood behind Emerson's literary experiments was not the past but a critical method that took history and nature into full account, and endlessly transformed them.

Emerson came back to America to found himself as an institution of private research and public presentation much like the Muséum itself. It became his life's work to gather specimens methodically from the exotic frontiers of experience, and to set them out, in their multiple dark affinities, on common ground. But it was not just his enterprise of writing that was "scientific." The centrality of Emerson's project rested on his insight that all experience labored consciously or unconsciously under conditions that made science (which for him was another word for criticism) life's most necessary clarification.

Already I am arguing that Emerson's revelation in the Muséum was more than a technical one. Perhaps it would be more precise to say that, in Paris, the domain of the technical was revealed as encompassing much more than institutional science. Besides offering a model for composition, the Muséum demonstrated to Emerson a context—a context of public demand as well as of private urgency—in which he could address American audiences with the power he desired. In a strange way, then, Emerson's vision in Paris was a rediscovery of native place, his own and his nation's. He saw America in Paris, or at least an essential strand of the America of his own prospects.

The harder one looks at Emerson's vow—"I will be a naturalist"—the more it seems invested with the aura of a founding moment, not only in his own life as a writer, but, to a significant degree, in the life of an American national literature. It may seem odd that this scene should be staged in a foreign city and upon inspecting the techniques and products of a foreign science; yet the quality of foreignness comes along with all uncanny revelations, even as what is revealed lies closest to home.

The remainder of this chapter explores some of the less obvious features of natural history—and of science in general—that made Emerson's assumption of the role of the naturalist an enabling strategy for realizing his founding ambitions. It focuses on the foreign setting of Emerson's discovery—not just the scientific setting, but also the broader framework of necessity within which natural history held its preeminent place.

Techniques of Recovery

> I should like to keep some book of natural history always by me as a sort of elixir—the reading of which would restore the tone of my system—and secure me true and cheerful views of life.
>
> —Thoreau, *Journal* (1842)

The idea guiding natural history before Darwin—that techniques of research and display might recover the universal sense hidden behind the hieroglyphic scramble of visible nature—expressed the hopes and self-recognitions of cultures moving toward democracy. Natural history had not given up the utopic spirit of the earliest botanical gardens (such as the original Jardin du Roi), which sought to present the flora of the entire world and so, in effect, to reconsolidate the table of contents of the lost original Garden. The notion that one could contemplate a recovered prospect of Eden, even if it came into sight only through the booklike device of the botanical garden, assumed that an Adamic genius within the viewer could also be recovered, even if this genius only emerged in the act of reading or spectating.

The utopic and democratic implications of the Renaissance botanical garden carried over into the Jardin du Roi's wider representation of nature. Indeed, this utopic heritage was a major reason for the fact that the Muséum flourished after the Revolution of 1789 while other intellectual and academic organizations were suppressed. In 1792, when the revolutionary government dissolved the old Jardin du Roi and established the Muséum d'Histoire Naturelle, it understood that the new institution would serve as a place where citizens could behold for themselves the mutual identity of nature and reason, a mutuality that was one of the principles alleged to have guided the Revolution. Hence the gardens and cabinets became permanently open to the public, who found in the Muséum not a pastoral escape from the reticulated, commercialized world of the capital city, but "a sort of metropolis for all the sciences useful to agriculture, commerce, and the arts"—an exhibition, that is, of the intellectual technology of a renewed civilization.[43]

The public symbolism of the Muséum was not lost on Cuvier, who as keeper of the menagerie, the mammal collections, and the Cabinet of Comparative Anatomy, did much to promote the institution's popularity from his election in 1795 until his death in 1832. Coming up professionally during the revolutionary period, Cuvier dutifully praised his science as "d'accord avec les principes du gouvernement républicaine"; and yet, throughout his career, he also pointed to a less orthodox reason for natural history's prominence in modern culture.[44] Cuvier insisted that the study of natural history served to counteract the emotional ills of society—in particular, the bitterness and resentment unleashed in the Revolution, in internal and foreign

wars, and in the sudden turn to a laissez-faire economy. In his *Tableau
élémentaire de l'histoire naturelle des animaux,* a textbook published in
the deeply troubled year of Bonaparte's Egyptian expedition and of
the Floréal coup d'état (1798), Cuvier defended natural history's inclusion in the new secondary-school curriculum by pointing out not
only its importance as a field of knowledge, but also its soothing effect
on manners and morals ("l'adoucissement des mœurs"):

> Those who peacefully devote themselves to the study of nature will
> be less tempted to launch themselves on the stormy road of ambi-
> tion; they will succumb only reluctantly to brutal or cruel passions,
> the usual stumbling blocks of hotheads who cannot control them-
> selves. Pure as the objects they study, they will act toward all those
> around them with the same beneficence that they see nature exer-
> cising toward all its productions.[45]

By similar reasoning Cuvier justified his career in the preface to
The Animal Kingdom (1816): "If I have endeavored by every means in
my power to advance this peaceful study, it is because, in my opinion,
it is more capable than any other of supplying that want of occupation
[*ce besoin d'occupation*] that has so largely contributed to the troubles
of our age."[46] This practical hope, that natural history might be an
anodyne for the sorrows and temptations of life in the Republic, was
a far cry from the National Assembly's dream that a rationalized picture of nature, manifoldly displayed in the Muséum, would help il-
luminate the vistas of the revolutionary program. In regard to the
"want of occupation" afflicting his time, Cuvier saw his discipline as
a treatment or inoculation of the social world rather than an escape
from it. Instead of evading the present scene with bucolic fantasies,
natural history brought people closer to home by dissolving the opacities of life—including the opacities of social life—into realities more
clearly at work behind them.

A similar opinion of the healthful effects of scientific study pre-
vailed in America. John Quincy Adams and Edward Everett were
among the many advocates for the public dissemination of science
already happening in lyceums, common schools, and mechanics' in-
stitutes. Everett, like Cuvier, saw scientific pursuit as a corrective to
tendencies that otherwise threatened to break up the coherent structures of social life:

> The excited mental activity operates as a counterpoise to the stim-
> ulus of sense and appetite. The new world of ideas; the new views
> of the relations of things; the astonishing secrets of the physical

properties and mechanical powers disclosed to the well-informed mind, present attractions which, unless the character is deeply sunk, are sufficient to counterbalance the taste for frivolous or corrupt pleasures; and thus, in the end, a standard of character is created in the community, which, though it does not invariably save each individual, protects the virtue of the mass.[47]

Everett was concerned with more than the elevation of individual minds. A scientifically inspired "standard of character" would work in opposition to the greed and aggressiveness that he, like many New England politicians, perceived as characterizing the cruder, "frontier" spirit of the Jacksonian period. With the opening of the West and with the gutting of the central banking system, the forces of wild expansion and speculation suddenly appeared to have no natural limit. The casualties of unchecked appetite would be the forms of economic, political, and cultural integration so anxiously contended over during the decades before the Civil War.

Everett astutely recognized that, if science were to offer a democratic "counterpoise" to these tendencies, it would have to replicate, on a higher level, their energy and expansive ambitions. Thus he pictured science as an activity that also opened up a "new world," providing "new views" and disclosing new opportunities. Everett pointed to the discovery of America as an instance of scientific achievement, placing Columbus's voyage in the same category with the discovery of magnetism and the invention of the telescope, the printing press, and the steamboat. As useful as these advances proved to be, Everett attributed to science a prospect of expansion as transcendental as it was practical. Intellectual romance, rather than sensual cravings, would settle the American continent. The terms of Everett's vision anticipated those Emerson would later set forth in "Circles": "Each new truth that is found out, besides its own significance and value, is a step to the knowledge of further truth, leading off the inquisitive mind on a new track, and upon some higher path, in the pursuit of which new discoveries are made, and the old are brought into new and unexpected connections."[48]

By lifting America itself into the scientific register, Everett's rhetoric stood for a discipline that promised to reform centrifugal energies into a "progressive" activity that would consolidate rather than break up the national whole. The same project of sublimation and consolidation is reflected in later enterprises such as the coastal and geological surveys, the founding of natural history museums, and the systematic cataloging of American natural life by biologists such as Louis Agassiz and Asa Gray.

Agassiz offers a particularly moving example of this effort of scientific "counterpoise." I have already mentioned his *Contributions to the Natural History of the United States* (1857–1862), which aimed to classify and describe the animal life of the entire nation, relying on public subscription and on contributions by amateur naturalists from all sections of the country. (Thoreau contributed a specimen but would not spring for the subscription.) The project sought to combine democratic appeal with the highest disciplinary sophistication. "I expect to see my book read," Agassiz wrote in his preface, "by operatives, by fishermen, by farmers, quite as extensively as by the students in our colleges, or by the learned professors; and it is but proper that I should endeavor to make myself understood by all."[49] Agassiz's *Contributions,* a prime instance of American science's attempt to achieve a unifying representation of the natural and national whole, was doomed to practical incompleteness by the eruption of civil war. And it is not without analogous meaning that this work was doomed to theoretical anachronism, at just the same time, by the publication of Darwin's *Origin of Species.*[50] Agassiz's magnum opus never got beyond the classification of American turtles and jellyfish. In both practical and theoretical terms, the aggressive, open-ended tendencies it had tried to sublimate and contain left it standing behind as a broken monument to the consolidating hopes of antebellum popular science.

Cuvier's claims for the tonic virtues of his discipline help to account for the huge appeal of natural history in Emerson's time. By the 1830s natural history societies had appeared in most sizable communities in northeastern America. One of these was the Boston Natural History Society (founded in 1831), the audience of amateur naturalists before whom Emerson delivered his first four public lectures. The lyceum movement, bread and butter of Emerson's career, was expressly founded for the promulgation of scientific knowledge.[51] As in Europe, demand in America for books and lectures on science was based on more than fashionable curiosity: it reflected a hope that the intellectual procedures developed by scientists would have moral applications, that they could be used to explain and correct human institutions.

William Ellery Channing, in one of his last lectures, "The Present

Age" (1841), compared science to a religion that, after having long incubated among the elect, was at last ready for universal dissemination: "Science has now left her retreats, her shades, her selected company of votaries, and with familiar tone begun the work of instructing the race." Channing's term "familiar tone" describes the public rhetoric by which science was expounded in the lyceums; yet it also designates the intimate relation that seemed to connect scientific method with the domain of everyday life. Science was no deus ex machina in regard to the ordinary; instead its already familiar relation allowed it to clarify everyday life by addressing real issues already in effect, but not yet apparent, in the world at large. Hence the glamour of the prospects suggested by scientific method: "Above all, it investigates the laws of social progress, of arts and institutions, of government, proposing as its great end the alleviation of all human burdens, the weal of all the members of the human race."[52]

The audiences Emerson faced on his return from Europe were prepared to recognize in science a moral, intellectual, even political authority for which standard religion no longer clearly qualified. The ideal of the democratic progress of knowledge offered the public an optimistic narrative within which technological and social changes, disorienting in themselves, appeared to have a necessary, ultimately beneficial role. Given the drastic cultural adjustments called for by the Northeast's rapid mutation into a manufacturing society, popular science furnished a more persuasive and hopeful literature of consolation than the bland tracts of religious orthodoxy.

It is important to note, once again, that much of this anodyne effect was homeopathic; for, after all, the economic changes so disruptive of American life were themselves identified with "scientific" technologies. Thus in Channing's account of the "expansion, diffusion, and universality" of his age, science is interchangeable with capitalistic expansion and technological innovation: "It is sought as a mighty power by which nature is not only to be opened to thought, but to be subjected to our needs. It is conferring on us that dominion over earth, sea, and air, which was prophesied in the first command given to man by his maker; and this dominion is now employed, not to exalt a few, but to multiply the comforts and ornaments of life for the multitude of men."[53] Once clarified through scientific interpretation, the same forces that scrambled the surfaces of social life could be shown to be fulfilling, at least in a material sense, the utopian destiny that early Puritans had sought to realize in America. The natural "multiplication" within God's plan for Eden ("be fruitful and multiply") was to be achieved through manufacturing techniques such as mechanical labor, mass production, and standardization of parts.

There was, however, a strain of reservation in Channing's applause for science, as if what it was being sought for—the power to dominate and open up nature—did not quite correspond to its benefits. Science was indeed managing to multiply "comforts and ornaments," but it worked from a point beyond the sanctions of traditional values. Unlike Everett, Channing feared the coming dominion at least as much as he looked forward to it; for he saw that it would be, as Emerson had said, "beyond his dream of God."

I am alluding to the famous last sentence of *Nature,* which Channing's invocation of a new scientific "dominion" echoes either directly or by reference to a common scriptural source: "The kingdom of man over nature, which cometh not with observation,—a dominion such as now is beyond his dream of God,—he shall enter without more wonder than the blind man feels who is gradually restored to perfect sight" (*CW* 1:45). While "dominion" for Channing meant mastery, whether real or feigned, over a recalcitrant nature, Emerson had used the same Adamic term to denote both mastery itself and the reconstructed home, the new *domus,* where a human master could dwell in clear sight. This was truly, as Emerson saw it, a kind of dominion beyond the dreams of previous religions. But whether the dominion Emerson envisioned could still be called "nature" was another question. Paradoxically, Emerson had called for a domestication wholly within the extravagant, astronomical terms of "sight" demonstrated by the intellectual technologies that took natural history as their paradigm. *Nature* posed the scientific question more ecstatically, and more unanswerably, than ever: How was it possible to be at home within the very techniques of homelessness? How sustain the mastery and still dwell in the house?

Channing missed nothing on this score. He sharply noted the relation between scientific discipline and transcendentalism's dream of building a new Edenic household on the unsteady foundations of transformation itself. Thus Channing ended his account of the scientific nature of the present age with a warning: "Undoubtedly this is a perilous tendency. Men forget the limits of their powers. They question the infinite, the unsearchable, with an audacious self-reliance. They shock pious and revering minds, and rush into an extravagance of doubt more unphilosophical and foolish than the weakest credulity. Still, in this dangerous wildness we see what I am stating, the tendency to expansion in the movements of thought."[54]

"Wildness," "extravagance," and "self-reliance" are watchwords from Emerson. Indeed, Channing's anxiety seems almost dictated out of "Circles": "The new statement is always hated by the old, and, to those dwelling in the old, comes like an abyss of skepticism" (*CW* 2:181). But there was more in Channing's warning than a hoary rebuke to his younger friends. Channing was also taking account of forces that, behind banners of the new dominion, were breaking up old economic, political, and religious integrities. The effects of these forces appeared through new manufacturing and transportation technologies, but they might also be felt in the ruptures spreading through the fabric of national union. Many of the age's antagonistic political and religious movements tended, from one extreme or another, toward more totalized dominion; many of them involved extravagances of both skepticism and faith; and all of them loosened the texture of established forms of cultural organization.

Such issues loomed on the borders of the "perilous tendency" Channing saw as preeminently scientific. He identified this tendency with what he read in essays such as "Self-Reliance" and "Circles" (the first edition of *Essays* was published that same year); and it would be hard, given the ensuing course of events, to discount his criticism. For Channing's complaint about both science and the new literature was not just that they made Americans unwilling to "dwell in the old," but that they threatened, in their "expansion, diffusion, and universality," to dissolve the basis for dwelling together at all.

∾ ∾ ∾

Emerson showed a complex understanding of the therapeutic appeal Cuvier's "peaceful study" had for American audiences. Even as he was delivering his first lecture series, "The Uses of Natural History," Emerson suspected that America's craving for lectures and books on natural science was not simply a matter of healthy appetite. In a letter of January 1834, he hinted at a diagnosis: "Is it not a good symptom for society this decided & growing taste for natural science which has appeared though yet in its first gropings? What a refreshment from Anti-masonry & Jacksonism & Bankism is in the phenomena of the

Polar regions or in the habits of the oak or the geographical problem of the Niger" (*L* 1:404).

While different in many respects, the hysterical populism of the anti-Masonry movement and Andrew Jackson's demolition of the Second Bank of the United States had something fundamental in common: they were fueled by a widespread suspicion that organized systems of control lay hidden behind the confusion and unfairness of contemporary economic life. The rage to expose and neutralize such supposedly undemocratic forms of organization ran parallel to the American rage for natural history. Pursuit of natural history, it would seem, also exercised the popular drive to expose hidden systems of order, but in a benignly speculative manner. The same suspicion that craved conspiracies could be lifted to a higher and safer point of view, a disciplined point of view from which the truly hidden order of things could be seen.

On the other hand, Emerson understood all too well that the political "exposures" of the 1830s—and particularly Jackson's attack on the central banking system—only exacerbated the mystery and unpredictability that already characterized the face of economic life. Cuvier, in the *Tableau d'histoire naturelle,* had declared that he would be "more than rewarded" if his discipline was able to "make people forget, for a few moments, their hatreds and their resentments [*les haines et les ressentiments*]."[55] Emerson expresses a similar hope in the letter just cited; but his flighty list of the sorts of science topics offered in lyceum lecture courses ("the phenomena of the Polar regions or . . . the habits of the oak or the geographical problem of the Niger") throws an ironic shadow over the apparent cheer of his statement. The irony is explained by his medical analogy, in which taste for natural science is a "good symptom." Society was ill and needed a dream, at least, of health. The "refreshment" audiences were finding in presentations on natural science was not a cure for the real contamination, even if it helped the patient to go on. Emerson saw clearly what Cuvier had hinted at: that the refreshment given by the naturalist to the public was no less a "symptom" than the ills it treated.

Emerson began his lecturing career with the insight that natural history comprised something more than a pristine realm of cool reason and research. Sophisticated as it was, natural history was part of a larger condition that included such social phenomena as Jacksonism, anti-Masonry, and bankism. Indeed, its very technical sophistication made natural history not only a path for spiritual recovery, but also a way of indexing other social and intellectual "symptoms," a means of exposing, laying open to public speculation, the disturbingly opaque conditions of contemporary life. Emerson's recognition and seizure of this immense technical capacity prepared the groundwork for his later accomplishment. The self-consciousness with which he managed this appropriation is reflected in a journal entry from July 1834, where he reaffirms the vow ("I will be a naturalist") he had made a year earlier in the Jardin des Plantes: "I will study Natural history to provide me a resource when business, friends, & my country fail me, that I may never lose my temper nor be without soothing uplifting occupation. It will yet cheer me in solitude or I think in madness, that the mellow voice of the robin is not a stranger to me, that the flowers are reflections to me of earlier, happier, & yet thoughtful hours" (*JMN* 4:290–291).

Given that he had already launched his secular career with a lecture not just on natural history but on "The *Uses* of Natural History," it is fitting that Emerson conceived of his new vocation as a "resource" rather than a refuge. Natural history was no retreat from the failures and perplexities of social life: on the contrary, it offered a means of practical recovery within the very environment that tested his optimism. As Cuvier had predicted, Emerson's activities as a naturalist—his botanizing, his deep reading in all fields of natural history, and his discovery of the compositional uses of the discipline—gave him a private resource that enabled a vigorous return to the public world. Natural history, itself a kind of therapeutic research, made it possible for Emerson to conceive of a ministry adequate to his age.

∾ ∾ ∾

Emerson's aperçu in the Jardin des Plantes was a revelation of the public context in which he, as a natural historian of the intellect, would become a necessary figure. The same framework of demand that linked audiences with the compositions of natural history also gave urgency to an array of other disciplines that took natural history as their paradigm. It is worth pausing for a moment to note that the strategy of representation Emerson discovered in the Jardin des Plantes also coincided, in significant ways, with the projects of realist novelists, whose works were beginning to appear in France during the early 1830s. The seamlessness of natural history's relation to contemporary life, at least as Cuvier expounded it, helps to explain why Stendhal and Balzac made a point of uniting the framework of the historical novel with the methodologies of natural history. Stendhal was an aficionado of Cuvier's, while Balzac advertised his *Comédie humaine* as the sociological counterpart to the work of Geoffroy Saint-Hilaire. In fact, Balzac, during the very summer of Emerson's stay in Paris, had also hit on the idea of his systematic fictional project while contemplating the displays at the Jardin des Plantes.[56]

The methods of natural history became increasingly germane to novelists and social theorists as the nineteenth century went on; Darwin's massive and well-documented impact after 1859 only continued an established trend.[57] The importance of the science for Stendhal and Balzac was due to their sense that the novelist's subject, the social world, was structurally closer to the natural world (at least as it appeared through the exhibition media of naturalists) than to purely human models. In terms of both its multifariousness and its need for experimental reclassification or reform, life in France—especially life in Paris—approached the condition of a zoo. Hence French realism emphasized not merely the odd and anomalous in people, but also the *types* of characters evident in society. "There have always been, and always will be, social species just as there are biological species," said Balzac in his 1842 preface to the *Comédie humaine*. "If Buffon achieved a great work when he put together in one book the whole scheme of zoology, is there not a work of the same kind to be done for Society?"[58]

Balzac and Stendhal anatomized, classified, and arranged humanity in its opulent speciation. While the descriptive or critical techniques with which they penetrated and characterized their subject matter bore obvious resemblance to those of Cuvier's comparative anatomy, the deeper connection between natural history and realism lay in the common drive to expose organizational forms invisible to everyday perception yet ultimately more important than the colorful but scrambled surfaces of external life. These hidden forms, whether they underlay the natural or the social environment, constituted the "history" that was the real subject of both sciences.

To be sure, the same general claim can be made in regard to novelists from periods and nationalities other than those being considered here. But the difference between, say, the historical novels of Walter Scott and those of French realists is not merely that the latter authors chose to write the history of the present instead of the past; rather it consists in the fact that, for the realists, classification had become a problem in its own right. In turning to natural history, Stendhal and Balzac aligned themselves with a discipline that was, almost by definition, in perpetual anxiety over the status of its means of analysis, identification, and display. For the realists no less than for late pre-Darwinian naturalists, the urgency of the enterprise of classification, reflected in an increasingly sophisticated array of technical options, became acute when classification itself became almost impossible to take for granted. "This is an age that confounds all distinctions!" Stendhal's Marquis de la Mole exclaims in *The Red and the Black* (1830).[59] It was an age, in other words, that could be addressed only by a literature that sought out the real nature of what was so confounding in it.

The urgency of Stendhal's and Balzac's projects, like the urgency of natural history projects in general, derived from the way social facts, with a revolutionary momentum of their own, were overwhelming older forms of coherence. The facts of ordinary life in the nineteenth century were no less outlandish—no less a challenge to ordinary classifications—than the masses of biological specimens flowing into the Muséum from exotic frontiers. But this profusion of strange facts in the Muséum, in the streets of Paris, New York, and even Emerson's Boston, was only a symptom of the disappearance of the wholeness of the social order. When the idea of the whole became impossible to see, then the means by which its parts had once been joined—ligatures formerly taken for granted—came glaringly into view.

They came into view as problems whose solutions were to be found only in the specialized, controversial realm of experiment and theory. Classification itself, the technology by which individual facts are integrated into dependable orders, had become a permanent problem. The solutions proposed, in all areas of scientific inquiry, were as numerous as they were unstable. It was this new compulsion to classify, founded in an anxiety over the very possibility of meaningful integration, that drove the projects of Balzac and Stendhal. This is no less true of Marx, who also insisted on comparing his "scientific" project of reclassification to that of natural history.

There is unexplored common ground between fictional realism and Emerson's "transcendental" writing project. The path to this common ground lies through the representational projects of pre-Darwinian natural history, which served as a quickening paradigm for both Emerson and the early realists. If we recall that French realism (from Balzac and Stendhal all the way to Zola's "experimental novel") conceived its disciplinary focus by identifying itself with natural science, and if we recognize the deep degree to which scientific models informed not only Emerson's arguments but also the very invention of his career, then we must revise conventional wisdom as to the origins of that postbellum genre set apart as "American realism."

Though realism is usually associated with prose fiction, Emerson's literary enterprise—not only the essays, but also the journals, lectures, and poems—stood more firmly on "realist" ground than did the work of any his fiction-writing American contemporaries. Certainly the miscellany of antebellum American fiction included striking new versions of gothic, sentimental, historical, and romance models. These versions were distinguished by the same anxious attention to the unreliability of social arrangements that led Emerson to warn, "This surface on which we now stand, is not fixed, but sliding" (*CW* 2:186). Among Emerson's literary contemporaries and near-contemporaries, however, only Thoreau was formally determined by the "scientific" writing project Emerson discovered in Paris. Yet we should not be misled by the gap that at first glance seems to separate Emerson from later novelists in America. The gap is bridged by recalling the superseded but still compelling assumptions of nineteenth-century science. Even though the lines of affiliation have become by nature hard to see, American realism, like so much else, starts with Emerson.

‿ ‿ ‿

The power of bringing to light invisible but real forms of natural organization was only the beginning of natural history's significance in the half century before Darwin. It was also a project that struck contemporaries as representing, in an expository rather than a merely analogical sense, invisible features of social reality. As they participated in the realm of ideal meanings, these features pertained as much to the future as to the present: they pointed—past the present—toward a future suggested by the scientific "history" of the present. In France and America, natural history invested itself with the medical or ministerial role of treating the ills of postrevolutionary society. To explore more precisely how this homeopathic treatment claimed to work, I must return to the Jardin des Plantes.

As I have indicated, the primary aim of the Muséum's displays was not to divert its visitors but to engage them in a special discipline of seeing. Gardens and cabinets exercised Parisians in the very same intellectual methods that informed the naturalist's tasks of research and display. Beyond the success of these methods in translating exotic natural objects into the registers of natural history, however, Cuvier argued that natural history techniques offered uncannily efficient ways of managing ordinary affairs. In *The Animal Kingdom,* he claimed that "the art of method" could provide a conceptual and technical foundation for all disciplines, including those of the marketplace:

> The habit one necessarily acquires in studying natural history, of the mental classification of a great number of ideas, is one of the advantages of that science which is little spoken of, and which, when it shall have been generally introduced into the system of common education, will become, perhaps, the principal one . . . Now this art of method, once well acquired, may be applied with infinite advantage to studies the most foreign to natural history. Every discussion which presupposes a classification of facts, every research which demands a distribution of matters, is performed according to the same laws; and he who had cultivated this science merely for amusement, is surprised at the facilities it affords him in disentangling all kinds of affairs.[60]

While it was obvious that natural history had perfected techniques of classification used traditionally by rhetoricians, librarians, and compilers of encyclopedias, Cuvier claimed that his method was the perfection, just as clearly, of techniques belonging to other fields: not only those belonging to the science of political economy, but presumably those belonging to practices such as banking, bookkeeping, market speculation, wholesaling, and currency regulation. Such practices regarded the market economy in the same way the specialties at the Muséum regarded nature: analyzing, interpreting, quantifying, aiming to "disentangle" *(débrouiller)* and recompose the hieroglyphic features of their subject. Cuvier's point was that if the affairs of these disciplines remained tangled (only their *embrouillement* made them seem "foreign" to natural history), it was due to their imperfect grasp of "method." Natural history, Cuvier declared, would cure this lack of efficiency with a dose of methodological insight.

The context for this surprising fit between natural history and modern economic and political life is more vivid today in theory than in experience. We are hardened to the notion that the facts of social life comprise a subject matter calling "naturally" for scientific research. It takes some effort to appreciate the relatively fresh sense of dislocation and perspectival estrangement that animated the projects of natural and social science in the early nineteenth century. In order for social life to be something permeable to scientific methodologies, in order for it to appear urgently as subject matter in the first place, it had to present a certain opacity to everyday means of interpretation. (When common sense loses sight of clarity and wholeness, their existence as features of an invisible totality becomes a matter of scientific faith.) This opacity consisted both in the subject matter's seeming independence from the observer and in its hieroglyphic veneer, in the way its tangled surface seemed to beg for systematic interpretation.

While such opacity had always, in various degrees, characterized the phenomena of nature, it seemed a quality only recently manifested in many departments of social life. In France, it was recent life, postrevolutionary life, as opposed to the remembered or fantasized life of the past, that had recast the human world into an object only science could claim to comprehend. Thus the cure or *débrouillage* promised by scientific method was never simply a matter of launching society forward into an unprecedented human condition: it was also, and perhaps more compellingly so, a matter of restoring what seemed, in retrospect, to have been an earlier and clearer sense of things. This earliness or clarity was "historical" in relation to the present, even though it could not convincingly be located in any single period in the past.

Emerson viewed precisely such a combination of prospect and retrospect in the Jardin des Plantes, where exhibitions of scientific progress lay within the unfinished tableau of a restored Eden. This aura of Edenic restoration went far beyond the Muséum's surface features: it emanated from natural history's desire (and from the novel techniques serving that desire) to recover the original plan concealed by nature's everyday facade. Similarly, utopian social scientists such as Fourier, Saint-Simon, and Marx placed their analytical methods within visions of ultimate systems of human relations that were not to be simply achieved but also recovered, restored, *won back,* by virtue of scientific progress.

This condition had a peculiar edge to it in America, where democracy and scientific rationalization had been joined from the beginning. The new need for science coincided with the newness of America; and any longing for earliness was bound to lead back to scientific or philosophical conceptions, rather than to the immemorial estates of tradition. Only a few decades before Emerson's trip to Paris, Americans had broken free in a revolution justified in scientific terms. Subsequently, Americans drew on the same resources of scientific rationale to contrive a federal structure that united disparate regional units into a common whole. The long, ultimately disastrous debate between advocates of disintegration, who in both the South and the North found authority in the Declaration of Independence, and advocates of federal union, who found authority in the Constitution, was not merely a debate about whether to favor idealism or expedient compromise (there were idealism and expediency on both sides); rather it was a contest playing out the double tendency, toward breakup and toward consolidation, that informed the scientific context in which America had been originally brought forth.

The same technical innovations Edward Everett celebrated as promoting national integration—steamboats, railroads, printing presses, cotton gins, carding machines—also magnified impulses antagonistic to established social forms. Such scientific advances made it possible to envision the practical fulfillment of the manifest destiny that came into view with the agitations in Texas and Oregon; at the same time, the real prospect of geographical consolidation antagonized Americans into what their integrative efforts strove to avoid—total war. Popular science, with natural history in the vanguard, essayed forward as an optimistic resolution of this emergency; but the very terms of its promise betrayed the fact that, in the most fundamental sense, science *was* the emergency. Science was out to solve itself. Thus in each of its inventions or provisional solutions, science could only add to its own problematic subject matter. In spite of its rhetorical prospect of a clear common ground, science fought fire with fire, disease with disease; and in reforming the impulses it opposed, science gave them greater power.

∾ ∾ ∾

One of the troubling features of the scientific condition in which Emerson founded his career was the necessary detachment of scientific perspective from the subject matter it was compelled to treat. In his late lectures "The Natural History of Intellect," Emerson observed that "the intellect that sees the interval, partakes of it, and the fact of intellectual perception severs once for all the man from the things with which he converses" (*W* 12:44). Emerson had been contemplating the price of such severence, and of the distances it opened up, ever since he had recast his writing project in the scientific mold. The chapter "Discipline" in *Nature* (as well as such essays as "Compensation," "Circles," and "Experience") assesses the inevitable losses in our histories—even the worst losses—as illustrations of how far into life's heart the fatal imperatives of detachment and revision can be seen to reach. For Emerson, loss inhered in the experimental situation, which was also the situation of venturing toward higher recovery. Essay after essay traces a constitutional pattern of loss and recovery. This pattern affects the very appearance of the material world, since to the scientific eye the initial opacity of a natural object becomes the unacknowledged sign of its having been somehow lost already. The subsequent realization of that loss, in the event of the objects going transparent before the scientific eye, consists in recovery not of what was initially lost but of some higher object. Hence Emersonian recovery appears to share in and perfect the process of loss. Opacity, obscurity, and tangle are parts of this process; and Emerson sought them as assiduously as he sought their clarification.

In a journal of 1835, Emerson compared himself to an astronomer "in his private observatory cataloguing obscure & nebulous stars of the human mind which as yet no man has thought of as such" (*JMN* 5:359). The "as such" in Emerson's sentence strikingly qualifies his terms of detachment and objectification. It was not just that people had never "thought of" the objects Emerson observed; they had also never consciously grasped how "obscure & nebulous" those objects really were; in other words, they had never properly thought of them *as* objects. Emerson suggests that first it is essential to lay hold of the obscure sense in objects in order to recover their luster, to restore their clearer function as "stars," pointers, or principles. Thus his "cataloguing" enterprise, even as it strains for clarification, must discover or create previously unrecognized opacities in ordinary things.

As I have noted, the scientific eye requires opacity as the pretext for its discipline of transparency: the opacity of subject matter expresses the distance of the observer, just as that same distance expresses the observer's prospective power over opaque subject matter. Without the opacity, without the distance, there is no prospect of power.

This rapport between transparency and opacity informs the lapidary prose style Emerson perfected in his essays, where seemingly simple statements provoke the reader to strenuous efforts of critical focus. The Emersonian sentence uses everyday words yet occludes their facade of easy clarity in order to restore the brightness, or at least the bright expectation, of an original language, of communication of the first importance. It is no accident that the most illuminating recent treatments of Emerson have come from the most exacting readers of his sentences, Richard Poirier and Stanley Cavell. These readers manage strong recoveries of the original by training their critical focus precisely on the least transparent (in the everyday sense) places—on statements Emerson has thickened through hard ambiguities of syntax and diction. The success of Poirier's and Cavell's methods is the result of their observance of what I am describing as the rule of the scientific in Emerson's plain style, a style that makes the reader seek critically specialized communications within terms of common language. Emerson's plain style works to present both the opacity of nature and the critical science of transparency. It is all the more scientific for the fact that the truly common, the prospect most difficult to establish, is the goal of its own specialization.

Yet opacity, new or old, is still opacity. While scientific disciplines responded to the opaque cast of the world, the very specialization of their techniques tended to add new layers to what was already dark to everyday interpretation. Ever newer removals of perspective became necessary as the scientific perspectives themselves fell automatically into the realm of subject matter. A particularly striking instance of this telescoping of perspective was taking shape during the period of Emerson's visit to Paris. In a series of investigations culminating in *A Treatise on Man and the Development of His Faculties* [*or, an Essay in Social Physics*] (1835), Adolphe Quételet first employed statistical techniques, which had been developed to measure uncertainty in astronomical and geodesic observations, for the purpose of describing characteristics of human populations. Quételet, an astronomer by training, propounded the stunning concept of "the average man" *(l'homme moyen)*, whose physical and moral qualities he derived through statistical analysis of data provided by the records of an increasingly bureaucratic society: censuses, birth and death reports, and files from hospitals, prisons, and the military.

"Having observed the progress made by astronomers in regard to worlds," Quételet asked, "why should not we endeavor to follow the same course in respect to man?"[61] The undermeaning of this innovation is a dramatic one: the human world, in order to be subject matter for a "social physics," must appear as distantly to the scientist's eye as do planets and stars. Quételet illustrated the necessity of his approach with the example of an observer whose everyday point of view showed him only "a small portion of a very large circle":

> But, placing himself at a greater distance, the eye embraces of necessity a greater number of points, and already a degree of regularity is observable over a certain extent of the segment of the circle; and by removing still farther from the object, the observer loses sight of the individual points, no longer observes any accidental or odd arrangements amongst them, but discovers at once the law presiding over their general arrangement, and the precise nature of the circle so traced.[62]

The adjustment of perspective called for by a statistical social physics brings to light several crucial points. First among these is the sheer force of Quételet's metaphor, which turns Galileo's telescope upside down by setting the facts of ordinary life in a place previously occupied by the stars. Statistical science analyzed the human world from an unprecedented distance. Yet it would be a mistake to conceive of statistics merely as a vehicle carrying Quételet into orbit over the social world. On the contrary: statistics was a hopeful path of return, a means of coming more closely to grips with a subject matter "by nature" remote and disturbingly unpredictable.

As a scientist, Quételet found himself in an epistemological situation no different from that of an ordinary citizen: he was already in orbit; his social physics merely aimed to negotiate an astronomical distance built into the given condition of things. Statistical method measured that astronomical distance and, in the pattern of all social sciences (especially those with utopian longings), served inadvertently to speed up and darken the very condition it had sought to clarify. Thus Emerson, after reading Quételet in 1849, identified "the new science of Statistics" as "one more fagot of these adamantine bandages" (*W* 6:17) comprising the body of fate. In spite of science's promise to overcome fatal limitations, Emerson understood that new scientific vantage points—including his own—also created new and higher circumscriptions, which themselves were bound to appear as horizons limiting the field of possible action.

A further component of Quételet's statistical orbit needs to be considered in order to gain a useful sense of the scientific matrix reflected in such compositional methods as those of natural history, political economy, realism, and Emerson's writing. This has to do, once again, with the "opaque" cast of human phenomena and their appearance as scientific subject matter. The removal of perspective formalized in a statistical social physics points to a peculiar aspect of its atomic subject matter. The astronomical distance Quételet celebrates reflects an infinitely increasable field of data ("all things being equal, *the precision of results increases as the square root of the number of observations*"); yet it also depends on the scientist's ability to find a purely quantitative form in all possible informational units. Indeed, distance is a metaphor indicating both the condition and the consequences of such quantification. For Quételet, it was not only the case that facts were significant insofar as they yielded themselves to classification and mathematical combination, but that *all* things, given a sufficiently general perspective, were liable to fall into the domain of statistically measurable facts. Quételet's "average man" epitomizes this condition: "The *social man,* whom I here consider, resembles the centre of gravity in bodies: he is the centre around which oscillate the social elements—in fact, so to speak, he is a fictitious being, for whom every thing proceeds conformably to the medium results obtained for society in general. It is this being whom we must consider in establishing the basis of a social physics, throwing out of view peculiar or anomalous cases."[63] This "centre of gravity" is mathematically determined; so it is "fictitious" in terms of ordinary perception. But in regard to scientific means of understanding, *l'homme moyen* is more real, more accountable to the given remoteness of perspective, than any individual we might encounter on the street or even at home.

The atomic units Quételet tabulated—individual bodies, intellectual attributes, moral tendencies—yielded themselves to mathematical interpretation. But it was not merely that the social physicist superimposed mathematical forms over human elements; it was rather the case that Quételet discovered averages as forms *already there* as the essential nature of the subject matter. Quételet's technique dissolved the opaque, occlusive surface of things as they ordinarily appeared and then revealed them in their truly human sense. That human sense consisted in the identity between the latent reality and the technical means of recovering it. The latent reality was the history of the subject matter in just the sense that the history of nature un-covered by pre-Darwinian natural science existed already in the tele-scoping order of classificatory forms signified by biological individ-uals—an order that, at least ideally, was identical with the technically established prospects in the naturalist's eye.

In the cases of both natural history and Quételet's statistics, ordi-nary perception was inadequate for the purpose of discerning the real nature of facts as they appeared: there was no satisfactory way of looking at things; the eye always seemed either too close to its objects or too far from them. (Cuvier's double project of dissection and hi-erarchical classification, which forced the spectator to shuttle be-tween extraordinarily close and extraordinarily remote focuses on natural objects, duplicated this instability of perspective even as it sought to resolve it.) But this very perspectival inadequacy furnished the mobility of perspective that was the condition essential to scien-tific adjustments of focus.

Of course, mobility of perspective was also symptomatic of the problem science aimed to solve: ordinary ways of looking at things failed to explain things adequately, so perspectives were set free by virtue of their own groundlessness. While science claimed to resolve this puzzling groundlessness by introducing new perspectives—new ways of looking at the subject matter—it actually depended upon and, as it were, replicated the very condition it sought to clarify. Hence it was that, if things seemed, to the ordinary citizen, strange and remote in regard to comprehension, Quételet's answer was that, indeed, things were not quite remote enough. What I have been calling the homeopathy of early-nineteenth-century science consists in the fact that scientific discipline, through its techniques of refram-ing and revising subject matter, offered not just to resolve but to regulate, even domesticate, the very mobility of perspective that made the social and natural world so hard to bring into ordinary focus.

It is difficult today to separate the science of political economy from that of statistics. Indeed, the ease with which Quételet's astro-nomical innovation became part of economic analysis points to the fact that a similar assumption about human subject matter was al-ready implicitly at work in the perspectives of Quesnay, Smith, Saint-Simon, Malthus, and Ricardo. The assumption was that the subject matter was already technically constituted, so that all methods of re-covering a human prospect were really only clarifications of technical processes already in play. In a manner fully visible in the cabinets and gardens of natural history, the subject matter of both economics and Quételet's statistics maintained its identity entirely through technologies of classification and exhibition. As with the species represented in the Muséum, the atomic form of this subject matter—in this case, the human subject—had become indistinguishable from the containers or vehicles of delivery that opened it up to the eye of science.

∾ ∾ ∾

This brings me back to Cuvier's claim, seized upon by Emerson, that natural history offered citizens a therapeutic means of disentangling the opacities of emotional and practical life in contemporary society. In France no less than in Jacksonian America, commercial disciplines seemed increasingly arcane to lay citizens, whose tangled affairs were expressed in relationships with bankers, brokers, accountants, and other technicians of the marketplace. Certainly the methods attached to the market economy were getting more complex as it grew and diversified. But the enigmatic nature of commercial practices was merely one of the more glaring aspects of a condition that, by the 1830s, had become the object of a tradition of critical focus in Europe and America. The basis of all things was becoming rationalized or mechanized according to business and technical principles.

Many of romanticism's horrors (and some of its hopes) centered on the realization that the prime element within social life was not the given human being, idiosyncratic and irreplaceable, but was instead a sort of technical module only contingently bound to the human. This technical form might be either totalized or combined infinitely; its elastic circumference might with equal integrity comprehend, coincide with, or be comprehended by the human individual. Such a form could come to light only in a social context distinguished, on the one hand, by the breakdown of dependable classifications and, on the other, by extravagant new proposals for reclassifying things.

It was precisely this form, itself already scientific and hence permeable only to scientific insight, that founded the specialized responses of economics, statistics, and realism. Observers as distinct as Blake and Dreiser were to be united in their fascination with this new common denominator, inhuman yet humanly made. For Marx the shift of ground from human individual to technical monad resulted from "the disintegration of all products and activities into exchange values."[64] But Marx's "exchange value" was only one of a number of candidates, hypothesized in the nineteenth century, for the uncanny technical element that seemed to project the present order. Emerson, reflecting on natural science after his experience at the Jardin des Plantes, relied on Cuvier's more fundamental term, "classification," to mean the same compositional element.

Whatever the chosen term, the condition it signified was one that Blake, Coleridge, and Wordsworth had already indicted under the rubric of the "mechanical." Carlyle extended their lament in "Signs of the Times" (1829): "Truly we may say, . . . 'the deep meaning of the laws of Mechanism lies heavy on us'; and, in the closet, in the marketplace, in the temple, by the social hearth, encumbers the whole movements of our minds, and over our noblest faculties is spreading a nightmare sleep."[65] The outlines of mechanism looked particularly stark in the first half of the nineteenth century, when memories or fantasies of precapitalistic times were strong and when new technologies were magnifying capabilities beyond the human scale. Whether, as Marx would claim, the mechanical appearance of all things was symptomatic of society's failure to come to grips with current conditions of material production or whether, as British and American thinkers tended to claim, mechanism was an external projection of decisions made consciously and unconsciously by individuals (each of whom was ultimately responsible for the problem), the fact remained that the human world seemed to exceed human comprehension.

Marx's theory of alienation, which, after all, only revisits a romantic commonplace, provides one picture of the circumstance I am describing:

> The social character of activity, as well as the social form of the product, and the share of individuals in production, here appear as something alien and objective, confronting the individuals, not as their relation to one another, but as their subordination to relations which subsist independently of them and which arise out of collisions between mutually indifferent individuals. The general exchange of activities and products, which has become a vital condition for each individual—their mutual interconnection—here appears as something alien to them, autonomous, as a thing.[66]

This syndrome of alienation and fetishism, which Marx saw spinning outward from the very heart of commodity production, helps illustrate natural history's centrality as a model for a whole array of technical responses, in literature as well as in social science. When it becomes possible to imagine that a purely technical form—say, the form of exchange value—has become the fundamental unit of social relations, and when it appears that laws inherent to that technical form have come to govern all things, it follows that people have granted natural, even biological status to means they have devised for dealing with one another.

The result, Marx says, is a secular animism: "The productions of the human brain appear as independent beings endowed with life, and entering into relation both with one another and with the human race."[67] Not only the enigmatic contrivances of the marketplace, but all forms of social activity seem to work automatically, "independently," exactly like the things and systems of things one comes up against in nature. Emerson's favorite line from Horace—" 'Drive out nature with a fork, she comes running back' " (*CW* 2:61)—sums up the pattern of renaturalization Marx describes. In supplanting the feudal system of classes, capitalism had silenced the traditional appeal to nature, the claim that social relations were as set within the natural order as the relations between species. Even as it broke up the old natural integrities, however, capitalism's triumph brought home the puzzling image of nature as a mask for new human expediencies. It was only by virtue of the wild exfoliation of what would ordinarily be considered most unnatural—human device—that social life took on the new veneer of the natural. And if social life was thus transfigured before the eye, nature also was forced into transfiguration.

As Emerson saw it, "Nature is overflowed and saturated with humanity" (*EL* 2:33). Nature, in short, had turned into the subject matter of natural history as Emerson found it in the Jardin des Plantes and as he soon reinvented it in America. The venerable domain of nature persisted only as a veneer: its interior reality, its history, opened up under the naturalist's eye into a labyrinth of design that, whatever its theological attributions, was only another account of human doing.

As human life was naturalized in the nineteenth century, economists, sociologists, and realist novelists—all following the preeminent example of natural history—became important as classifiers of a new ecology. Cuvier was responding to this condition when he advocated the naturalist's "art of method" as the formal perfection of all compositional practices (including those of the market), and therefore as the best means of mediation between citizens and everything that was most tangled, most "foreign" in the world they inhabited. The real subject matter of Cuvier's discipline, like that of the other disciplines discussed in this chapter, was not raw nature but the remanufactured mask of the natural. It was precisely what Emerson called "this shadow of the soul, or *other me*." For the natural historian no less than for Emerson, ordinary nature was a mask that concealed and encrypted agencies and techniques that were intimately "one's own," and yet were recoverable only through scientific discipline. Emerson's hope in *Nature*, like Cuvier's hope in the Jardin des Plantes, was that transcendental insight might point the way back home, and so work to instruct, if not cure, a world becoming more and more exotic in its own eyes.

Passage to America

The earth is a museum, and the five senses a philosophical apparatus.

—Emerson, "The Uses of Natural History"

The conditions uniting natural history with the therapeutic needs of contemporary France and America were strikingly visible in the Jardin des Plantes. Since its reconstitution in 1792, the Muséum had sought to maintain a balance between its roles as a research facility and a center for public display. By the 1830s, however, French natural science had lost much of its groundbreaking vitality; meanwhile the Muséum steadily shifted its efforts from research toward satisfying public appetite for spectacle.[68] The institution Emerson visited was not, in other words, an island of pure reason in the middle of an otherwise commercialized Paris. On the contrary, it was a public spectacle entirely continuous with the rest of the city.

Accordingly, Emerson's reports of the Jardin des Plantes in his journals and letters lie sandwiched between anxious, often hostile descriptions of an urban culture that seemed wholly oriented toward the exhibition and consumption of commodities. "Paris abounds in all conveniencies for leading an easy, fat, amused life," he noted sourly a week after arriving; "it is like a Liverpool or New York all alive with an Exchange & new gloves & broadcloths" (*L* 1:386–387). Paris, it seemed, was "a vulgar superficial unspiritual marketing community" (389)—even the tombs at Père-Lachaise reminded Emerson of "advertisements" (*JMN* 4:201).

On the other hand, he was astonished by "the splendour of the shops—such endless profusion of costly goods of every sort that it is a constant wonder where they find purchasers" (*L* 1:391). To Emerson, the spectacular displays of the city were as affecting as the displays of nature in the Muséum, but in a disconcerting, suspect manner. He was especially intrigued by the Parisian use of mirrors, which counteracted the narrow subdivisions of urban space by tricking the eye into impressions of multiplicity and expanse: "Ah they understand here the powers of the lookingglass; & all Paris is a perpetual puzzle to the eye to know what is object & what is reflection. By this expedient reading rooms & cafés have all a bewildering extent & the wealth of the shops is multiplied. Even on the dessert service at the dinner table they set mirrors into the fruit-stands to multiply whips cherries & sugar plums, so that when I took one, I found two were gone" (390). In describing the "perpetual puzzle" and "bewildering extent" of these mirrored spaces, Emerson was discovering some of the key terms he would use four days later, when he responded to the Jardin des Plantes by declaring, "The Universe is a more amazing puzzle than ever as you glance along this bewildering series of animated forms" (*JMN* 4:199). Emerson's bewilderment, in the Muséum as in the cafés and shops, derived from the way such spaces made objects seem to disappear into media of display, so that multiplicity appeared less an attribute of nature than a product of how one looked at or reflected on nature. Whether it was a classified specimen or a commodified good, the fact itself had become indistinguishable from the form it found in reflection.

But there remains the strong contrast in Emerson's reactions to these two reflective situations, the Muséum and the city; and surely his ambivalence toward the urban displays was more than a matter of native prudishness. In the Muséum, exhibition media served to *contain* the profusion of individual facts by transforming them into specimens of classes, thus replacing natural multiplicity with a history constituted by three-dimensional sequences of stacked classificatory forms. Sheer quantity and variety were overcome by emphasis on reference and on the transitive acts of mind that made such reference clear. The Muséum brought referential sequences into visibility by its exhibition of containers and groupings of containers—armoires, parterres, herbaria, display tables—but in the city, Emerson found that similar display techniques produced a contrary effect. There, reflection increased the field of subject matter in a mainly quantitative manner, multiplying either spatial extent or the number of objects along a flat conceptual plane. The result, in the shops and cafés, was a kind of optical mass production rather than the dialectical process whereby visible objects went transparent before higher organizational forms. If both the Muséum and the city produced vertiginous effects, they can be distinguished from one another by noting that the Muséum's "sublime effect" was akin to the Wordsworthian or "egotistical" sublime, in which vast reaches of nature seemed subordinated under the power of an idea; while, on the other hand, the sublimity of the city suggested nothing so much as the Kantian "mathematical" sublime, whereby vistas of great extent, quantity, or duration astonished the mind with the prospect of an infinitely repeatable, endless calculus of measurable units.

In spite of these differences, however, Emerson described both the Muséum and the city as "bewildering." The word implies that, in both scenarios, it was not only objects that disappeared into media of display—not only plants, animals, whips, and sugarplums—but also the spectating subject, who fell into the mirrors and was multiplied just as wildly. The mirrors in question did not present images of the spectator's bodily face, as in Narcissus's reflection; instead, reflected images fit together with a disjunctive coherence, not unlike the analyzed, boxed elements in a Cézanne landscape or a cubist portrait. These mirrors were outstanding features within environments that were themselves workshops of reflection, factories of intellectual production. Each of the great speculative models Emerson encountered, the Muséum and the city, was an "amazing puzzle," a modern instauration of nature, a place to get lost in or to be guided in, but also a place for active dwelling, a new technological and textual household.

One must appreciate the continuities between the Muséum and its urban setting in order to make full sense of Emerson's ultimate revelation in the Jardin des Plantes. He had already been in Paris for more than three weeks before he finally entered the Cabinet building on July 13; he would leave the city four days later. That was more than enough time to become saturated in the larger Parisian scene. Indeed, he had lamented the length of his stay only ten days after his arrival: "I wish I had not taken my place here for a month. I am quite satiated and ready to leave for London tomorrow" (*L* 1:388).

During those weeks, Emerson took walks through the grounds of the Jardin des Plantes and even attended public lectures given there by the scientists Thénard and Gay-Lussac. But these experiences merely ran together with his other, rather painfully confused impressions of Paris. Alienated, listless, trapped in a consumer's heaven, Emerson blankly listed the Jardin des Plantes (two weeks before his epiphanic visit to the Cabinet) as simply another Parisian spectacle: "I go to the Sorbonne & hear lectures. I walk in the Jardin des Plantes. I stare & stare at the thousand thousand shop windows. I go to the Louvre, the King's Library, the Theatre" (387–388).

Unlike most tourists in Paris, Emerson did not enjoy the role he found himself playing: that of the flâneur, the idler whom Walter Benjamin characterized in his study of Baudelaire.[69] Against his will, Emerson tasted something of the endemic "want of occupation" Cuvier had hoped the study of natural history would cure. The city, "a loud New York of a place" (*JMN* 4:197), showed Emerson an image of a condition of things he both feared and eventually came to complex terms with in America: the assimilation of all aspects of life to the forms of commercial practices. The image was all the more uncanny for being French; and its recognition by Emerson makes another moment in the tradition of Americans and French recognizing themselves, darkly and brightly, in one another.

Tocqueville, who was in Paris writing the first volume of *Democracy in America* at the time of Emerson's visit, had already recorded thoughts like Emerson's, but in reverse terms. The Frenchman previewed in America a condition corresponding in certain ways to the condition Emerson responded to in France. America persuaded Tocqueville that political democracy and the market economy were fatally bound up one within the other. Meditating in 1831 on recent events in France (the "Bourgeois Monarchy" of Louis-Philippe, a political projection of the new economic and social order, had come to power in 1830), Tocqueville wrote in a letter from Yonkers, New York, that "we ourselves are moving . . . toward a democracy without limits. I am not saying this is a good thing; what I see in this country convinces me, on the contrary, that France will come to terms with it badly; but we are being pushed toward it by an irresistible force."[70] The "irresistible force" abroad in America was also at work in France, though as a dark tide beneath the "apoplectic torpor," the rigid surface of disoccupation and indifference, that Tocqueville found everywhere in French political and intellectual life.[71] Tocqueville, along with Cuvier, Stendhal, and Balzac, anxiously recognized that the energies behind political and economic democracy were themselves uncontainable, more akin to natural forces than to ethical persuasions.

Cuvier was, of course, the least pessimistic of this group. He promoted natural history as a means of channeling and binding those energies. He understood that the link between natural history and the forces of contemporary economic and political life was only initially expressed by the Muséum's role as public spectacle. The deeper relation lay in natural history's methods of transformation and production, in the very transcendentalism of its mappings of nature.

～ ～ ～

The fact that Emerson's revelation in the Muséum took place at the end of his month in Paris suggests that it came as a kind of relief or release from pressures that had been building throughout his stay. This relief was not a flight from the urban context, however, any more than dreams are a flight from mental life. The spectacle of the cabinets offered Emerson rather an expression and experimental resolution of those pressures. It should be seen, in fact, as an instance of just the sort of homeopathic therapy that natural history aimed to provide. Emerson's revelation, coming as it did in the contained, concentrated formats of the cabinets and the menagerie, then extending out into the botanical gardens where he had previously strolled without illumination, was a condensation and resolution of the "nature" at large in Paris. Some version of this same nature— and this same prospective cure—also constituted America's future, at least insofar as Emerson was to determine it.

Even as it led Emerson to his discovery of a new career in America, then, the Cabinet leads us back into the city, where commercial life cast up a far wilder array of compositional experiments. We look for some point where the city exhibited itself, using its own explicitly urban terms, in a microcosm comparable to the microcosm of the Muséum. We find it, most vividly, at street level beneath Emerson's own Paris address: "I live at *pension* with Professor Heari at the corner of Rue Neuve Vivienne directly over the entrance of the Passage aux Panorames" (*JMN* 4:201).

The Passage des Panoramas was the first important *passage*, or shopping arcade, built in Paris; its location enabled it to exploit the crowds who came to see the famous dioramas on the Boulevard Montmartre. The Paris arcades—Emerson guessed there were about fifty in the city—were the great forerunners of present-day shopping malls and department stores.[72] "Few things give more the character of magnificence to the city," Emerson observed, "than the suite of these passages about the Palais Royal" (*JMN* 4:201). Stretching through the middle of city blocks, they were closed to boulevard traffic, protected from weather by glass-covered roofs, and glamorously lit by gaslight. The *passages* had the look, in the words of a contemporary guidebook, of "a city, indeed, a world, in miniature."[73]

Everything that shocked and excited Emerson in Paris found its image in the microcosm of the arcade bustling beneath his pension. Shop windows full of commodities shimmered with the strong combination of color and transparency that marked the exhibits in the Muséum. In fact, the arcades duplicated the compositional structure of the Muséum in a number of ways.[74] Each institution combined gaudy multiplicity with rigorous organization, making a show of the processes of abstraction and representation that transformed all things into specimens of classes of things. Just as the exhibition spaces in the Muséum tended to reproduce the rectangular shape of a page (each page displaying the juxtaposed "characters" of specimens), the interiors of the *passages* were uniformly subdivided into transparent shop-fronts filled with samples of things for sale. The Muséum demonstrated techniques of analysis, preservation, and composition; on the other hand, the mercantile spectacle of Paris, compressed within the *passages*, advertised the living technical processes that projected the hieroglyphics of the urban world.

A ground plan of the Galeries Colbert and Vivienne (see figure) illustrates the resemblances of the Paris arcades to the encyclopedic, librarylike formats of the cabinets and gardens of the Muséum. These two opulent *passages*, extending side by side, opened on the route between Emerson's pension and the Palais Royal. Their design was typical in its strategy for reconciling the multiplicity of categorized subject matter with the spectator's capacities in regard to inspecting that subject matter. The main corridor of each *passage* formed an axis of vision penetrating into the interior of the city block; the corridor itself was composed of specifically framed possibilities of vision on

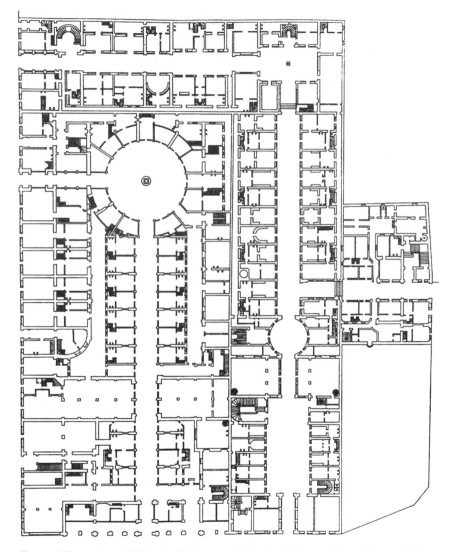

Ground floor plan of Galerie Colbert and Galerie Vivienne. From Johann Friedrich Geist, *Arcades: The History of a Building Type* (Cambridge, Mass.: MIT Press, 1983).

either side: these were the transparent, serial box-spaces of the shops bordering the corridor.

The *passages*, like the compositions of the Muséum, were complex visionary totalities built up out of subordinate deeds of vision. While the sequence of commodity categories lining the *passage* reflected the laws of the marketplace (as opposed to the classificatory laws that dictated the sequences of specimen displays in the Muséum), the identity of format in both places suggests that the compositions shared a common foundation in the assumed nature of the spectating eye, if not in the higher invisible structure of the reality (mercantile and natural) represented in microcosm by both frameworks. The compositional models Emerson encountered treated the spectator not as a substance existing alongside other natural substances so much as a nature made up of sheerly technical capablities. Both the Muséum and the *passages* hypothesized a spectator who was, by "nature," an active set of means ultimately productive of the surrounding material world.

It follows that these models were not only designed for the uses and entertainments proper to such a "scientific" spectator, but that they themselves also appeared, at least in a provisional and utopic manner, as blueprints *of* such a spectator. For although the visitor initially stepped into the Muséum and the *passages* from a louder, more scrambled world, these were actually privileged vantage points from which to look out at the world. The axis of vision defining such places belonged less, in other words, to the passerby who paused on the road to peer in than it belonged to the spectating identity posed ideally in the center of the *passage*'s rotunda or on the steps of the Cabinet building that rose over the linear vistas in the grounds of the Jardin des Plantes. These clear vantage points, like the grand eyeball in Emerson's *Nature*, were metaphors for a subjectivity that realized its world through the dynamics of transparency. From the speculative centers they proposed, it would be possible to look out into the opaque world of the street through, as it were, an optical or cognitive instrument whose techniques of organization laid a saving foreground for the present and a clear promise for the future.

Against the clarifying designs within the *passages*, however, there remained the bewildering impression one could have looking into them. In *Nana*, Zola provides a picture of the way the Passage des Panoramas, above which Emerson had slept in 1833, looked at night during the 1860s:

Under the windows, white with reflected light, the pavement was violently illuminated. A perfect stream of brilliancy emanated from white globes, red lanterns, blue transparencies, lines of gas-jets, gigantic watches and fans, outlined in flame and burning in the open. And the motley displays in the shops, the gold ornaments of the jewelers, the glass ornaments of the confectioners, the light-colored silks of the modistes, seemed to shine again in the crude light of the reflectors behind the clear plate-glass windows; whilst, among the bright-colored disorderly arrays of shop-signs, a huge purple glove loomed in the distance, like a bleeding hand which had been severed from an arm and fastened to a yellow cuff.[75]

Like the mirrored shops and cafés that puzzled Emerson, Zola's Passage des Panoramas is a clutter of dissociated signs, with advertisements multiplied through reflection and detached behind plate glass. The scene is empty of direct human elements save for the figure of the hand, which Zola's simile forces into the *passage* as a kind of stigma within the glover's logo. Luridly disclosed in the image of the commodity that covers up hands, Zola's bleeding hand restores to visibility the sacrifices entailed by the "invisible hand" at work in the marketplace: the division of labor, the mechanization of the body, the severance of instrumentality from any larger human integrity. But, more interesting, this description of the Passage des Panoramas is also a point where *Nana* reflects upon the terms of its own production, since the hand, mutilated as it is, raises the question of design within the fragmented scene, a design necessarily shared by both the urban environment and the novel itself. The *passage* compresses all the material of Zola's naturalism into a single tableau. The writer's eye confronts this tableau and compels the image of his own authorship to appear. As it looks to Zola, the hand of his writing is both lost and found in its subject matter—in a new nature, as it were, whose real history becomes clear only through a specialized version of the same "scientific" way of working that essentially, if darkly, projected this nature in the first place.

With its emphasis on fragmentation and severance, Zola's nightmare vision of the *passage* compares with Emerson's well-known picture of "the *divided,* or social state" at the beginning of "The American Scholar." There Emerson also invokes the hand as a figure for the division and multiplication of labor: "It is one of those fables, which out of an unknown antiquity, convey an unlooked-for wisdom, that the gods, in the beginning, divided Man into men, that he might be more helpful to himself; just as the hand was divided into fingers, the better to answer its end" (*CW* 1:53).

The primal hand, for Emerson, attests to unity's transformation into practical integrity. This was the original deed of division or analysis, generating both human community and individuality within supernatural technique. Agassiz would have seen it as an instance of design. In Emerson's technological fable, the genesis of individuals is nothing more than the disclosure of human nature as an index of means; yet it also reveals human nature, in its wholeness and in its individual parts, as raw material or scientific subject matter. This image of the human, which may be integrated and disintegrated through reflection, is born in science, in strategies of inhibiting and redistributing the whole.

It seems a relatively small step from the hand's initial condition of integrity to the modern phase of fragmentation, ruin, and bewilderment. As in the passage from Zola, the original hand of human authorship falls away from the systematic human body and loses itself in a heap of dissociated parts:

> The fable implies that the individual to possess himself, must sometimes return from his own labor to embrace all the other laborers. But unfortunately, this original unit, this fountain of power, has been so distributed to multitudes, has been so minutely subdivided and peddled out, that it is spilled into drops, and cannot be gathered. The state of society is one in which the members have suffered amputation from the trunk, and strut about so many walking monsters,—a good finger, a neck, a stomach, an elbow, but never a man. (53)

With Zola's example in mind, it is worth experimenting briefly with the notion that Emerson's fable observes "the state of society" just as he had previewed it in Paris—as though, in other words, looking out into an American street were like looking into a cabinet, a botanical garden, or down the receding corridor of a *passage*. We must recall the lessons taught by natural history and by the sociological and literary disciplines allied with natural history: these are the lessons of transparency, clarification, perspectival mobility, and the reference of objects to invisible histories of production. What such scientific disciplines attacked in their subject matter was the uncanny quality of apparent surfaces, the sense of dismembered or forgotten familiarity that lingered within the opacity of things and fixated attention upon them.

For Cuvier and Agassiz, the puzzling surfaces of animal bodies encrypted the disjunction between human understanding and the higher ongoing designs of the Creator. For Quételet and Marx, the "natural" veneer of social life symptomized the mind's alienation from modes of production that were fully human, but whose significant features had multiplied beyond the range of ordinary, unscientific comprehension. The speculative techniques of all their disciplines aimed to redeem the ruins and fragments of visible nature, reorganizing all the scrambled parts as members of an original human integrity. This was the ultimate task of the naturalist, who, as Emerson said, "should domesticate me in nature" (*JMN* 4:214).

Emerson joined the prospects of natural history to those of urban life because together they taught the lesson that integration and disintegration are moments within the same circuit of technical activity. In the fable from "The American Scholar," the state of society looks like an inversion of Cuvier's Cabinet of Comparative Anatomy. (It also brings to mind Emerson's journals, which were places for assembling fragmentary passages of writing, the broken-up hands of future compositions.) The grotesque "members," putative individuals in America, strut about as anatomical parts dissociated from any larger organic integrity, which now may be projected only as an aggregate or mechanical combination. They manifest the uncanniness of what I have discussed as a renaturalized nature: that is, they appear not merely as inanimate ruins but as "walking monsters" that somehow mimic the effect of having life in themselves.

The saving irony, however, comes in the fact that the very monstrosity of both contexts—nature and the human world—shows itself as such only by contrast with whole compositions that abide either in retrospect or in prospect, just as the original systematic hand stands in prospective or retrospective relation to the broken-up hands of the present age. "Every thing is a monster till we know what it is for," Emerson declared in "The Uses of Natural History" (*EL* 1:17). As the ultimate science of uses, natural history can solve monstrosity because natural history, or something primordially like it, made the monsters apparent as such in the first place. So what Emerson describes in "The American Scholar," what Zola describes in *Nana,* is not raw nature but a museum turned inside out. Reorganizing the museum will entail shifting the vantage point from a place outside the spectacle to a central place within it, and remembering its elements in a newly conceived prospect or project of the whole.

This brings me back to the speculative model presented in the format of the *passage*. Like any architectural form, the *passage* was a metaphor for habitation in the most vivid sense. Its shape not only reflected rules of optical subjectivity but also the body's ability to pursue and inspect at first hand the eye's prospects. These prospects were transitive and instrumental rather than static and substantial; hence, as its name suggests, the *passage* was an environment of artfully sustained transition. Neither in nor out of doors, but flanked by windows on either hand, these walkways were collective thresholds through which the spectator could move without necessarily crossing into the fixity of a specific place of exchange.

Like present-day malls and gallerias, the *passages* can be seen as architectural projections of an idea that preoccupied Emerson in all his work—the famous idea that "power ceases in the instant of repose; it resides in the moment of transition from a past to a new state" (*CW* 2:40). What Emerson said of Plato's dialectic, he could as well have said of the *passages:* that they were "adroitly managed to present as much transitional surface as possible" (*CW* 4:32).[76] Passing by the serial windows prolonged a consumer's sense of unconstrained possibility. One could behold the spectacle of goods and people while feeling invisible to others, unfixed by any single determination. Emerson perceived that such commercial spaces created a kind of freedom characteristic of the age:

> Young men are very fond of Paris, partly, no doubt, because of the perfect freedom—freedom from observation as well as interference,—in which each one walks after the sight of his own eyes; & partly because the extent & variety of objects offers an unceasing entertainment. So long as a man has francs in his pocket he needs consult neither time nor other men's convenience; wherever in the vast city he is, he is within a stone's throw of a patissier, a cafe, a restaurant, a public garden, a theatre & may enter when he will. (*JMN* 4:201–202)

Emerson's term "unceasing entertainment" precisely details the strong mix of his experience among the rows of shop windows. There was a certain pointlessness in the repetition of display frames, a sense of merely substitutive rather than progressive arrangement. On the other hand, "entertainment" implies a pose of in-betweenness, an exhilarating state of being both sheltered and in the open, held and still let go. This fostered in the spectator a kind of distracted individualism. Suspended indefinitely between the demands of specific purchase, Emerson discovered himself walking "after the sight of his own eyes"; and yet this mode of optical passage was full of involuntary turns or distractions of attention, as he also found that the "dazzling shops" made it "very hard for a stranger to walk with eyes forward ten yards in any part of the city" (203).

Among the displays of the city, not only things but subjectivity itself dissolved and reappeared following the rules of the reflective and transparent media. By virtue of these rules, the purely optical latitude Emerson discovered in Paris compensated him for darker reductions, as commodious prospects also brought home the limits of consumers' abilities to spend.

"They had a right to their eyebeams," as Emerson would say in another context, "and all the rest was Fate" (*W* 6:19). In the *passage* "all the rest" amounted to the francs in one's pocket. Strolling through a shopping mall will illustrate, cartoonishly, the Emersonian notion that, beyond our limited options of how much to spend or save, the only unlimited power we have is our sense of power in speculating on our prospects. Since these prospects must (in order to come into conceptual focus) acquire some figurative character or other, we cannot help reframing them in terms of their "cost"; and so we are returned, perhaps unhappily, to the matter of our "capital" or ability to spend.

The sense of power entertained in such cross-references between prospects and capital is more complicated than what we feel in simply gazing at an array of things, or in looking forward to something that might come. It derives from the interventions of serial acts of framing, acts that comprise the history of natural subject matter. Hence the window is an apt figure for the conditions of sight Emerson would soon investigate in *Nature:* "The beauty that shimmers in the yellow afternoons of October, who ever could clutch it? Go forth to find it, and it is gone: 't is only a mirage as you look from the windows of diligence" (*CW* 1:14). In Emerson's economy, prospects only appear when the eye converts opaque boundaries into transparent media and thus sees through one defining, restricting form—a shop window, a zoological cabinet, a page—to the image of more attractive things on the far side.

The *passage,* within the very shelter it offered from the streets, opened up what the Muséum attempted to contain. I have already, in assessing the "reflective" aspects of natural history and urban displays, suggested that they presented distinct models of sublimity. It should now be apparent that the two models showed alternative and complementary perspectives on the same subject matter. The "nature" of this subject matter consisted in its fusion of material substance and reflective technicality. Its elemental form—the form of its invisibility as well as its visibility—was that of the classification, which was as clearly bodied forth in transparent display frames as in particular specimens or commodities.

The Muséum offered relief from the ennui of urban reflection by subordinating its classific subject matter within hierarchical, progressive frameworks. Yet the Muséum also made patent what was assumed at large within its urban environment: it not only presented nature as idea but, more astonishingly, it dissolved both ideas and natural facts into the activity of device. The Muséum exposed *logos* as *technē,* demonstrating that the idea or meaning of nature was identical with techniques of production and delivery. The *passages* echoed the Muséum's claims to total representation just as they mirrored its strategies of display. Beyond such correspondences, however, the *passages* showed that the forms of containment at work in the Muséum could themselves be held within no outer limit. The classifying frames of the *passages* disappeared into the distance, into the future, toward a vanishing point whose apparent finality was nothing other than the temporary limit of the spectator's line of sight.

Having isolating the technical form of the classification as the fundamental element within the Muséum and the *passage,* one should be able to gain an idea of the peculiar sort of shelter these institutions offered the public. Such shelter was no asylum from urban life; on the contrary, it was a synoptic clarification of the reality that otherwise proliferated in confusing variety throughout the city. The Muséum and the *passages* housed the very means by which citizens perpetually unhoused themselves and, generously enough, they invited citizens to make themselves at home there. They made a display of the power that created "nature" and left it open to the critical inspection of the human creator.

Just as the corridors of the *passages* penetrated city blocks, the shelter I refer to could only be found within the anatomical core of Paris. But "core" is a misleading term, since I am speaking of something that was not so much a place as it was a technical process generative of places. Certainly it is paradoxical to suggest that there could be real shelter inside the double heart of classification itself, the deed that detaches and dismembers its subject matter even as it composes new unities. Even though it involves finding or making a "place" for a natural fact, classification also depends upon severe displacements of conceptual focus, so that the relation between categories, even in hierarchies of classes, appears as discontinuous as it is continuous.

This double sense of location and abandonment of place was reflected in the fact that the Muséum and the *passages,* shelters though they were, discouraged spectators from reposing long in a single spot. Even within these contexts of restless abstraction, however, the spectator enjoyed a kind of membership not easily felt elsewhere in the city. This was, to use a word covering both the Muséum and the *passages,* "museum" membership, a membership that might be defined in terms of "unceasing entertainment." It eloquently proposed a new model of human integration founded on principles of sheer transition.

Emerson experienced this new urban membership as "boundless domestic liberty" (*L* 1:390), a state of being conveniently inside his own household yet without the orthodox constraints of home. Such was his freedom to walk "after the sight of his own eyes." Within the grand museum of Paris, he found himself invisible to others to precisely the extent that he subordinated the world of objects under his gaze. The museum, in the city, in the Jardin des Plantes, and finally in Emerson's writing project, was the best available model for the innermost speculative self, a self unknowable by others and accountable for all otherness. Beyond the colorful distractions of subject matter, Emerson the spectator beheld himself, in his clearest possible reflection, as still another instance of the museum.

3

∽ ∽ ∽

Life's Writing

O bright dark, or Dark Day of Genius—still secret to thyself,
because there is an excess before, which hides from thee the
thing done.

—Emerson, *Journals* (1842)

The path leading from the Muséum to the *passages* and then to the
workshop of Emerson's writing introduces a practice in which forms
of containment become instrumental, vehicular, loosened up without
sacrificing their power to mark precise circumferences in the world
at large. This was the dynamic prospect illuminated by the Muséum,
even though Cuvier and Agassiz insisted that their classifications
merely recovered an immutable system of identities in nature.

For Emerson, classifying came to mean finding new uses for things.
By the same logic, looking critically at already existing classifications—in books, religions, philosophies, whole frameworks of
thought—meant reading them not as fixed truths but as catalogs of
prior uses. A classification, he said, is "used by the Scholar as a help
to the memory, or a bare illustration of his present perception of the
law of nature, the memorandum only of his last lesson, and in the
face of it, only a makeshift; merely momentary; a landing place on
the staircase, a bivouac for the night, and implying a march, a
progress, a conquest tomorrow" (*EL* 3:129–130). Emerson appropriated tools and methods from the natural history of his time; he
married himself to the naturalist's project; but it was all for the pur-

poses of "conquest," for the trials of fresh pursuit, rather than for mapping out some static external reality. Hence natural history, which gave him the means of bringing his project as a whole to bear on each new act of writing, also freed him from the authority of prior classifications—his own as well as those of other writers—and sent him outside institutions into the world of experience, experiment, and what he called "biography."

In an 1839 journal entry that reappears as a central statement in "History," Emerson describes his practice as not history at all, but biography:

> There is no history: There is only Biography. The attempt to perpetuate, to fix a thought or principle, fails continually. You can only live for yourself: Your action is good only whilst it is alive,—whilst it is in you. The awkward imitation of it by your child or your disciple, is not a repetition of it, is not the same thing but another thing. The new individual must work out the whole problem of science, letters, & theology for himself, can owe his fathers nothing. There is no history; only biography. (*JMN* 7:202)

Of course contemporary disciples of history will find little to agree with in the initial sense of Emerson's refrain, "There is no history; only biography," since it seems to reverse the normal view that any life story is at most a telling fragment of the much larger story known as history. Still less would they accept the refrain's practical implication, as Emerson draws it out in "History," that individual experience offers the original scripture against which historical records are to be reviewed in the way of commentary: "The fact narrated must correspond to something in me to be credible or intelligible. We as we read must become Greeks, Romans, Turks, priest and king, martyr and executioner, must fasten these images to some reality in our secret experience, or we shall see nothing, learn nothing, keep nothing."[1]

Emerson promotes a narrow egotism, it would seem, a domestication or personalizing of Carlyle's grand presumptions in his book *On Heroes and Hero-Worship*. Understanding history becomes something like the selective identification with heroes, criminals, or victims enjoyed by the novel reader in fireside raptures. Or perhaps, in a more generous view, Emerson argues a kind of readerly Platonism, whereby historical events gain meaning when they ferry us back to the soul's transcendent realities, and reading history prompts us to recall what we already know. Emerson's stress, however, falls on the word "experience," which for a Platonist is the last place to seek reality. Individual experience makes up the ground for history just as it comprises all achievements of seeing, learning, and remembering. Yes, Emerson does affirm a reality transcending history, but he indicates that it hides somewhere in empirical activity, in the sort of activity that absorbs our lives and makes subject matter for biography.

The nature of this activity becomes less obvious when we observe that Emerson calls it *secret* experience, which we must regard not as the cherished and largely squalid personal realm of fantasies, memories, and self-conceits (these are shadows of conventional genres, merely held close), but as a strain of activity he elsewhere insists is "impersonal," an ineffable but nevertheless empirical work of probing, suffering, tracing paths, making memories. It is the individual's own work; but the individual person ultimately has no more authority over it than a stranger has. This secret experience may not itself be the same as the realities it leads up to, yet it shares the spontaneous quality attributed to every incursion of reality. As Emerson writes in "Intellect," "In the most worn, pedantic, introverted, self-tormentor's life, the greatest part is incalculable by him, unforeseen, unimaginable, and must be, until he can take himself up by his own ears. What am I? What has my will done to make me that I am? Nothing. I have been floated into this thought, this hour, this connection of events, by secret currents of might and mind, and my ingenuity and wilfulness have not thwarted, have not aided to an appreciable degree" (CW 2.191 195).

Prophecy derives from what lies at hand in everyday life: "this thought, this hour, this connection of events." While Emerson speaks of his experience in terms of ecstasy and revelation, it has little of the world-annihilating quality of the conversion of Paul or the rapture of Ezekiel. Emerson's spontaneous, "secretly" produced vision remains decisively empirical. As I have already indicated, even Emerson's most extreme rendering of ecstatic experience, the transparent eyeball passage from *Nature,* describes instrumental procedures that never stop devising new ways of getting through the world. The empirical nature of eyesight somehow conspires with incalculable breakthroughs, and we lose our way if we try to separate ordinary perception from revelation. Emerson says as much in "Self-Reliance": "Every man discriminates between the voluntary acts of his mind, and his involuntary perceptions, and knows that to his involuntary perceptions a perfect faith is due. He may err in the expression of them, but he knows that these things are so, like day and night, not to be disputed" (37).

This connection of unconscious experience with actual perception is significant, since terms of eyesight—focal detachment on one side and focused objectification on the other—also furnish a traditional model for conscious knowledge. Emerson anticipates Freud by treating thinking as a kind of second sight superimposed over a primary perceptual process in which encounters with new things, while actively sought out, still strike us with the sense of involuntary experience.[2]

The claim that the empirical work of perception makes up a common ground for both knowledge and experience suggests that detached consciousness corresponds, "from far and on high," to patterns of experience it cannot directly acknowledge. These patterns are always being knit before us in the texture of nature. The knitting happens in the most everyday activity, in the impromptu, largely unappreciated experiments of perception. So the passage from "Intellect" continues: "Our spontaneous action is always the best. You cannot, with your best deliberation and heed, come so close to any question as your spontaneous glance shall bring you, whilst you rise from your bed, or walk abroad in the morning after meditating the matter before sleep, on the previous night. Our thinking is a pious reception" (*CW* 2:195).

Our thinking, if devoted to perception, piously receives the quick of our seeing, which itself is both passively open and aggressively outgoing, as in the glances that bring us closest to our questions. Perception offers immediate answers in its dealing with things, even if the answers do not translate into the rhetoric of the question. "The soul answers never by words," Emerson says in "The Over-Soul," "but by the thing itself that is inquired after" (167). And once again, in "Intellect": "How can we speak of the action of the mind under any divisions, as, of its knowledge, of its ethics, of its works, and so forth, since it melts will into perception, knowledge into act? Each becomes the other. Itself alone is. Its vision is not like the vision of the eye, but is union with the things known" (193). Emerson's picture of mental life revives the manual sense of grasping or taking *(capere)* buried in the word "perception." Vision has a hands-on dimension, as it were, in which worker and material come together. Holding such union in mind, we do well to set aside easy separations between spirit and the physical world. With perception as our example, we might infer that if part of experience or experimental life seems transcendent, this is not because it belongs to another world, but because it works, in this world, at a point ahead of all our capacities for direct inspection. It is what we do before turning to take stock of things, and what we do, in advance of ourselves, even when taking stock of things.

Are we really engaged in a strain of experience not just kept secret from others, but that by nature works secretly ahead of our own conceptual grasp, unavailable in any direct sense to knowledge, reflection, or evaluation? Such a claim would contradict the central claims of the empirical tradition in philosophy; for in restricting the ground of knowledge to experience, the empiricists also forbid the possibility of any *experience* that does not coincide with the conditions of knowledge. Empiricism outrages rationalist positions by claiming that knowledge has no resources outside experience. On the other hand, Emerson upsets empiricist epistemology with a more extreme empiricism, asserting that the leading edge of experience cuts its way through the world at a point beyond the direct grasp of knowledge. For all we know, our secret experience leaves knowledge somewhat mournfully in its wake: "Thoughtless people contradict as readily the statement of perceptions as of opinions, or rather much more readily; for, they do not distinguish between perception and notion. They fancy that I choose to see this or that thing. But perception is not whimsical, but fatal" (38). The distinction between perception and notion is crucial. Taking perception as the prime instance of spontaneous activity, Emerson's American empiricism finds the question of what we do far more to the point than any questions of what we know.

Perhaps it is ironic that such a severe reliance on experience revives a sense of the transcendental; yet Emerson's way of transcendence is far from Plato's or from that of Christianity. Emerson argues a visionary empiricism, or an empirical transcendentalism, in which transcendence obtains not through dialectics, whereby thought rises through discrete categories of being, but by virtue of our "reception" of the secret yet practical work going on ahead of us in the course of time and events. The work is ours; it goes on assiduously in the most casual glance. The challenge in receiving it is to make our notions or reports of it faithful to the standard it sets, secretly, for everything that actually pertains to us.

Here I come back to the enterprise of biography, which addresses Emerson's demand for some reality to which we might "fasten" the detached records of history. Emerson's claim for biography is hardly Carlyle's—that the meaning of human history concentrates into the life stories of a few great men. Nor does he mean that all historians are covert autobiographers rehearsing their own cherished notions of themselves no matter what the purported topic. The deepest thrust of "There is only Biography" is that, before all endeavors of understanding and recovery, *life writes*. Consequently life makes up the ultimate resource for reading: "The student is to read history actively and not passively; to esteem his own life the text, and books the commentary" (5).

It is untrue that only a few eminent lives become the subjects of biographies. We are all biographers, *bios*-writers, writing ahead of our limited notions of who we are whether we are illiterates or professional historians. Our biography, which is as much a work as a text, remains at once both private and impersonal; nevertheless, it offers a necessary model for what we gather in the way of notions, a way that includes both our notation of life and the rules governing its interpretation. In notions, we report biography indirectly through the metaphorics of retrospection. In regard to the initial writing of biography, normal history and autobiography are doublings back, strategic detours in what is really our ongoing quest for authority, a quest to coincide with a primary authority, our own spontaneous authoring, already at work in experience. Our habitual deference to historical notions only masks, and blindly apes, our constitutional deference in respect to this primary authority.

The secret, continuous life of every individual affirms the ground of biography as a democratic basis for all essays in history. It gives Emerson the opening statement for his first essay, "History"—"There is one mind common to all individual men" (3)—as well as the founding stake for a lifelong series of essays. "There is only Biography" means that writing first coincides with life, a life we hold in common even while keeping it to ourselves. When we seek to write the notional history of life, as of course we must, we are bound to try our utmost to reproduce that original coincidence.

❧ ❧ ❧

The great difficulty of making history vital—of making it something more than professional duty, hero worship, or a respectable means of passing off challenges currently at hand—consists in recovering evidence of the past in ways that address our own vitality. No doubt we first need confidence in our own vitality. If we have it, if we rely on experience as biography, we have a model resource for history writing. In "History," Emerson lays claim to this resource with images that anticipate the moral soundings of *Moby-Dick:* "The primeval world,—the Fore-World, as the Germans say,—I can dive to it in myself as well as grope for it with researching fingers in catacombs, libraries, and the broken reliefs and torsos of ruined villas" (14).

The origins that archaeology digs for make up one kind of foreground; but Emerson values such research only as an inverted reflection of the work of disciplined abandonment that dives forward into a realm lying ahead of (in time and in priority) the manifold fragments of the present world. Biography takes interest in origins because they instruct us in the originality of the life in question. The same holds for our own onward biography: all interests in historical origins are conscripts in our own drive for originality. And originality, as opposed to origins, always lies ahead of us, in our prospects; it consists in what we are capable of achieving rather than in anything we have already done or been.

However it strains the present and rewrites the past, original work must turn to the future for the perfection of its ends. Of course, subordinating origins to originality does not mean giving up the critical methods used to uncover origins. Emerson abandons the direction but not the techniques of historical inquest: he seeks to replace backward pursuits with something like an archaeology of the future or a natural history of prospects. Looking backward, we can set particular original deeds within one historical narrative or another. In its own terms, however, originality will be history's consummation. In getting to the whole of it, to the Fore-World ahead of us, we must in our private experience go over all the narratives that lead up to it: "Every mind must know the whole lesson for itself—must go over the whole ground. What it does not see, what it does not live, it will not know" (6).

"History" calls for founding historical insight on resources of seeing and living; we are to recover historical facts by raising them toward the condition of direct perception. Again, it is characteristic of

Emerson that such a position derives from an extreme empiricism rather than from idealism or from a restrictive phenomenology. Emerson would concur with Hume's argument that intellectual notions merit belief to the degree they approach the liveliness of perceptions.[3] (A similar criterion may also be found in Blake's views on poetic imagination and, later, in Freud's views on dreaming.) But to Hume's empiricism Emerson adds the crucial point (and this allies him with both Blake and Freud) that perception is an outgoing enterprise, meeting and transforming nature in such a way as to *be* nature so far as the individual is concerned.

The secret import of such perceptual work is signaled back to us by our obliquely intimate relation to the unconsciousness of what we see around us in nature. Even in its secrecy this import offers a model reference point for evaluation; hence it can be spoken of as a kind of primary writing, the vital biographical text commented on by books and organized reflections. "Civil and natural history, the history of art and of literature, must be explained from individual history, or must remain words" (*CW* 2:10).

This imperative points to Emerson's major format for explanation from individual history, the serial essays inaugurated in "History." Granting biography's authority, Emerson founds history writing on the novel, experimental basis of the individual essay. The essay is the vehicle, partly literary, partly scientific, that most closely pursues the trials and revelations of empirical life. Unafraid of contradictions, encompassing both critical commentary and experimental stances, Emerson's essays pursue biography equally by reporting on it and by provoking readers aggressively to further perceptions.

"History" opens the enterprise of Emerson's essays much as Emerson had opened his eyes in Paris in 1833: by restoring the prospect of history to the original sense of the word, the sense preserved in the term "natural history." This means subordinating records and facts to the present work of perception. As Emerson says, the effective historian "must attain and maintain that lofty sight where facts yield their secret sense, and poetry and annals are alike" (6). But there is a practical dimension to such seeing, since Emerson also treats history (here again evoking natural history) as study of the facts gathered presently before us in respect to our decisions about what to do with them. The doing itself, performed partly in the transparencies of "lofty sight" and partly in the hands-on engagements of physical life, makes up the invisible Fore-World ultimately heralded by those facts. Certainly, the records of past events comprise one aspect of the facts at hand; hence in Emerson's time (before Lyell's and Darwin's geological model came to dominate the life sciences) geological history spoke to one aspect of the whole history of nature also studied in synchronic disciplines such as mineralogy, zoology, botany, and astronomy. In the Jardin des Plantes, Emerson beheld a model (really a model environment, for it established nature as a methodical context for his own biographical enterprise) that demonstrated possibilities for the encyclopedic recomposition of nature's history. It was a new model, boasting a contemporary genesis that neither literature nor chronological history writing could match. On the moment, Emerson saw how writing natural history would go: it would include the history of the past, of contemporary times, and of his own life. But this prospect also gave urgency to his pursuit of the Fore-World already alive in his own secret experience. From that point on, the work of extended composition, which could only find shape through essays in the natural history of the intellect, had to be continuously derived and rederived from the even more thoroughgoing project of diving forward into biographical foundations.

Emerson pursues biography most closely in the endlessly repeated instances of foundation worked out in his journals. These instances were themselves founded in spontaneous perception, perception inseparable from writing and from revising what, in the past, he had already left in writing. The result is impersonal biography, or at least a series of renewed experiments in approaching impersonal biography. Anything has possible value in such a project, so nothing is categorically excluded. Revelation shares the page with routine details; quotations jostle alongside new insights; hard facts border on dreams of the night before. It is inevitable that significant patterns emerge across the range of experimental findings, and that these patterns themselves become new findings, each one shaping a more focused interest or expectation in regard to future efforts. In working over his journals, Emerson cataloged these higher patterns in the form of topics or classifications; and, as I have noted, he relied on them as both indexes for research and as preliminary modes of organizing the more extended experiments of lectures and essays.

The form that emerges throughout this work is the vehicular form of the topic itself, the clear open place of invention. In terms of

Emerson's writing practice, the topic was his "bare common" crossed and recrossed in new deeds of perception, the open public place that yielded scope for individual history. Emerson built up his lectures and essays from topics; then again, each higher composition was itself a new essay upon a topic, generating a more capacious circumscription of field. I have suggested that models for Emerson's topical practice appeared in natural history classifications and in their public display places as well as in new commercial formats, like the Parisian *passages,* which displayed numerous classes of commodities (in which each specimen appeared as the representative of its commodity species). The examples of these organizing forms opened up possibilities for remaking history; at the same time, their transcendental technology also pointed ahead to the place where mind and material creation converge and depart from each other in the immediate, secret experience of the individual.

We identify this secret, common place (recalling how the metaphor of place informs the notion of the topic) as the Fore-World of biography, the scene of life's automatic writing. We might also identify it as nature, though not as the nature we normally take for granted. "To speak truly," writes Emerson, deadpanning in *Nature,* "few adult persons can see nature. Most persons do not see the sun" (*CW* 1:9). This statement recalls the Platonic–New Testament paradox of the sighted blind, those mundane souls who "seeing see not" (Matt: 13:13). Yet for Emerson it is not some otherworldly reality most people fail to see: he is concerned about our literal failure to see nature.

Emerson's rhetorical bias toward spirit can often make us forget the quite literal, material implications of many of his points—which is to say we too easily overlook the intimate degree to which his transcendentalist enterprise coincides with attention to actual things and deeds. The Platonic notion that ordinary vision imprisons thought, offering at best a negative reflection of where real insight stops, cannot describe Emerson's appraisal of nature. To be sure, *Nature*'s catalog of its subject's "uses" includes the prompting of the mind to the negative stance of idealism; but this occurs as a "noble doubt," an advantageous skepticism rather than a world-denying faith. Idealism, like nature's other uses, creates leverage for the real essays of faith—actions—which take practical effect in the arena of natural life.

Success in seeing nature depends on our inventiveness, our ability to turn things to use. Matter and spirit meet in uses. Hence even the most sophisticated invention cannot discredit the materiality of things; it only refines the material for more ambitious purposes. Toward the end of *Nature,* in the chapter "Spirit," Emerson writes: "All the uses of nature admit of being summed up in one, which yields the activity of man an infinite scope" (*CW* 1:37). Human activity needs scope: not just latitude to see, but also material and opportunity for getting new things done. American nature presented scope for invention on a grand scale (Whitman spoke of it as "vista"), but Emerson finds scope just as reliably in words and phrases.

An example occurs in the sentence just cited, where he uses the verb "yields" to draw together senses of relinquishing and bringing forth. The word's doubleness qualifies one-sided views of use by implying that human activity does not simply wrest its achievements from nature as from a recalcitrant medium, but that even the most antagonistic actions cultivate in nature the supernatural harvest of a common practical and intellectual scope. Nature, recognized as a material process of using, working, and acting, yields *to* human activity by yielding human activity. The yielding, integrating edge between material nature and human effort keeps generating the biographical original for all essays in history.

What we say about nature we must also say about language. Emerson insists that our relation to nature tallies with our relation to language; and one of the effects of this claim is to democratize the ancient tradition that compares poetic work to the earth's cultivation. The deep reluctance of language to submit to the need for originality is a vital factor in poetic work; for it takes this natural reluctance, along with inspired cultivation, to yield poems that are as much a produce of the common language as of the individual poet.[4]

Like New England soil, the American idiom made for harder lessons on this score than did the rich fields of Latium. The mills lining the Merrimack were not the only sites where a reluctant nature gave grounds for invention: Emerson's writing, by its style as much as by the images and ideas it calls up, also turned natural limits into more refined, "transcendental" uses. Emerson grounded his refinements through special devotion to the places in language and in nature where limits force themselves into clear view. We might think just as readily of Thoreau's Katahdin, Whitman's sterile beaches, Melville's Nantucket, Dickinson's blank snowfields, and Frost's desert places. These American places of invention follow Emerson's essays in holding hard to a certain native poverty, where it takes the reluctance of bare ground to yield the transparencies of copious invention. Only from a historical point of view does this confrontation appear to take place between incommensurables, as though raw nature and refined spirit could be no more than juxtaposed. From a biographical perspective, it must be granted that the yielding happens where we live, along that sharp edge of experience from which both invention and native ground are even now being derived.

Emerson had many words for the boundary I am rather tendentiously speaking of as nature's "edge": scope, circumference, limit, form, character, fate. All of them name not just a fixed external boundary but also a principle of definition exerting itself within actions and indeed in contradiction to seemingly unbounded first impulses. As much as this principle complicates considerations of freedom and originality, it also acts as the graphic element within biography, since life constantly makes itself legible through new determinations in one fact after another. As Emerson states in *Representative Men,* life always comes to issue graphically: "In nature, this self-registration is incessant." Hence he presents Goethe as the epitome of the writer because Goethe, for whom being a man of letters also meant becoming a naturalist, was most systematically responsive to nature's total sense as life's automatic writing:

> Nature will be reported. All things are engaged in writing their history. The planet, the pebble, goes attended by its shadow. The rolling rock leaves its scratches on the mountain; the river its channel in the soil; the animal its bones in the stratum; the fern and leaf its modest epitaph in the coal. The falling drop makes its sculpture in the sand or the stone. Not a foot steps into the snow, or along the ground, but prints in characters more or less lasting a map of its march. Every act of the man inscribes itself in the memories of his fellows, and in his own manners and face. The air is full of sounds, the sky of tokens, the ground is all memoranda and signatures, and every object covered over with hints, which speak to the intelligent. (*CW* 4:151)

Like Emerson's journal project, nature is at once graphically full yet also constantly enlarging itself by writing over its own topics: "Nature is intricate, overlapped, interweaved, and endless" (*W* 6:36). Its text records past actions and anticipates future ones. Each graphic element is ready-made for natural history, as nature's spontaneous biography offers blueprints for the naturalist's critical methods. Early botanists believed that all plants displayed "signatures" indicating their practical uses; by the same token, the "memoranda" and "hints" Emerson sees in nature are designed to prompt new actions in regard to them. Intellect takes these hints by subjecting biographical facts to its own uses; as Emerson goes on to say, it selects, classifies, and "disposes them in a new order," making up a "second creation" (*CW* 4:151–152).

Even when informed by intellectual remove, however, the primary writing of life continues; we cannot be conscious of it without fixing a new record and going on, unconsciously, still further. We might well take the touchy memoranda of our own lives as subject matter and dedicate ourselves to the special genre of autobiography; but we still do the unconscious writing of life, which registers its own style in spite of all the ways we construe ourselves and our objects. Life will always be ahead of its subject matter, perhaps never so vividly as when that subject matter is what we take to be ourselves.

For Emerson, biography prescribes both history and nature, and makes them exchangeable. Nature absorbs the stratified memory of history; history assumes the phenomenal plasticity of nature. We depart from Emerson in separating these two categories from one another (natural history insists on their marriage), yet if for a moment we try the separation, we will find that history and nature indicate two poles between which Emerson found himself oscillating. He often represented these as poles of memory and immediacy, retrospect and surprise. Taken by themselves, they presented Emerson with the alternatives of exiled, spectral observation, on the one side, and lethean abandonment on the other. Brooding on the patterns of his own mental experience in his 1837 journal, Emerson famously defines individual being as a process of "contradiction" sparking these two dead ends into antagonistic but mutual life:

A certain wandering light comes to me which I instantly perceive to be the Cause of Causes. It transcends all proving. It is itself the ground of being; and I see that it is not one & I another, but this is the life of my life. That is one fact, then; that in certain moments I have known I existed directly from God, and am, as it were, his organ. And in my ultimate consciousness Am He. Then, secondly,

the contradictory fact is familiar, that I am a surprised spectator &
learner of all my life. This is the habitual posture of the mind,—
beholding. But whenever the day dawns, the great day of truth on
the soul, it comes with awful invitation to blend with its aurora.

Cannot I conceive the Universe without a contradiction? (*JMN*
5:337)

This passage appears to treat beholding and being, memory and
immediacy, as alternating stages in a binary pattern of experience.
Emerson invokes this same pattern in many places, perhaps most
prominently at the opening of "The Over-Soul": "Our faith comes
in moments; our vice is habitual" (*CW* 2:159). Yet closer inspection
shows that the journal passage describes something more complex
than an up-and-down toggle. In fact, elements of either beholding or
being seem to infiltrate what ought to be the exclusive instances of
each opposing condition. Even in moments of faith, Emerson's sense
of divine immersion is buffered by a persistent framework of seeing
and knowing: "I have *known* that I existed directly from God, and
am, *as it were,* his organ." These traces of objectifying consciousness
hold off the annihilation of "the great day of truth," replacing its
apocalyptic immediacy with a less literal approach, an "awful *invitation* to blend."

Similarly, Emerson describes the static detachment of "beholding"
as a condition to some degree fractured, destabilized by surprise: "I
am a surprised spectator & learner of all my life." By virtue of this
mutual contamination of opposites, memory becomes unsettled and
immediacy stretches across an expanded temporal frame. The apparent fixities of retrospection, for all Emerson's detachment, remain
shaky and factitious; and in spite of his faith, he puts off headlong
immersion in favor of its auroral prospects. It follows that the answer
to his anxious question—"Cannot I conceive the Universe without a
contradiction?"—is *no,* which is itself a contradictory way of saying,
"Yes, even in your most extreme moments, it is precisely through
contradiction that the universe is to be conceived."

Even though Emerson often emphasizes his preference for immediate being over retrospection by opposing the two in biased di-
chotomies such as faith and habit or enthusiasm and repose, his writing conceives a middle passage probing unevenly, experimentally
between extremes. In this sense, writing imitates the patterns of both
experience and the dynamic texture of nature, which Emerson tells

us is "thoroughly mediate" (*CW* 1:25). But he also insists that nature's mediateness consists more in contradiction than in compromise, and that the force of every contradiction derives from powerful extremes. This is one of the chief ways in which nature corresponds to biography and leads into writing.

Emerson himself is perhaps most contradictory when he ventures definitions of nature, as he does on almost every page. In "The Method of Nature" he claims that "nature is the memory of the mind. That which once existed in intellect as pure law, has now taken body as Nature. It existed already in the mind in solution: now, it has been precipitated, and the bright sediment is the world" (123). In spite of this picture of crystalline fixity, where all beholding is necessarily retrospective, where all traces only memorialize past events, Emerson offers a contradictory account of nature only three paragraphs later:

> Its smoothness is the smoothness of the pitch of the cataract. Its permanence is a perpetual inchoation. Every natural fact is an emanation, and that from which it emanates is an emanation also, and from every emanation is a new emanation. If anything could stand still, it would be crushed and dissipated by the torrent it resisted, and if it were a mind, would be crazed; as insane persons are those who hold fast to one thought, and do not flow with the course of nature. (124)

It would appear that nature itself thrives by contradiction, arguing its case now from memory, now in melting revelation. But as such contradictions accumulate they also force our attention to a point ahead of every particular argument. We read nature, as Emerson teaches us to read his essays, in a permanent attitude of expectation. Emerson's contradictions build up the implicit sense of an activity at work in advance of all its rhetorical positions, which seem most partial when they make the most absolute claims. The activity itself is mediate and practical even though it works at the transcendent edge of the writing of life.

Conceiving of nature as biography, as life's writing, is one way of negotiating passage between the twofold aspect of nature as a rigid text, with meanings dictated by history's authority, and nature as a torrent of pointless immediacy, with no definitions in which meaning can reside. Either aspect, taken by itself, has deadly implications for the human spirit, which in the first extreme would find itself superannuated from the start, haunting the sepulchres of a finished world;

while in the second, this same spirit would be buried in a flood of evanescence, unable to find itself at all. Between these poles of life-in-death and death-in-life, mechanical fate and meaningless freedom, our secret experience blazes its way. The life that takes effect with transcendent authority in fact moves contradictorily among extremes.

Emerson catches this double ply of transcendence and practical negotiation in his well-known phrase from "Self-Reliance": "This one fact the world hates, that the soul *becomes* . . ." (*CW* 2:40). By leaving open that particular transitive verb, Emerson pictures an identity that is unassignable to any particular object precisely because of its inclination to transform itself in regard to any number of objects. And if any number of objects will serve, this means that no particular object can be fastened permanently to the soul's becoming, which "forever degrades the past, turns all riches to poverty, all reputations to a shame, confounds the saint with the rogue, shoves Jesus and Judas equally aside."[5]

Emerson's passage experiments with the harsh thesis that, if all the landing places of becoming (moral oppositions, for instance, such as Judas and Jesus) are superimposed in rapid enough succession, they dissipate in torrential immediacy. This is history's narrative in diabolical fast motion; as "Experience" pictures it, "The parti-colored wheel must revolve very fast to appear white" (*CW* 3:34). The picture of subject and action persists, by repetition if not by continuity, while that of their specimen predicates pales into the blankness of an open topic. It is not hard to see why Nietzsche kept a translation of the *Essays* close at hand. But as powerfully as such nihilistic positions must have struck Nietzsche, he nevertheless had to acknowledge about Emerson that "his spirit always finds reasons for being satisfied, and even grateful."[6] Seen at a more humane speed, a speed appropriate to the material work of writing, "the soul *becomes* . . ." is a statement that appreciates each of its possible points of orientation. It is like one of the anaphoras or refrains that both breaks up and replenishes Whitman's catalogs in *Song of Myself*. In this view, the opened-up form of Emerson's phrase becomes a figure for life at work, for life always freshly emerging into the common world by turning to new tasks, becoming or defining itself by virtue of one ordinary thing or the next.

∞ ∞ ∞

That little phrase, "the soul *becomes*," is one of many moments when Emerson makes his words "do" something very much like what they seem to be stating. The effective deed takes place in our own reading as much as in his text. There are many other moments when his words do a great deal more than, or other than, what they seem to state. Still, we grant to Emerson both the overt statement and its covert implications. Ambiguity, contradiction, and excess of meaning contribute to the impression of a biographical character whose power to engage us exceeds its statements, even while that power is in one view defined by its statements. A few pages earlier in "Self-Reliance," Emerson gives the word "pass" much the same edge as that of "becomes": "We pass for what we are. Character teaches above our wills. Men imagine that they communicate their virtue or vice only by overt actions and do not see that virtue or vice emit a breath every moment" (*CW* 2:34).

The first sentence seems to say that we get by in the world by impersonating ourselves, passing ourselves off as something other than ourselves. The point has a hortatory air; it fits with Emerson's broader indictments of consistency and conformity. Even so, "Self-Reliance" also teaches that transition, passage, and becoming are crucial features of life, and that *anything* that enables us to move forward serves the authentic principle of "what we are." The ways of becoming pass through all our better and worse self-fabrications; and real and provisional identities must conspire to get ahead. We might be left once again with the sheer open-endedness of becoming if not for the next sentence, which indicates that a significant figure appears across the superimposed historical layers of everything we pass for. Emerson calls it "character," a kind of password we give without knowing it. As something pertaining to others as much as to ourselves, character works above our overt aims and intended legacies; it stays secretly ahead of us and out of our own reach. Character is the way we pass for what we are; it is how what we are performs in the common world. As such, character is bound to be a topic that dominates Emerson's reflections.

It would be hard to find a more comprehensive name for life's writing, since "character" combines the material element of writing with the vital boundaries of ethical possibility. Emerson insists on character's graphic aspect, which for him underscores the fact that it always comes to bear in the world as a whole form. "A character is like an acrostic or Alexandrian stanza," he says in the same paragraph from "Self-Reliance"; "read it forward, backward, or across, it still spells the same thing" (34). Again, in "Spiritual Laws," Emerson describes character as "like a quincunx of trees, which counts five, east, west, north, or south; or, an initial, medial, and terminal acrostic" (86). This graphic sense (a sense absent from the Greek concept of ethos) drives the ancient equation of character and fate into a more precise figure, for a character is by nature a sign in a history-writing (or journal-writing) representational system. A character may be an elemental sign among others or it may be the whole configuration of someone's mark in the world. The literary tradition of character sketching, going back to Theophrastus, shows that these whole configurations are themselves classifiable as parts of a larger but still limited system. Character's written nature makes it an impersonal concept, even though the rules for its normal significance hold locally and not universally.

On the other hand, character unifies the traces of a daimonic, unconscious pressure that escapes control, or rather that forces its own controlling implications into the world. We are accustomed to hunting this daimonic aspect of character in the dark basement of personality. Emerson, however, finds no reason to look for it outside the rather practical issue of "publication," an event qualified by the rules of local graphic conventions. Hence in "Spiritual Laws": "Human character does evermore publish itself. It will not be concealed. It hates darkness,—it rushes into light. The most fugitive deed and word, the mere air of doing a thing, the intimated purpose, expresses character. If you act, you show character; if you sit still, you show it; if you sleep, you show it."[7]

Emerson speaks of character as a whole effect whose significance includes not only obvious actions but also "the most fugitive deed and word." "Fugitive" here may mean either fleeting or covert, yet it seems Emerson uses the word to name those covert but pointed actions that pass themselves off under the guise of what is fleeting, inadvertent, or merely transitional. Character shows itself at least as much in style as in direct statement. (It is worth noting that, in our critical moment, discussions of "style" are not considered very stylish. We need the word, however, if only because "character" compels us to think of sentences as styluses, instruments marking impressions as well as formal written accomplishments.)

Emerson's own writing style, where ambiguous locutions and tricky syntactical bridgings persistently score points against the more obvious thrust of the sentence, makes for a supreme example of character's fugitive effect. What he admits in "History"—that "it is the fault of our rhetoric that we cannot strongly state one fact without seeming to belie some other" (*CW* 2:22)—becomes the rule in "Spiritual Laws": "The sentence must also contain its own apology for being spoken" (89). "Nominalist and Realist" carries the point even further: "No sentence will hold the whole truth, and the only way in which we can be just, is by giving ourselves the lie" (*CW* 3:143–144). We give ourselves the lie by contradictions; and we do so as well by accepting, as a kind of gift or gratuity, the peculiar geography of the sentence. The famous contradictions between Emerson's statements also take place within his individual statements: through ambiguity, his sentences admit their rhetorical faults, the partial meanings they at first seem to pass off on us; but they also justify themselves (the alternate sense of "apology") by offhandedly publishing their several internal faults or divides of meaning. These semantic faults, which are evident in each of the Emerson sentences just cited, mark the character of the apology. In an almost geological sense, the faults between fugitive and more enfranchised points expose not only the genius but also the natural history (the "lie") of the sentence; for the sentence publishes itself as a whole, as nature does, to the discerning critical eye.

The whole effect, which may be defined as character, is not so much the silently unifying effect of irony, where partialities point to an unspoken or impossible rhetorical unity, as it is an engagement in an arena of debate, argument and counterargument, an arena where the disposition of the whole truth is not in the background but ahead of us, at stake in our contentions. As "apology" implies, the whole effect of character, with all its contradictions and fugitive implications, is a matter of public issue.

The character of Emerson's sentences makes it hard to pass on from them, as fugitive effects keep disputing our grounds for departure. Almost always it seems there is another sense vitally at work in the statement beyond the senses already noted. This is never so much the case as when we feel we have already tried our hardest to understand everything the sentence says. When Emerson says, "The sentence must also *contain* its own apology for being spoken," he means, as I have noted, that the sentence should encode its apology, its characteristic reason for being. But he also suggests that the sentence must restrain or hem in a force that threatens to break it open or perhaps erase it altogether, a force that in its very dilemma of being contained recounts the natural history of the sentence or indeed of any sentence.

So it is not just that contradictions and supplementary points nicely play out a fugue within Emerson's sentences. His sentences, for their own sakes *as* coherent sentences, must drive powerful contradictions into something of an underground life. The sentence's fugitive sense, however, "will not be concealed": it shows itself characteristically in offhand meanings of words and phrases. For Emerson's reader, the effect can feel like a certain groundlessness, with statements threatening to come unhinged from one another and to open up into fragments of competing significance within their own grammatical boundaries. Instead of groundlessness, however, it would be more precise to speak of a ground that is contested, and that offers no hold for the stakes of meaningful foundation other than the challenge of contest. As Emerson says in "Circles," "this surface on which we now stand, is not fixed, but sliding" (*CW* 2:186).

Yet against this effect we must acknowledge something in the stubborn materiality of Emerson's sentences, with their stony words and spare Americanisms, that does in the hardest possible way "contain" the expansive pressure of their fugitive meanings. In Emerson's writing a rugged second nature gets rebuilt on the sliding surface of contest. By reproducing native limits—what "Fate" worships as "the Beautiful Necessity"—his writing hands down to us the character of the land and the language, "that plot of ground which is given to him to till" (28). So despite his fondness for western vistas, Emerson stays home in the bleak rocks and bare commons of his particular corner of America: "Thus all concentrates; let us not rove; let us sit at home with the cause" (41). This is not to deny the fugitive strains of romance everywhere in Emerson's writing; it is only to say that he manages to bear excess in one hand by keeping the bare necessities in the other. As his readers, we need some such hard common ground, even if it holds together only in words and sentences, before we can appreciate our possibilities for passing on.

❧ ❧ ❧

A kind of psychology, or something supplanting psychology, emerges from the wild coherence of Emersonian character—that is to say, from the whole impression of Emerson's writing style. Like most American accounts of mental life it boils down to an ethics, though not necessarily a prescriptive ethics and certainly not a morals.

Emerson's idea that character works against concealment, showing itself offhandedly in hints and airs, invites comparison with the analysis of seemingly unintentional behavior that Freud began undertaking in *The Psychopathology of Everyday Life*. Freud has made us vigilant to find meaningful patterns in slips, misreadings, faulty rememberings—fugitive deeds that appear to be mistakes in regard to the execution of normal purposes. We suppose these mistakes betray repressed intentions working at odds with the rules governing conscious activity. Emersonian character resembles Freud's unconscious intentions in that it affirms itself against a context of resistance, a normal context in which characteristic signs are most likely to be misunderstood or passed over. Yet the graphic nature of character also means that the resistant context, oddly enough, is character's own property as well as something containing it for the sake of coherence or identifiability. Thus in his essay "Character" Emerson describes his subject not in terms of a transcendental self, a pristine Me struggling to express itself against layers of factitious surface, but as a whole effect, a "masterpiece" of nature: "Character is nature in the highest form. It is of no use to ape it, or to contend with it. Somewhat is possible of resistance, and of persistence, and of creation, to this power, which will foil all emulation" (*CW* 3:61).

Such a statement jars strongly against Freud, for whom character appears as a pattern of symptoms whereby unconscious intentions insinuate their claims against a more superficial, uniform context of resistance. Emerson has no use for intentions per se: he defines character as the whole form of what one manages to do in the world. This includes all the contradictory effects of resistance, persistence, and creation; it includes the norm as well as the deviation. For Emerson as for many other Americans, character is not what we intend in spite of what we do, nor is it what we do to spite our intentions; it consists in what we actually *effect* independently of whether we plan it, approve it, or even know it. Questions of latent and patent motives, along with the layered mental apparatus they imply, simply fail to pertain. The meaning of character, like that of any fact in nature, consists wholly in its results.

Emerson's theory of character casts aside the dichotomy between instinctual self and inhibiting external form that European romanticism both nourishes and impossibly complicates, and that Freud, at least in his earlier publications, tends to conserve. The dichotomy becomes especially popular (in our time as much as in the nineteenth century) when assimilated to Rousseauistic sentiments that make a hero of the natural but sadly furtive human self, a self oppressed and corrupted by fraudulent social conventions. Following Nietzsche, Freud superbly resisted such moralization by reversing its orthodox terms of value.[8] But Emerson, with his stress on action and its consequences rather than on motives, simply leaves behind the sentimental picture of the self as a titan struggling against his chains, or as an oppressed victim hunting for small but intense avenues of self-dignification or revenge.

Instead of reading human nature as a battle between normative text and daimonic subtext, Emerson reads it as a matter of deed and counterdeed or even, in a phrase he favors, cause and effect. The result is no less agonistic, but now all sides contribute with equal daimonism to life's characteristic writing. This means that nature's text is indeed the true measure of the human self, though most people find it unbearable to deal with as such. "A man passes for that he is worth" (*CW* 2:91), Emerson repeats in "Spiritual Laws"; and also: "That only profits which is profitable. Life alone can impart life; and though we should burst, we can only be valued as we make ourselves valuable" (89).

Emersonian character does not apologize for a whole life that diminishes or loses itself as it appears in the world; instead it represents a wholeness already actively at work in the world, in the way of biography, as the full writing of life. There is a paradox here, just as there is a paradox in what Emerson, following Goethe and Carlyle, liked to call the "open secret" of nature. Nature is open because it turns out toward interpretation; and yet its interpretation has no end. It is the fact of the openness itself, its endless yield of possible uses, that keeps the larger part of nature a secret. Thus nature's real secrecy abides in its future rather than in its historical identity. We may say the same about our biography, which marks its impressions openly and publicly but nevertheless stays secret or unconscious in the main. Writing natural history, Emerson realized, is an enterprise responsive to this open secret. The disposition of the future's conscious recovery is at stake in natural history, as well as in critical contentions and historical inquiries. All such essays at recovery are important, even as they keep giving us the lie, since they try to survey our common basis for going on together with things.

I must keep insisting, even if somewhat tiresomely, on this difference between Emerson's and Freud's pictures of character. It shows Emerson renouncing a certain masterplot of romanticism (with roots reaching back to Plato and the New Testament) that still continues to attract true believers.[9] Many of Emerson's most influential stances—his championing of instinct, his attacks on conformity and consistency, his demands for originality—can make it tempting to confuse his self-affirming argument, which draws so much else from European romanticism, with the strain of piety that cheers for the underdog self in its mostly unsuccessful battle against a world of enthralling facticity.

To prefer this confusion, however, is to lose sight of much of what is most distinctive, not to mention most American, in Emerson's work. At the worst it can lead readers to equate Emerson's optimism with business ethics or else with a kind of Panglossian moral idiocy. At the very least, the old standard disables us from understanding how Emerson can declare that character always presents itself successfully—which is to say *wholly*—not just in spite of its manifold ostensible defeats but, when necessary, by virtue of them.

If the ghost of Prometheus lingers in Emerson, it does so in the Fichtean transcendental Me that haunts the opening of *Nature* and that enables Emerson to strike the initial pose of regarding everything else—"nature and art, all other men and my own body" (*CW* 1:8)—under the category of negation. Like most initial stances, this one soon comes to pieces and gets abandoned. In "The American Scholar," the "NOT ME" reappears as something more intimate, an "*other me*," and in the same breath Emerson identifies the self as something inseparable from its practical, empirical work in the world: "So much only of life as I know by experience, so much of the wilderness have I vanquished and planted, or so far have I extended my being, my dominion" (59).

More and more, as Emerson's body of work grew, self extended into character. This extension took effect not only in the lengthening series of Emerson's essays, but inversely by a kind of contraction and crystallizing—that of Emerson's increasingly sententious style, whereby character exercises its true dominion. I have described how his style shows us at least as much of character's nature as his definitions of character tell us: his style redefines his definitions. It takes style to prove that redefinition can work earthward toward concreteness and materiality just as well as (and for most purposes more practically than) outward toward abstraction and association. Were it not for the hard containment of Emerson's sentences, we might lose our concrete grasp of things in the prospects opened by the sentences' fugitive effects. Containment is half of style's work; indeed, it is what makes the work local and memorable. Writing that is fit to keep must remind us of the common place where insight becomes interwoven with its body, its language, and its world, and where it is no less impatient with its own possessions for being so.

❧ ❧ ❧

Emerson's theory of character asks us to see meaning in terms of actions and their consequences instead of by reference to intentions, which lie buried in the strata of personal history. We may use this fact to distinguish an Emersonian "psychology" from European ones, though for Emerson turning away from intentions was also a liberation from the inquisitorial sifting of motives perfected in the attitudes of his Puritan forebears. Though it anticipates Freud in some ways, Emerson's natural history of intellect is in no way just another symptomology of persons: it is an ethics at once individual and impersonal. With this in mind, I would suggest that character, whose wholly public sense relies on what remains secret in it, offers an account of human action defined from the point of view of secular democracy. (Note that this reorientation—away from the archaeology of personal history and toward evaluating actions—corresponds to the other quite American reorientation enacted by Emerson: the shift of focus away from origins and toward originality.)

Emerson's unyoking of character from personality is a founding distinction not unlike the founding separation of church and state: it establishes a common realm where suspicions of why a person might do or say something vanish before practical questions of the nature, limits, and consequences of individual activity.[10] We must look for meanings where they are presently yielded—in original actions— and not in the underworld of intentions where we dig forever for authoritative origins. Thus Emersonian character, in what it excludes as well as what it affirms, gives us another application of his opening challenge, "There is no history; only biography."

It is a challenge met with equal force by both writing and reading. Character presents itself textually, but the fact that its showing relies on interpretation proves that character is a great deal more than a text. Character also generates authority, which Emerson locates in what readers look forward to rather than in what readers literally read. In "Character," Emerson argues that the respect usually granted to imposing authorities is never really based on the facts or textual evidence gathered under their names:

> We cannot find the smallest part of the personal weight of Washington, in the narrative of his exploits. The authority of the name of Schiller is too great for his books. This inequality of the reputation to the works or the anecdotes, is not accounted for by saying that the reverberation is longer than the thunder-clap; but somewhat resided in these men which begot an expectation that outran all their performance. The largest part of their power was latent. This is that which we call Character,—a reserved force which acts directly by presence, and without means. (*CW* 3:53)

What sets this statement apart from hero worship is his insistence on the transitivity of latent power in relation to the authorities in whom it "resided." As might be expected in a discussion of character, this transitivity has both semiotic and genealogical aspects. Emerson reposes the structural separation between sign and meaning (just the separation Coleridge also refused to accept) in terms of the practical relationship between text and reader. The characters on history's page confront the character over or ahead of the page. Stress falls on the latter, supervisionary character, which Emerson compels us to speak of as an event rather than as a person, a reading event drawing together the author's authority and the reader's freshly authorized expectations.

Authority and expectation mirror each other in the deed of reading. But this fertile correspondence generates a new separation—our newfound superiority as readers—because the old sense of constrained respect will not stay confused with the freshly realized sense of our own capability. As Emerson says in "The Over-Soul," "the great poet makes us feel our own wealth, and then we think less of his compositions" (*CW* 2:171). Inventive reading makes it apparent that the author's authority is a facsimile, bearing the seal of earliness, of our own characteristic genius. Latent power acts directly when the seal breaks open, and we turn away to make a new mark.

With this it becomes clear that there is a kind of genealogy implicit in Emerson's account of character. Like an authoritative parent, character "begot an expectation," which is not only a stance of looking out for something but also an aggressive, competitive offspring bent on outrunning its parent. Expectation's alternate meaning of pregnancy strengthens the emerging point: that genius, like originality, characteristically reproduces itself over generations of authors and readers. Its significant patterns become legible to the eye that reads across a series of historically discrete biographical instances. These biographical patterns may appear in the history of literature or of events; or they may appear in the immense scope of a journal project such as Emerson's or Thoreau's, where history and biography are made the same. In either case, we seize the characteristic genius in expectations we half receive and half create. We must expect it will be seized again, as genius will not stay sealed in our work any more than it does in the work of our authorities. The lesson this teaches about biography is that, insofar as life writes, life reproduces. Character is the transitive outline of this incessant reproduction.

The fact that character begets itself on the world "above our wills," and that its authority generates material marks as well as indefinite expectations, leads back to the point that life's writing in some way must originate in the experimental, unpredictable essays of action and perception. For Emerson, this is not just an account of what happens, but a directive as to the conduct of life. It demands that we appreciate the work of character in a fuller scope of activity than that of officially recognized deeds.

I have already discussed the way "Intellect" depicts empirical activity as walking "abroad in the morning after meditating the matter before sleep, on the previous night." Emerson anticipates this picture in "The American Scholar," where he declares: "The preamble of thought, the transition through which it passes from the unconscious to the conscious, is action. Only so much do I know, as I have lived" (*CW* 1:59). Our attention sticks on the word "preamble," which implies something more independent and mobile than just an introduction or a prologue. Like Wordsworth, Thoreau, and Stevens, Emerson maintained the habit or discipline of taking long walks to gather his thoughts even while, in another sense, he was resting from them. Preambling, strolling abroad in the morning before sitting down to write, is something like dreaming, where spontaneous perception bridges between the torrential lapse of sleep and the detachment of conscious reflection. It also resembles reading, which Emerson describes as another sort of daydreaming, "for the scholar's idle times."

As it applies to reading, dreaming, or walking, an amble is an excursion taken within the precincts of domestic life, a constitutional with no outward destination but whose open-endedness is reliably contained in the circuit that brings the walker home to work. Ambles take us abroad while sparing us the cost of those more extreme excursions (of thought, writing, or physical deeds) in which action opens the door to unpredictable consequences even as it directs itself to the most pointed aims.

Certainly there is a tame and prudential element to this picture of outgoing activity. It stands rather modestly against those famous polemical moments when Emerson exhorts the reader in purer terms of wildness, abandonment, and self-forgetfulness. But for Emerson even the wildest actions must happen within the experimental framework of a larger project. His real interest lies in the way actions lead home to thought, and then beyond thought to characteristic communication.

In "Heroism," for instance, he finds much to celebrate in spectacles of headlong activity, but he adds: "There is somewhat not philosophical in heroism; there is somewhat not holy in it; it seems not to know that other souls are of one texture with it; it has pride; it is the extreme of individual nature. Nevertheless, we must profoundly revere it" (*CW* 2:148). Heroic action does not bother to ask for reverence; it simply compels it. As "an obedience to a secret impulse of an individual's character" (149), heroism accords with something profound in every one of its witnesses; it has the power to compel us because we identify it with our own most powerful compulsions, which protest against the constraints we love as fiercely as against those we hate.

There is no denying the sanative force of Emerson's calls for heroic abandonment in a social world made tedious by conformity and consistency; but neither can we dismiss his almost reluctant warning that heroism is "not philosophical," and that its heedless pride makes it unsharable with others. As action that cannot be communicated but only obeyed, heroism denies the common texture of human life and casts community into the same pit with conformity and consistency.

Emerson had plenty of such heroic examples to ponder, having recently read Carlyle's *French Revolution*. Closer to home, he could see them erupting in infant form in the antislavery movement, in Texas (*Nature* was published in the year of the Alamo), and in the sectional extremism that kept threatening to end political debate. Of course these were only shadows pointing forward to the fully daimonic heroism of civil war, an unphilosophical extreme to which Emerson, when the time came, also paid his full measure of reverence.

So we might say Emerson looks ahead as well as backward when he writes that "times of heroism are generally times of terror" (154). We might also say that times of terror are hospitable neither to literature nor to the regenerative work of character. The "reserved force" character needs to make its impressions gets spent entirely in the triumph of the individual will; thus heroism presents others with a spectacle at once all text and no text at all, for it allows no room for unauthorized reading: "There is somewhat in great actions," Emerson says, "which does not allow us to go behind them. Heroism feels and never reasons, and therefore is always right" (148).

Against this calamitous extreme in which action lacks a domestic or constitutional horizon, and in which self-reliance turns compulsively to hero worship, it is crucial to recall "The American Scholar" and its homely picture of action as "the preamble of thought." Like heroism, this preambling activity works in solitude; but its paths circulate within a constitutional realm where individuality is both guaranteed and turned into something for solitary individuals to hold in common. (On the other hand, "The heroic cannot be the common, nor the common the heroic" [154].) This path toward the common can be traced in the characteristic details of Emerson's writing. When he writes, for example, that action is the preamble *of* thought rather than *to* thought, he makes the old Promethean antithesis between action and formal thought somewhat harder to maintain. Action doesn't just lead up to thought: it belongs to thought. Emerson implies that thought has legs, as it were, though it cannot feel them; at the same time, he implies that action is too busy to acknowledge the incipient thoughts that are directing it.

This interanimation of thinking and acting reappears often in Emerson, though he is also quick to separate them for his argument's sake. "Intellect," for example, makes us consider questions of physical as well as conceptual difficulty when it asks, "What is the hardest task in the world? To think" (196). Whether it goes with or against the grain, thinking works in nature with nature's own materials. It is a "task" imposed by action; or it is a duty, or tax, compensating for action. "Spiritual Laws" is more straightforward about the matter: "To think is to act" (94). Finally, Emerson's well-known chiasmus in "The Poet" indicates not a standard ratio but an inworking of contraries: "Words are also actions, and actions are a kind of words" (*CW* 3:6). If we look at actions characteristically, they seem to be akin to words; by the same view, when we read inventively we make words do what they say, and more than what they say. The very pervasiveness of action throughout nature and language warns us away from glorifying it as moral energy liberated from human circumferences. On the contrary: Emerson's preamble teaches by experience that the circumferential points of words and thoughts are bound into every one of action's fresh turns.

For all these reasons, "The American Scholar" celebrates action as a "resource" or, more precisely, as the recovery of character in its infant form. As a matter of course, Emerson can only do this by contradicting standard ideas of what constitutes real action:

> The mind now thinks; now acts; and each fit reproduces the other. When the artist has exhausted his materials, when the fancy no longer paints, when thoughts are no longer apprehended, and books are a weariness,—he has always the resource *to live.* Character is higher than intellect. Thinking is the function. Living is the functionary. The stream retreats to its source. A great soul will be strong to live, as well as strong to think. Does he lack organ or medium to impart his truths? He can still fall back on this elemental force of living them. This is a total act. Thinking is a partial act. Let the grandeur of justice shine in his affairs. Let the beauty of affection cheer his lowly roof. Those "far from fame" who dwell and act with him, will feel the force of his constitution in the doings and passages of the day better than it can be measured by any public and designed display. Time shall teach him that the scholar loses no hour which the man lives. Herein he unfolds the sacred germ of his instinct, screened from influence. (*CW* 1:61)

I must dwell a moment on this remarkable passage. The continuing influence of Transcendentalism—and, more particularly, the pow-

erful example of Thoreau's experiment at Walden Pond, a trial undertaken on Emerson's advice—makes it harder to appreciate the
perversity with which Emerson's recommendations must have first
impressed his audiences. In a time of strenuous political debate,
when it was becoming apparent that the stakes were nothing less than
the nation's survival, and in a time of spectacular exploration and
national expansion, Emerson pictured *action* as a return to life under
the "lowly roof" of the private household. He keeps the impression
of perversity alive by insisting on the word. "Action" is too public a
term to identify this withdrawal as just another rehearsal of the old
Puritan imperative of self-examination; nor does it have anything in
common with the personal ablutions urged by latter-day Puritans
such as William Lloyd Garrison and his nonresisting circle. For Emerson, action takes us home; but it does so in order to turn us back out
into the public world.

Locating action's original in life at home seems perverse only if an
exclusive distinction is maintained between the domestic and the
public world. Today's social historians tend to treat this distinction as
axiomatic for the antebellum period (though they usually disapprove
of it); and they find ample evidence for this view in popular and
sentimental publications of the period. These scholars follow the
quite respectable path of accepting conventions as concrete forms of
history. One might conclude, from reading most historians, that history's picture of the world loses little by remaining dead to what literature shows to have been original in it.

What passes in history writing, however, will not pass in the pursuit
of biography, for in biography wholesale patterns of conformity and
consistency make up the least, and the least interesting, part of the
story. The conventional image of home as an island of sanity apart
from public life, of home as a refuge where action is both more important and less important than what one does in "the world," is
easier to credit in Lydia Sigourney and Harriet Beecher Stowe than
in writers such as Emerson, Thoreau, and Dickinson. Whatever their
perversities, these latter writers developed deep interests in home life
because of its uses for their own projects of living and writing originally. And originality, even for a writer as homebound as Dickinson,
turns on the prospect of yielding new character in the world at
large.[11]

In the passage from "The American Scholar," Emerson's very claim that domestic action offers a "resource" implies that it finds meaning in regard to a wider field of contest, abroad in the common realm of public eyes and ears. "Each fit reproduces the other" means not only that thinking and action lead into each other, but that each in some way replicates the other. The same holds true for public and domestic activity. For all its apparent modesty, domestic life reproduces characteristic aspects of the public arena.

We should remind ourselves of Emerson's pattern of professional activity, in which extended and exhausting lecture courses (these took him increasingly farther away from Concord) were offset by whole seasons of life at home, where he stayed busy with domestic matters—raising children, gardening, hosting visitors—as well as with the discipline of new reading and writing. His "doings" at home may mainly have fed the metabolism of ordinary life, but his "passages of the day" were also fresh journal, lecture, and essay passages. Nor did staying at home exempt Emerson's writing from being "measured," as he made a practice of reading new passages aloud to his circle of family and friends.

But in a larger and more piercing sense, Emerson suggests that only the trials of domestic commitment can judge character's "total act," its real biography, a fraction of which is taken up in writing pages. These are trials themselves examined in the biographical register of the journals; they include not just the heartening aspects of home life, but also the tedious guest, the fruitless gardening, the wife's despair, the child's death—all of which furnish their parts toward Emerson's larger outcomes. As he says in "Prudence" "Whoever sees my garden, discovers that I must have some other garden" (*CW* 2:131). The other garden was, of course, the weatherproof *hortus siccus* of the journals. By the same token, looking into the journals, where promising and abortive germinations lie side by side and where writing's devices are left out in plain view, suggests in turn that this garden also defers to a field of greater finish. After domestic life's "grandeur of justice," essaying again into the public world turns out to be a necessary repair.

Emerson affirms character's generational or genealogical pattern when he notes the procreative uses of homebound action. He speaks of home not so much as his castle as his incubator: "Herein he unfolds the sacred germ of his instinct, screened from influence." The purposes of the study, the nursery, and the bedroom overlap in this picture. Against the privacy of those places, however, the word "unfolds," with its mixed senses of intimacy and openness, points forward to public revelation; indeed Emerson's sentence is a fitting description of the characteristic effects he worked for in lecture halls and in his published pages. So it is not just that domestic activity (ambling, reading, writing) shelters and fosters a public future: home life already is, in germ form, that characteristic future.

Recognizing all this, we can see how the lifelong series of essays Emerson began publishing in 1841 relied on his cultivation of a certain wholeness of domestic ground. This project demanded the most effective technologies of invention, criticism, and composition. But it also demanded a special carefulness, like that of a farmer or a naturalist, in regard to the nature of his own given field of production. The end of *Nature* recommends precisely this: "It will not need, when the mind is prepared for study, to search for objects. The invariable mark of wisdom is to see the miraculous in the common" (*CW* 1:44).

In his life at Concord, Emerson worked to teach himself the hardest thing: how to stay awake at home; how to keep on the lookout without altogether overlooking his own vantage point. Thoreau carried the enterprise even further by trying deliberately to build and keep a house that was only barely a home, with so little comfort that he could not help but stay awake. In Concord, the characteristic way to power in writing involved waking up to life's secret writing and cultivating that wakefulness, in oneself and ultimately in others, with further writing. As Emerson declared in 1840, while looking after two small children and preparing the "other garden" of his *Essays:* "I sit at home with the cause grim or glad" (*JMN* 7:404). The responsibility he accepts is as maternal as it is paternal. Passages of writing, like the characters of children, are to be unfolded from within the home disciplines, which include in their initial scope all future deeds of both criticism and creation.

We can deny neither the privacy of this enterprise nor the framework of community that houses such privacy. Because we start by living together, our "secret experience" is already biography—writing's original—the essentially communicable experience (secrets are made to be told, whether we do so or not) that we hold in common and keep to ourselves. We should be able to see why Emerson pictures life at home as action, as returning to the source, and as a preamble to some greater constitutional whole. What we build by reworking words and other natural materials keeps alive a common ground where more individual life will find more ways to dwell. Even if the outbuildings fall, because they cannot pass for the life itself, the ground will have been carried forward.

4

ᘡ ᘡ ᘡ

Practical Power

Reality is the beginning not the end,
Naked Alpha, not the hierophant Omega.

—Wallace Stevens, "An Ordinary Evening in New Haven"

If among Emerson's many refrains there is a single dominating image, an image at once so common and synoptic as to seem ubiquitous,
it is that of an opening eye. I can say without exaggeration that all I
have been doing, in looking at Emerson's approaches to natural and
mental life, to reading and writing, and to the frontier between the
Old and New Worlds, has been to consider how he managed to conceive of opening the eye. This is a practical task as much as a stirring
image, and it needs readers and listeners in order to take place. It
may be a matter sheerly of mental life, as pictured in "Intellect": "We
do not determine what we will think. We only open our senses, clear
away, as we can, all obstruction from the fact, and suffer the intellect
to see" (*CW* 2:195). Or it may signal Emerson's prophecy of a national
awakening or new birth, as in "The American Scholar": "Perhaps the
time is already come . . . when the sluggard intellect of this continent
will look from under its iron lids and fill the postponed expectation
of the world with something better than the exertions of mechanical
skill" (*CW* 1:52). Whether we consider the eye's unsealing in its private or in its public sense, however, it will always be an event hugely
resisted by what Emerson calls "circumstance" or, more archly, "our
age."

202

He means two things by this last term: our physical and mental debility and also the elaborate system of conveniences, physical and mental, by which we negotiate life in a given historical period. Since these conveniences provide us with a shared world of language, utilities, and institutions, we use them to communicate with our age. Yet they cannot be relied on primarily to communicate with our youth, which passes judgment from its own, far less settled sense of a common ground. From the standpoint of age, life's possibilities are contained by the system of the epoch; its manifold distribution of limits and entitlements appears to dictate all flights and resistances, as well as the more patent conformities. But from youth's vantage, the boundaries of historical age reflect the latest exhaustion or betrayal of our innate power; the age's instrumentalities, like Captain Ahab's whalebone leg, appear to substitute prosthetically for what we can no longer stand to do ourselves. These instrumentalities become "iron lids" over our eyes when we resign our possibilities wholly to their charge, a resignation Emerson often compares to sleep, the refuge of age.

But it will be a sleep greatly troubled with dreams; for whether we think of age as the condition of being far along in history or being far gone in an individual life, "our age" cannot account for the impulses of youth. Of course youth matches this incapacity with its own incapacity, since youth cannot, in terms properly its own, take advantage of the material prospects available to it. In spite of all wishes for an absolute awakening, for a final rejuvenation, the newly opening eye can no more do without age's instruments than the young writer can do without the currencies of language. Like nature, with its mixed presentation of formal closure and openness to invention, only our age can offer the practical opportunities necessary for realizing our youth. As far as possible, then, our youth must redeem our age's instruments, not in the ironwork of their institutional establishment, but in the promise of new transformation that we begin to see, by youthful device, through them and beyond them.

The three sections that conclude this book examine some of the ways Emerson finds for realizing youth, or power, through the instruments of age. As these ways involve coming to terms with limits, Emerson appears, from one point of view, to be striving to bring himself into coincidence with the larger work of fate. This holds for his approaches to abandonment—the *amor fati* of heroism, the ecstasy of

revelation, his recurrent dream of throwing the reins on the horse—
as much as in his concentrated devotion to the home disciplines, his
sitting "at home with the cause."

Perhaps Emerson's largest way of making terms with limits, though,
comes by accepting that he lives in the age of criticism, "the Reflective
or Philosophical Age." "This time, like all times, is a very good one,"
he says in "The American Scholar," "if we but know what to do with
it" (67). For Emerson, criticism itself becomes the discipline by which
we manage to do something further with our age. Criticism transforms fatal limits not into unconditional Promethean power but into
what, in "Experience," he calls "practical power."

The idea that we realize power through concrete purposes, that
power means getting something done in the world, suggests that a
literature of the critical age should bring us closer to the world we
share. It will aim for supreme realism rather than supreme fiction.
Since this literature is by nature practical, we will find no use in separating its vital meanings from its discipline, remembering that discipline of any sort—athletic, literary, scientific—seeks the point
where power and limit, youth and age, coincide to such a degree that
for a moment we forget their distinction, and afterward find our
images of both to have been transformed.

Compensation and Criticism

Emerson gives his age its due in *Nature*'s first sentence, which summons the eye's fresh opening by indicting what would seem to be its
historical foreclosure: "Our age is retrospective." As opposed to reflective, cataracted age, youth looks forward to its future; and in *Nature* Emerson promises a world worth looking forward to, if we can
somehow manage to open our eyes. This turns out to be a hard demand, since the devices of opening must be recovered from from the
rigid machinery of closure. The baldly impossible transparent eyeball, which follows up on the beginning of *Nature,* avers itself too
absolutely to be a practical picture of the eye's unsealing, for it expels
all the devices of both opening and closing. *Nature* leaps so suddenly
and prematurely to its apotheosis—"I become a transparent eyeball"—that for a moment we forget the discipline required to raise
our lids on new perception when the weight of all circumstance is
bearing down on them. There is no eyelid in the picture, no pupil,

no focal instrumentation; in fact there is hardly a picture at all. Perhaps this is why Emerson's most famous image occurs only once in a body of writing that otherwise welcomes repetitions, for clear sight can never float loose from the work of opening. "Of what use is genius," he asks in "Experience," "if the organ is too convex or too concave, and cannot find a focal distance within the actual horizon of human life?" (*CW* 3:30). At any rate, we overlook the impatience of the transparent eyeball because it comes at the beginning of a long "*Nature*" series of arguments that instruct us, on every page, in the discipline needed for drawing out more perfect sight.

Taking a harder look at our brightest moments is something we do in the course of keeping awake. In *Nature,* Emerson rather quickly blinks his optical afflatus by recalling his own shrunken prospects after the recent death of his brother Charles: "Nature always wears the colors of the spirit. To a man laboring under calamity, the heat of his own fire hath sadness in it. Then, there is a kind of contempt of the landscape felt by him who has just lost by death a dear friend. The sky is less grand as it shuts down over less worth in the population" (*CW* 1:10–11). The phrasing of these sentences makes it hard to say whether the loss of "worth" is due to death's subtraction or to a diminishment in the speaker, who may feel as contemptible as he feels contemptuous in respect to the landscape. Nature's shutdowns happen in the heart as well as in the sky. Like the fall into knowledge of death, the calamity weighing upon labor is also the imperative of labor itself; its burden shapes all the compensating effects of invention's fire. A similar lowering sky has made up the foreground for the grandiose hypothesis of the transparent eyeball ("Crossing a bare common, in snow puddles, at twilight, under a clouded sky . . ."); and in this, transparency's aftermath in contempt, nature itself returns as darkly as if it were the iron eyelid left out in momentary abandon. Our freest insights, if we bear with them, instruct us in what Emerson calls "the natural history of calamity" (*CW* 2:72), which predicts that lids will keep falling shut, and that there is no rest from the challenge of new openings.

Emerson never loses sight of this compensatory pattern of natural return. It is the costlier side of our secret experience and claims at least half the yield derived from any effort at cultivation. He warns us about it with the Horatian proverb in "Compensation": " 'Drive out nature with a fork, she comes running back' " (61). The essay clinches the point a couple of paragraphs later: "There is a crack in every thing God has made. It would seem, there is always this vindictive circumstance stealing in at unawares, even into the wild poesy in which the human fancy attempted to make bold holiday, and to shake itself free of the old laws,—this back-stroke, this kick of the gun, certifying that the law is fatal; that in Nature, nothing can be given, all things are sold" (63).[1]

This compensatory or natural character rules as sternly over reading and writing as over experience. In all cases, shutdowns of local "circumstance" are prices endured as the larger project reaches a critical stopping point and then picks up again under new bearings. The "old laws" score and punctuate all stances of freedom in Emerson's writing. They break up continuity between statements in his argument; they also inscribe the characteristic "crack" (a report as well as a fissure) within each of his strong statements, as it opens up by ambiguity into contradictions its grammar can hardly contain. We need to think about this compensatory pattern, for it may offer a means of accounting for the special character of Emerson's essay style, the way his statements turn out to be at once "spheral" and fragmentary, with "paragraphs incompressible," as he told Carlyle, "each sentence an infinitely repellent particle" (*CEC*, 185).[2]

℘   ℘   ℘

Compensation is the oldest of Emerson's spiritual laws. His theory of "the absolute balance of Give and Take" (*CW* 2:67) persists unchanged from his first journals to the very end of his writing. He was well aware that it only repeated an indefinitely older formula—he copied it down in an early journal as *"Nothing can come of nothing"* (*JMN* 3:364)—which flows forward through Anaximander, the Delphic inscriptions, Epicurus, and Lucretius.[3] Compensation assesses gains and losses, growth and change, by reference to the new equations they represent in the whole order of things. As a critical principle, it is a way of reading across time and difference, of seeing whole meanings in partial effects. Emerson suggests all facts can be read as issues of action and reaction, regardless of whether they appear in physical, moral, or linguistic realms:

> Polarity, or action and reaction, we meet in every part of nature; in darkness and light; in heat and cold; in the ebb and flow of waters; in male and female; in the inspiration and expiration of plants and animals; in the equation of quantity and quality in the fluids of the animal body; in the systole and diastole of the heart; in the undu-

lations of fluids, and of sound; in the centrifugal and centripital gravity; in electricity, galvanism, and chemical affinity. Superinduce magnetism at one end of a needle; the opposite magnetism takes place at the other end. If the south attracts, the north repels. To empty here, you must condense there. An inevitable dualism bisects nature, so that each thing is a half, and suggests another thing to make it whole; as spirit, matter; man, woman; odd, even; subjective, objective; in, out; upper, lower; motion, rest; yea, nay. (*CW* 2:57)

It is not hard to see why sweeping lists such as this have contributed to Emerson's reputation for philosophical soft-headedness. But Emerson fully intends that his conflation of multiple types of polarity—a kind of "bold holiday"—will generate skepticism. None of his examples should be taken at face value, and there lies the point. Any unit of significance is partial and has its meaning only by being partial. The meaning appears not in the form of its identity, however, but as its consequence, as the compensation it brings about; and that too will be partial, though it expresses the work of the whole.

Compensation, for Emerson, is a kind of automatic criticism governing nature: "The world looks like a multiplication-table or a mathematical equation, which, turn it how you will, balances itself. Take what figure you will, its exact value, nor more nor less, still returns to you" (60). All compensations, all meanings, are critical events; and the supreme critical principle is the whole reality—"the present action of the Soul of this world" (55)—that effects their transformations.

This idea of meaning as a reactive *event* separates Emerson's compensatory theory both from the traditional notion of meaning as identity and from the structuralist notion that particular meanings are posed within a fixed constellation of differences. Emerson treats meanings as historical events recording the pressure of wholeness as it comes to bear in or against the assertion of any part. Sometimes the event looks like retribution, sometimes like a surprising reward. Its pattern includes the cycle of rapture and dejection that romanticism makes so familiar—the cycle that plays itself out in the transparent eyeball episode and its aftermath. Strangely enough, it also includes the laws of magnetism and the periodic errors in planetary orbits. The cosmic dimensions of compensation indicate the degree to which criticism, for Emerson, has absorbed the full outline of reality.

However he pictures it, compensation is the compositional work of fate over time. There is nothing providential or tritely optimistic about it. Indeed, a hunt for its analogs would lead onward to Freud's psychic economics or to Nietzsche's universe of "dynamic quanta," in which the will to power is "not a being, not a becoming, but a *pathos*."[4] My interest, though, lies in its relation to Emerson's writing, where each significant unit, he says, works like "an infinitely repellent particle."

Every approach to Emerson must reopen the issue of his stylistic discontinuity. His writing seems most characteristically his own where his sentences pursue one another in ratio rather than in progression; where, instead of filling out a scheme of argument, each new claim makes its own stab at stating the whole; and where the next revision is so fresh and severe that it looks like a total supplanting of what preceded it.

In the past, critics often attributed this pattern (not always admiringly) to Emerson's practice of writing up from material collected in the journals. The argumentive and tonal discontinuities in the essays, by this view, betray Emerson's juxtaposition of fragments lifted from a wide range of initial contexts. Carlyle, who knew how Emerson composed, complained of just this quality after reading *Essays: Second Series* in 1844: the writing was incompletely synthesized, "the paragraph not as a beaten *ingot*, but as a beautiful square *bag of duck-shot* held together by canvas!" (*CEC* 371). More recent critics have, of course, found virtue in what Carlyle saw as a defect. They persuasively read Emerson's gaps and contradictions as key features of his strategy for dealing with uncontainable meanings. By their account, Emerson's writing anticipates the disjunctive techniques found in a poet such as Dickinson or seen at large across the broken canon of twentieth-century modernism.

No doubt the latter view comes closer to the "faulty" character of Emerson's writing considered in the last chapter. But we cannot dismiss the other, more Coleridgean criticism, which reads Emerson's gaps as evidence of an incompletely consummated history of writing, the very history that disappears in smoothly fused literary "ingots." From this view, discontinuities in the essays repeat the open distances separating journal entries, distances that are in fact historical, since in the journals they come between discrete moments of time, mood, and topic. This suggests that the journals (for Emerson the workshop and archive of writing's history) persist in the essays not only in the concrete materials reproduced from them but also in the less visible but no less transferable mode of their practice. The journals persist, in other words, in the mode of just what Emerson *does* across their open distances.

I have already discussed this as a kind of natural history including the critical practices of analysis, classification, and arrangement. The most striking evidence of this transtextual practice appears in Emerson's indexes, though the journal entries themselves come to take up similar work of analysis and revisionary composition. Emerson founded his career on the realization that, while he could not deliver the wholly synthesized, encyclopedic presentation of nature called for by natural history, he could still do the critical work of a museum. It is the intellect, not its aggregated products, that "must have the same wholeness which nature has": "Neither by detachment, neither by aggregation, is the integrity of the intellect transmitted to its works, but by a vigilance which brings the intellect in its greatness and best state to operate every moment" (*CW* 2:201).

So Carlyle was right: the essays are far from beaten ingots. But what he saw as unfinished in Emerson's essays we should see as evidence of something ongoing and unfinishable. The essays break up where critical work has taken place and where, in our reading, it keeps taking place. Thus Emerson's gaps and contradictions are not conceptual building blocks (like the transparent containers in natural history displays), nor do they point only to multiple relations that hold simultaneously between concrete units (as is arguably the case with the gaps in Dickinson's poems). Instead they are places of exchange and transformation belonging equally to the reader's present and to the natural history of the essay.

And this is precisely where the aphoristic nature of Emerson's style converges with the theory of exchange he calls compensation. Emerson's literary discontinuities, like the "inevitable dualism" bisecting nature, are not so much structural as they are historical; or perhaps I should say "biographical," since they remind us of where life writes—"the present action of the Soul of this world"—breaking down and rebuilding, posing and reposing. They signal transformation rather than static relation; their meanings derive not from what is seen at any given moment, but from what happens by force of a "vigilance" larger than any particular text or reader.

∾ ∾ ∾

In the essays, Emerson brings his "repellent particles" to issue in a
series. He could not do so if their partiality itself did not somehow
attest to a power, in the reader as well as in the text, more central
than any of its productions. Thus in his strongest passages Emerson's
statements appear as distinct effects of a common cause; one statement contributes to the next not directly but only after being taken
back, as it were, and projected again from the source. It would be a
mistake to say that they serve, in the European manner, as moments
in some punctilious dialectic wherein a preordained totality com-
pletes itself. For what Emerson gives us is not thesis and antithesis,
but hypothesis versus hypothesis. Nor does the trope of magnetic
repellency by which he pictures his writing bear much resemblance
to the Coleridgean ideal of organic outgrowth and cooperation of
parts: rather, it suggests the mutual warding-off of like units, whose
resistance to contact is best proof of any identity they might share.

We learn to read Emerson's aphoristic statements as products "certifying that the law is fatal," that a whole economy or constitution is
in play. They strike us in their sequence as prices paid, the effort of
one compensating for that of the other while, at the same time, each
one entirely disregards the other. In fact, his statements speak out as
individuals speak, or by rights should speak, in America. It is not
surprising that Emerson invokes the principle of "repellency" to describe both his writing style and the nature of human individuality:
"Man is insular, and cannot be touched. Every man is an infinitely
repellant orb, & holds his individual being on that condition" (*JMN*
5:329). If these stylistic or political individuals contribute to a pro-
gressing line of conversation, they do so in spite of themselves, as a
consequence of debating over common ground. The shutdowns and
withdrawals that close them off reaffirm the critical ground between
them, which is not empty or merely formal, but full of contentious
force.

Perhaps it overstates the case to say that *all* Emerson's writing in
the essays comes off in this aphoristic, fragmentary manner; yet a
certain compensating economy shows itself at work within the seams
of even his smoother passages. Emerson's reliance on compensation
is his way of insisting on himself, which means insisting as severely
on natural limits as on supernatural capabilities. While the compensating swings of such a style make the progress of Emerson's argu-

ments a matter of constant question, they also make digression impossible, since "God re-appears with all his parts in every moss and cobweb" (*CW* 2:60).

The essays encourage us to view this pattern under an involuntary, daimonic aspect, as when in Aeschylus and Herodotus we see character fatally emitted in a course of events. The same limits that force things apart are, from another point of view, instruments of a unifying power at work: "There is a third silent party to all our bargains" (69). Thus in "Compensation" Emerson turns around his favored trope of magnetism to picture the way competing, contradictory deeds can in fact hold together: "Our action is overmastered and characterized above our will by the law of nature. We aim at a petty end quite aside from the public good, but our act arranges itself by irresistible magnetism in a line with the poles of the world" (64). As a direction cutting across the indirect character of Emerson's writing, this meridian "line" is something obeyed rather than represented; it mani- *Compensation* fests itself in multiple corrections of error rather than in any terms of its own. "The voyage of the best ship is a zigzag line of a hundred tacks," he writes in "Self-Reliance." "See the line from a sufficient distance, and it straightens itself to the average tendency" (34). Particular passages of writing coincide with this true line, which is traced by critical oversight, only when they obliquely and momentarily cross it. As for the writer, immediate ends—not all of them so petty—must be forsaken with each new turn.

Emerson never stops phrasing and rephrasing the compensatory law. Its most memorable formulation occurs in "Power," where it is at once a challenge in the spirit of Franklin and an epitaphic brand worthy of Nietzsche: "Nothing is got for nothing" (*W* 6:54). Notice how the verb of willful grasping is struck passive by grammar, while nevertheless centering the equation. For Emerson, there is no finding ourselves outside this fatal grammar of loss and gain, of oblique stroke and backstroke. Yet it must be admitted that the laws forcing action into compensatory shapes pertain to powers that are our own—all the more so because they drive us in the manner of an irresistible dictation from without or from within. Like fire, wind, and water, they can prove useful for conveyance if we find the right devices for respecting them, if somehow we adopt necessity as the basis for method.

"All power," Emerson goes on to say, "is of one kind, a sharing of the nature of the world" (56). His work gives us the harsh exhilaration of reading compensatory retributions as fate seconded, as natural law assimilated by private technique. Hence power and limits constantly seem to be trading places in his writing. The compensatory pattern of shutdown and new opening, in which the endless war between age and youth finds its narrative, forms the measure of his style. "If Fate is ore and quarry," he writes in "Fate," "if evil is good in the making, if limitation is power that shall be, if calamities, oppositions, and weights are wings and means,—we are reconciled" (35). On this principle, Emerson's writing becomes a kind of experimental geomancy, seizing on natural limits to ride and override the greatness of nature, and celebrating the fact that in doing so it will summon up even greater retributions from the source.

∾ ∾ ∾

What concerns me most, however, about this graphic pattern of stroke and backstroke, of shutdown and new opening, is Emerson's claim that its compensations derive from the pressure of the whole. Our fatal errors, he insists, lie in the partiality of our deeds: "Whilst thus the world will be whole, and refuses to be disparted, we seek to act partially, to sunder, to appropriate" (*CW* 2:60–61). These partial deeds include not only petty ends but also the grandest attempts to circumscribe the whole, "the wild poesy in which the human fancy attempted to make bold holiday." We cannot avoid this partiality; nor can we avoid its consequence, that "what we call retribution, is the universal necessity by which the whole appears wherever a part appears" (60). The largest mystery of this statement will have to do with the one to whom this compensatory pattern "appears," the observer who can see the "average tendency" of its contradictory "tacks." Our way to that principle of observation, though, lies through the fate of facts, or "parts," for the whole seems to exert itself only in antagonistic regard to one constriction or another.

In Emerson's account, retributions for errors of partiality take effect in two closely related ways. Both of them may be found among the "lords of life" cataloged in "Experience." The first he calls "succession," "the onward trick of nature" (*CW* 3:32) by which objects follow one another in the way of substitution rather than in any continuously developing sense. New objects appear only at the cost of their antecedents; there is no filling the gap between the old and the new. The second mode of retribution Emerson calls "surprise" and, occasionally, "shock." These latter terms denote the way objects reveal themselves to be something other than, and more than, what they had initially been taken them to be. Every act of perception verges on surprise; but the strongest surprises come as total perceptual breakthroughs, calling into question former beliefs and their attendant systems of explanation. It must be admitted that this distinction between succession and surprise is only to be made heuristically, for the temporal and affective retributions they name tend to collapse into one another: succeeding objects surprise us; and the startling newness we find in a previously underestimated object itself congeals into a new object superseding the old one.

At the end of "Compensation," Emerson suggests that both these episodes result from conflict between the inexorable "growth" of life as a whole ("every soul is by this intrinsic necessity quitting its whole system of things") and our attachments to partial self-definitions, which imprison us in a "beautiful but stony case." The more extensive and adequate the "case" (a fate, an argument, and a container), the more calamitous will be its breakup:

> In proportion to the vigor of the individual, these revolutions are frequent, until in some happier mind they are incessant, and all worldly relations hang very loosely about him, becoming, as it were, a transparent fluid membrane through which the living form is seen, and not as in most men an indurated heterogeneous fabric of many dates, and of no settled character, in which the man is imprisoned. Then there can be enlargement, and the man of today scarcely recognizes the man of yesterday. And such should be the outward biography of man in time, a putting off of dead circumstances day by day, as he renews his raiment day by day. But to us, in our lapsed estate, resting, not advancing, resisting, not coöperating with the divine expansion, this growth comes by shocks. (*CW* 2:72)

Readers of Charles Sanders Peirce, William James, and George Santayana will recognize the issue of growth by "shock" as it first appears in Emerson. Emerson anticipates all these writers in identifying shock or surprise as a primary feature of life, and especially of life in America. We recover from surprises by reorienting ourselves; yet Emerson is less interested in the reorientation than in the constitutional necessity of it. In "Circles," he speaks of surprises as "the masterpieces of God, the total growths and universal movements of the soul" (189).

They may be pictured equally well as external force breaking in or as internal force breaking out. In either case, they come in endless series, and with costs so heavy as to make a dark paradox out of the value of life as a whole. "Life is a series of surprises," he says in "Experience," "and would not be worth taking or keeping, it if were not" (*CW* 3:39). If life is worth taking, it is worth keeping—and vice versa. Surprise, the way we hang in the gap between loss and gain, or between rejection and affirmation, is the preeminent moment for an American empiricism because it situates us where there is no established situation, in the crisis between a former and a succeeding set of bearings, each of which appears contingently in regard to the unconditional condition of being surprised.

In the long passage from "Compensation" just cited, Emerson imagines dwelling permanently in this crisis, in a mode of incessant revolution, with youth always coming forth out of age but never itself declining into age. The fact that this is hardly possible leads to the most urgent concern of the passage: once again, the issue of style or clothing. Emerson's images of loose-hanging relations versus rigid vestiture point back not only to *Nature*, where language is "the garment of thought," but to *Sartor Resartus* ("indurated heterogeneous fabric of many dates" not only sounds like Carlyle, it also describes his style), where Carlyle's clothes-philosopher declares: "The beginning of all Wisdom is to look fixedly on Clothes, or even with armed eyesight, till they become *transparent*."[5]

In contrast to Teufelsdröckh's peeping Platonism, Emerson wishes for an investment and divestment so rapid that the "living form" will exhibit itself "through" its garments—by means of them as well as in spite of them. This is his practical solution to "our lapsed estate," the fallen condition of having to present ourselves in an opaque, refractory medium and in terms of succession and surprise. (It was always Carlyle's deflective style, rather than his philosophy, that irritated Emerson: "O Carlyle! the merit of the glass is not to be seen, but every crystal & lamina of the Carlyle glass shows" [*TN* 2:169].)

Emerson would redress this condition with literary technique rather than with philosophical claims for certainty. "Tis a rule in rhetoric," he wrote in a notebook, "that the word used should never suggest the word that is to follow it, but the hearer should have a perpetual surprise, together with natural order" (164). Thus, in his essays, rapid shifts of statement make an instrument or vehicle out of the necessary "lapse" by which we are suspended in surprise between past and present, between resistance overcome and resistance to come. Spun across a series of surprising statements, these lapses generate their own virtual image; they display something irreducible and ungraspable. Emerson calls it "the living form," which for him is an oxymoron, unless one thinks of it as the place where life and limit coexist before departing in antagonism. But observe how Emerson's dream of fast living and fast writing turns into a vision of reading. This virtual image could only appear to a superhumanly fast reader, the reader capable of *seeing* transparency. Emerson writes to such a reader, whom he generously suggests anyone may be. In the lapsed estate of ordinary readers, however, "the divine expansion" will come in a discontinuous, startling series.

Now let me return specifically to the law of succession, which dictates that unaccounted-for facts will come along to supersede our achievements and to contradict our definitions. In "Compensation," Emerson pictures this event as the revenance of facts temporarily excluded in fancy's "bold holiday"; our partial deeds trigger the backstroke of the whole. So it is not simply that the future presents us with unanticipated materials. On the contrary, the future confronts us with those aspects of the present we have somehow rejected or excluded: "What we call retribution, is the universal necessity by which the whole appears wherever a part appears."

A strange fable about time lurks within this compensatory equation. Emerson suggests that the reason we have a future at all is because we have not measured up to the demands of the present moment. In contrast to the fullness of the present, our efforts to encompass the whole appear as the image of an inadequate past. Then the need to make a more adequate enclosure opens our eyes to the prospect of a future. This is never so painfully apparent as after we have tried, as Emerson constantly does, to capture the present in a grand generalization. "Nominalist and Realist" lays out the case with force: "Nature will not be Buddhist: she resents generalizing, and insults the philosopher in every moment with a million of fresh particulars. It is all idle talking: as much as a man is a whole, so is he also a part; and it were partial not to see it. What you say in your pompous distribution only distributes you into your class and section. You have not got rid of parts by denying them, but are the more partial. You are one thing, but nature is *one thing and the other thing*" (*CW* 3:139).

Nature lives as fully in the parts as in the whole; to find it as one means missing it as the other. Nature will resist us either way. The retribution for slighting nature's wholeness with our own exclusive claims happens in the very next moment, which presents us with an influx of unlooked-for parts. The impact of their return reduces what had seemed an absolute stance to the pathos of a fragment among fragments.

Dejection is an inevitable factor within this critical economy, for succession involves loss, failure, and sometimes disasters of the largest sort. If Emerson's essays nevertheless seem "cheerful," it is due to the rapid pace of their statements, which serves not so much to conceal dejected intervals as to compress them into useful energy. The technique of "perpetual surprise," like Emerson's compositional discipline as a whole, aims to reassume technical processes already at work in nature: "If we were not kept among surfaces, every thing would be large and universal: now the excluded attributes burst in on us with the more brightness, that they have been excluded. 'Your turn now, my turn next,' is the rule of the game. The universality being hindered in its primary form, comes in the secondary form of *all sides:* the points come in succession to the meridian, and by the speed of rotation a new whole is formed" (142).

It is hard to decide whether this extraordinary passage describes experience, or reading, or writing. The same critical principle rules over all these categories of activity. And the place to find it is in Emerson's idea of a "hindered" universality, in which the "primary form" of the whole has somehow been channeled into the "secondary form" of compensatory succession. Nothing gets lost in this hindrance: what is whole on the primary side seems to be fully distributed on the secondary side. It is the hindering itself that stands out as the great mystery in Emerson's passage. One cannot say whether this is some historical event, such as the Fall, or a counteractive pressure exerted automatically every moment. It interposes itself like a scene of initiation between the whole and the fatal economy of all the parts over history. As the word "hindered" suggests, Emerson is speaking of something that strikes universality into surface and depth, behind and before, past and future—in other words, something that dictates the terms and possibilities of human life. Not just special limitations but the fact of limit itself seems concentrated in this mysterious idea.

One might wish to invoke Freud here, since Emerson's treatment of power and limit suggests several of Freud's mutually contaminating dualities—primary and secondary processes, drive and defense, the instincts of love and aggression—yet the best Freudian analog lies in a speculative idea that remains no less mysterious than what we find in Emerson. This would be Freud's idea of "primal repression," the aboriginal event in which a limiting antagonism gets born out of instincts that seem by nature opposed to any limits.[6] As with "hindered universality," this event is not just the first in a ramifying series of cultural inhibitions (though it makes the basis for culture): instead it is an act of creation, a kind of troubled miracle by which power realizes itself in the instrumentalities of form. Emerson and Freud share the insight that creation coincides with a deed of criticism, with a spontaneous circumscription or determination of limit. Criticism stands at the beginning of things, though as a matter of course its dispensation will always be judged "secondary" to a previous state of unity.

So it is that an aboriginal criticism parses the whole life across time through the compensations of experience. Its method is artful as well as restrictive: "the excluded attributes," Emerson says, "burst in on us with the more brightness, that they have been excluded." This combination of violence and incandescent beauty informs a life where meanings are effects of endless activity. Furthermore, Emerson seizes the "universal hindrance" as a model for his own critical method, which, as I have noted, redresses the problem of succession with the stylistic technique of speed: "the points come in succession to the meridian, and by the speed of rotation a new whole is formed." Emerson imagines a technique that restores the original universality in the ideal measure of a line, a "meridian" whose polar diameter spans the whole but that also must appear to the perspective of an individual viewer. This virtual meridian, a line dividing what it also unites, is no particular line of writing, but the prescription for a writing discipline that would assume for itself the critical processes always at work in creation.

∽ ∽ ∽

Criticism is habitually associated with form, definition, constraint, discipline—terms often opposed to the creative lexicon of power, instinct, and freedom. But Emerson says "Life itself is a mixture of power and form, and will not bear the least excess of either" (*CW* 3:35). In his view, nothing is got for nothing, so far as criticism and creation are concerned. There is nothing life bears—nothing it can stand, nothing it will produce—that will not also show up as a balanced "mixture" of the two. Neither priority nor preference can be assigned to either side.

Poetry demonstrates this in endless contests between the expansive drive of voice and the constraints of verse form. The lesson goes further, for poets find that the very medium of language already mixes up every possible hindrance with all the stances of freedom. A word by itself makes the most penetrating criticism on any of its best uses, and the poet who seeks the full power of words also invokes determinations beyond any author's control. A "superior being," the critical reader, traces those unwilled determinations, which return the poet's "bold holiday" to a larger body of fate. There is something darkly creative in this as well, since, for Emerson, the reader's superiority to any text answers to the aboriginal criticism by which power gave itself form in the first place.

The line dividing criticism from creation has never been a stable one, but it vanishes altogether when we conceive of creation as something originally "hindered" into its multidimensional nature. Hard work teaches this lesson better than theory does. It was the working up of his own literary practice, which he held to be paradigmatic for his age, that led Emerson to declare in his journal that "literature is now critical. Well analysis may be poetic" (*JMN* 7:303). He found strength in the idea that criticism shares power with creation ("It is not when I analyze that I am unhappy," he says in the same journal entry). If criticism and creation coincide, however, it must follow that criticism submits to the same necessities creation submits to—the same necessities, in fact, that critical practice both enacts and takes into account. Again, this is the lesson of compensation, the critical rule of nature: our practices enmesh us in a fatal order of things that they reproduce but cannot master.

This peculiar relation to necessity is one of the chief qualities by which an Emersonian criticism may be distinguished from other late romantic models. Romanticism, of course, had always worshiped necessity. Notwithstanding its shallower rhetoric of liberation, it preferred the compulsions of dream and prophecy over the less binding options of judicious arrangement. With its theories of unconscious creation and organic growth, and in its hatred of arbitrary manners and ornaments, romanticism depreciated the voluntary element in literary practice. But criticism, at least according to one important line of thinking, seemed exempt from literary necessity: it enjoyed a freedom that made its secondary status preferable, in a way, to the more constrained situation of original literature.

This view belonged not to Coleridge or Carlyle, neither of whom (try as they might) could separate critical oversight from compulsion, but to Matthew Arnold, who in 1864 celebrated criticism's "independence" from the complex necessities that "genuine creation" relies on but cannot control. To Arnold and his followers, criticism offered a "disinterested free play of mind" that, though secondary to literary practice, "a man of insight and conscience will prefer to what he might derive from a poor, starved, fragmentary, inadequate creation."[7] Criticism, by this view, is the last refuge of literary freedom. It enjoys a simulacrum of the wholeness of being that creative literature finds itself unable to achieve, even though for the critic this would consist in the "play" of free options and possibilities rather than in any practical engagement. The Arnoldian critic has the universe at his fingertips, so long as he can keep his hands out of it.

Arnold's contrast with Emerson is instructive, since Emerson's "natural history of intellect," with its vast detachments and optical removes, also seeks to oversee the largest possible field of subject matter. For Emerson, however, what the critic ultimately beholds is a criticism already there at work in creation; and its disengagements and removals reflect decidedly practical costs and advantages. "Disinterestedness," which Arnold sees as the empyrean inhabited by criticism, becomes in Emerson a component of activity, an unstable moment within a compensatory series of withdrawals and reinvestments, with both the critical perspective and its subject field changing in real ways in every new deed of focus. Clearly, the voluntary will has little place in a practice modeled on compensation; nor can it have much meaning in a compositional method, like that of natural history, which claims to participate in real and ineluctable processes of nature. The only wholeness available to an Emersonian criticism consists in what it manages to share, moment to moment, with the compelling work of the larger system. It is ironic that Emerson, who drives so fiercely against the rocks of practical limitation, nevertheless strikes the freest imaginative sparks, while Arnold evinces a critical conscience compulsive to the last degree—precisely because of his balanced, disinterested liberality.

Arnold's devotion to a criticism that "maintains its independence of the practical spirit" would be impossible for Emerson, though Emerson also would detach the function of criticism from the meaner expediencies Arnold repudiates. The very fact that it cannot subserve a cause or ideology, and that its effect is to undo such partial devotions, makes an Emersonian criticism more, not less, practical. This becomes apparent, however, only when the notion of practicality is revised to include the darker, even destructive aspects of effective power along with the brighter ones. In other words, criticism's own hand must be recognized in what Arnold saw as the "fragmentary, inadequate creation" of romanticism's legacy.

Although he professed admiration for Emerson, it would be hard to imagine Arnold countenancing a criticism that identified its work with the cycles of universal destruction and re-creation hypothesized in catastrophist geology or with the boom-and-bust cycles that governed American economic life during the decades before the Civil War. But this was just the analogy Emerson made during the Great Panic of 1837:

> It is an epoch so critical a philosopher would not miss . . . What was, ever since my memory, solid continent, now yawns apart and discloses its composition and genesis. I learn geology the morning after an earthquake. I learn fast on the ghastly diagrams of the cloven mountain & upheaved plain and the dry bottom of the Sea. The roots of orchards and the cellars of palaces and the cornerstones of cities are dragged into melancholy sunshine. I see the natural fracture of the stone. I see the tearing of the tree & learn its fibre & its rooting. The Artificial is rent from the Eternal. (*JMN* 5:332–333)

He made much the same observation during the next financial panic, in 1839:

> And lo! how fast the great Critic, who now instructs,—discerns, separates the dead from the living, the flesh from the spirit! see the living veins & strata run detaching as bark & burr, what we thought was stock & pith. See laws to be no laws, & religions to become impieties, & great sciences mistakes, & great men perverters. (*JMN* 7:323)

Emerson saw "great scientific value" in these public disasters. He found himself similarly flooded with fresh perceptions following each of the private catastrophes that overturned his life in their own grim cycle. He viewed such events, large and small, as the necessary price of his work's growth. It was not that surviving them gave him the authority for a criticism of life, but that they affirmed in him the idea that life itself, in the severest and most literal sense, was a critical process. A literary criticism that would ground itself on the laws of such a life, no matter how amply it might record the scale of their demonstrations, would have to grant its own submission to their greater equations of power and limit: "The Supreme Critic on the errors of the past and the present, and the only prophet of that which must be, is that great nature in which we rest, as the earth lies in the soft arms of the atmosphere; that Unity, that Over-Soul, within which every man's particular being is contained and made one with all other; that common heart, of which all sincere conversation is the worship, to which all right action is submission" (*CW* 2:160).

Criticism, as Emerson presents it, makes up the parental nature whose laws we share, and to which the solitary work of the individual is the best tribute. Yet it is hard to imagine how the Supreme Critic could ever be cultivated. We can only keep cultivating ourselves in regard to it. It will certainly never be friendly to academies and canons of judgment, which seem set up rather to fend it off. Emerson identifies criticism as an "overpowering reality," like the revolutions of nature and history, that "confutes our tricks and talents, and constrains every one to pass for what he is" (160). By virtue of this power, the cracks in made things, the seams of artifice, open into wider faults; and the critic's eye confronts a ruined nature, a congeries of parts. But we are also left with the new openness, which is the best possible image of our "common heart," of the bare common we come to cross with stroke and backstroke. "Thus is the soul the perceiver and revealer of truth," Emerson goes on to say. "By the same fire, serene, impersonal, perfect, which burns until it shall dissolve all things into the waves and surges of an ocean of light,—we see and know each other, and what spirit each is of."[8]

The dissolved, broken-up field of criticism will always suggest greater possibilities yet to be realized. Chief among these is literature's own dream of communication: that we might "see and know each other, and what spirit each is of." Thinking back on Coleridge's secondary imagination or on the plowing and smelting of Los in Blake's prophecies, where the native ground of imagination is pictured as an infinite level plane, one remembers that romanticism had already fostered the sense that original literature begins nowhere but in this critical condition, which is also where the critical eye perceives literature itself, in all its partial formations, to have ended. To say, with Emerson, that literary artifice can only originate on a ground harrowed by a supreme criticism is not, of course, to deny criticism's need for literature, history, or its own age. It is to predict, however, that criticism's nature will lead it through its subject matter toward a vision of criticism itself, or something greatly like it, already there before any special deed of creation.

The Skeptical Return

If the work of criticism reflects our "common heart," it must bring us back to clearer perceptions of the world we share. At the opening of *Nature*, this world appears in the setting of the woods, "within these plantations of God" (*CW* 1:10), where Emerson recovers youth through solitude. It also appears in the image of the town common, the bare but not barren ground of democratic individuality. The crowded abundance of the woods and the openness of the common both attest to supremely critical processes that give us the shared world. In either instance, it is a thoroughly practical world, full of aims, instruments, and unrealized possibilities.

Following Emerson, the best that criticism can say for itself is that it takes account of life's practices, the historical uses and misuses of facts (private facts as well as public ones), and recalls them into intellectual nature, where new practices become imaginable. This requires not a departure from the practical order of things, but ever closer approaches to it. The transparencies and elevations encountered by the critic are intimate features of that practical order. Hence when Emerson describes worshiping the Supreme Critic in "The Over-Soul," he pictures a kind of homecoming: "But the soul that ascends to worship the great God, is plain and true; has no rose-color, no fine friends, no chivalry, no adventures; does not want admiration; dwells in the hour that now is, in the earnest experience of the common day,—by reason of the present moment and the mere trifle having become porous to thought, and bibulous of the sea of light" (*CW* 2:171–172).

In this sentence (whose syntax forecasts that of Whitman's prose) it is not unfocused ecstasy but the distinct perception of a thing that brings the soul closest to the whole sense of where it is. It may be the case that the enabling fact, the "mere trifle," goes transparent before the excess it welcomes (who can say whether the trifle disappears or only seems to do so in its convivial expansion?), but the common place where it was found persists. When things become "porous to thought," the world comes into its own as the soul's own place. This is the present moment, the common day, the hour that is now—and in this, by reason of the world's plain particulars, the soul "dwells."

Transparent

But notice how much gets rejected when the soul ascends to a "plain and true" vision of where it already is. The "Over-Soul" passage rejects literary charade: rose-color, chivalry, admiration. A more extreme picture of rejection appears in "Self-Reliance": "When good is near you, when you have life in yourself, it is not by any known or accustomed way; you shall not discern the footprints of any other; you shall not see the face of man; you shall not hear any name;—the way, the thought, the good shall be wholly strange and new. It shall exclude example and experience. You take the way from man, not to man. All persons that ever existed are its fugitive ministers" (39). The relentless *ex*'s in that passage—exclude, example, experience, exist—mark the aggressiveness with which a supreme criticism crosses out the signposts of prior authority. And yet, though these commandments seem to erase all human particularity, they also indicate a way to the common world. Perhaps we can find it in the sentence that makes the strongest exclusion of all:

You take the way from man, not to man.

Catching the meaning of this epigram is like trying to catch Proteus. If we can be persistent, though, its fugitive shapes will tell us something about the way criticism finds paths in and out of literature. Emerson's sentence addresses pathtaking; and its first sense is that, to have life in yourself, you must set out on a path away from others rather than toward others. But when we look harder at the sentence, we see that its terms of orientation, the prepositions "from" and "to," are troubled by the idiom of "taking the way." Why shouldn't "take" mean seizing or stealing a way instead of following one? (Letting plain idioms speak against their normal meanings is one of Emerson's characteristic tricks; and its legacy turns up in Thoreau, Dickinson, and Frost.) If we accept the sense of aggressive expropriation in "you *take* the way," the picture shifts from blazing a fresh trail to seizing the highway from others. With this change of sense, the sentence's grammar becomes sylleptic: taking *from* and taking *to* are different sorts of actions. This in turn puts pressure on the object taken, "the way," which now begins to shade from a path into a communication, a *logos*, as in the gospel message that haunts the entire passage from "Self-Reliance": "I am the way, the truth, and the life."

One fugitive effect gives rise to another, and it becomes harder and harder to keep hold of the sentence. If "the way" is a *logos*, then the "you" of the sentence has evolved from being a quester to being a speaker who apparently has a negative but corrective job to do: it might be paraphrased as "you do not bring the way to man, you take *away* the way from man." Emerson can play Antichrist just as well as Nietzsche does.

But a still harder point remains to be made: for what Emerson's little sentence takes away with one hand, it returns with the other, and an affirmative promise emerges from those orienting words, "from" and "to." The way from man, the way we take, is the positive of what Emerson demands that we cross out. In other words, we read the *logos* as "not to man": the negative way is itself a positive communication, spoken by this particular man, generated out of the cultural work of mankind. Speaking *from* and not *to* man is communication of the highest order, since it most faithfully expresses the originality of our human efforts. By the same logic, taking the way from and not to man is precisely what all true path-takings have in common. We share possibility, we share prospects, but each of us takes our own way. The common world is realized not by mutual obedience to a doctrine but by the recognition of a common place, the visionary place where manifold individual paths of departure can stand in mutual criticism and mutual respect.

I court tedium or implausibility, no doubt, in analyzing a brief statement at such length. But against the risk lies the other possibility, that a "mere trifle" might become "porous to thought, and bibulous of the sea of light." Analysis, Emerson says, "may be poetic"; and strenuous critical pathfinding, not broad summary of doctrine, is the best way to appreciate Emerson's own revisionary method—his resolve, when faced with the facts and trifles of the journals, "to throw myself into the object so that its natural history shall evolve itself before me." Not only words, but all objects are "fossil poetry"; and the protean nature of facts, their resistance to partial uses, is a key to their critical evolution. "Things refuse to be mismanaged long" (*CW* 2:59), Emerson says in "Compensation." Facts tend to turn in our hands and in our eyes; their fresh senses spur us to reject old estimates and to take new bearings. When we read, we see this happening more in spite of, rather than because of, literature's apparent mastery over its materials. Rich passages of writing betray the common world by leading us away from it into newly authorized beliefs and then, against their own persuasive drift, they betray it back to us through stubborn particulars that exceed rhetorical control, and that suggest our own greater possibility. This is why Emerson says, "I read for the lustres," the opaque but surprisingly reflective particulars marking where the author's management stops and where the real world, and our own prospects, begin.

◈ ◈ ◈

For all his stress on faith and belief, skepticism is a leading feature of Emerson's practice and cannot be separated from the work of new perception. As he says in "Montaigne," "The ground occupied by the skeptic is the vestibule of the temple" (*CW* 4:97). The temple itself— the world we share, the housing of a reality we can believe in— only comes into view when we take exception to what are usually considered the steady foundations of belief. These include customs, persuasions, political arrangements, and the canons of scripture, philosophy, and literature. They even include the plainer and more open-ended realm of material things. If such facts unite us, it is not by conditions they secure us in but by the challenges they present, challenges we overcome by taking any number of solitary paths. And all viable paths begin in doubt.

[margin note: Doubt about establishment causes us to become individuals]

Much of Emerson's hopefulness about human nature rests on his confidence that skeptical impulses are beyond our control. Skepticism befalls us, as surprising perceptions do, in spite of our best accomplishments and expectations. Against our wishes, the Supreme Critic leads us out of false or superannuated pieties back into the vestibule of the true temple. "People wish to be settled," "Circles" tells us; "only as far as they are unsettled, is there any hope for them" (*CW* 2:189).

Emerson's essays are remarkable for the way they keep themselves unsettled. Their gaps and contradictions, their ways of pursuing and rejecting eloquence, seem most often to take impulse from skeptical returns of one sort or another. Since so much rides on these hard returns, it would be worthwhile to consider one representative instance. It happens just after the swelling climax of "History," when Emerson has chanted ecstatically that "a man shall be the Temple of Fame," and that "I shall find in him the Foreworld," and that "he shall be the priest of Pan, and bring with him into humble cottages the blessing of the morning stars and all the recorded benefits of heaven and earth." Suddenly the essay recoils against its own uplift:

> Is there somewhat overweening in this claim? Then I reject all I have written, for what is the use of pretending to know what we know not? But it is the fault of our rhetoric that we cannot strongly state one fact without seeming to belie some other. I hold our actual knowledge very cheap. Hear the rats in the wall, see the lizard on the fence, the fungus under foot, the lichen on the log. What do I know sympathetically, morally, of either of these worlds of life? As old as the Caucasian man,—perhaps older,—these creatures have kept their counsel beside him, and there is no record of any word or sign that has passed from one to the other. What connection do the books show between the fifty or sixty chemical elements, and the historical eras? Nay, what does history yet record of the metaphysical annals of man? What light does it shed on those mysteries which we hide under the names Death and Immortality? Yet every history should be written in a wisdom which divined the range of our affinities and looked at facts as symbols. I am ashamed to see what a shallow village tale our so-called History is. How many times we must say Rome, and Paris, and Constantinople. What does Rome know of rat and lizard? What are Olympiads and Consulates to these neighboring systems of being? Nay, what food or experience or succor have they for the Esquimaux seal-hunter, for the Kanàka in his canoe, for the fisherman, the stevedore, the porter? (22–23)

Of all the abrupt disestablishments in Emerson, surely this is one of the most stunning. Critics have tended to pass over this moment, and they can hardly be blamed, given the passage's elusive rhetorical temper. How can we separate what Emerson rejects from what he affirms, since with the same hand he strikes keys of irony, satire, derision, and earnest encouragement? Yet this passage, with its deliberate impoverishment of the present, drives Emerson's opening essay to its close on a new note of discipline and chastened expectation. In doing so, it prepares the ground for his oncoming series of essays, a series that by its own terms has no definitive ends or extremes.

The scene of rejection enacted at the end of "History" will recur within the oncoming essays; it will also recur implicitly between many of the essays, holding the series together even as it strikes its members apart. The scene merits careful attention, because it promises to show the inner working of what proves "serial" in Emerson, the disciplined action and counteraction by which his pursuit of the whole turns, in one view, into a succession of competing fragments and experimental positions, and, in another view, into the realization of a life we hold in common, a life that somehow qualifies as whole where it gets broken up, renewed, then broken up again.

First, I should note the obvious: that here we witness the performance of the backstroke, the vindictive circumstance taking the measure of rhetoric's faults. As I observed in examining the idea of character, Emerson's style gives the lie to faults of rhetoric with greater faults, using contradiction and severe ambiguity to expose the cracks in everything made. Over the course of an essay, this provokes us into exercising one of the chief claims in "History," "that involuntarily we always read as superior beings." Confronted with a spectacularly faulty rhetoric, we not only look more skeptically at particular rhetorical claims but also recognize character at work in the cracks and divides of writing, where our critical superiority confirms itself in the intaglio of original authority.

Acts of reading turn out to be the vindictive circumstances that fancy's "wild poesy" calls down on its head. Backstrokes, which are necessary to complete character's graphic outcomes, take effect in the event of critical reception—by others, or by ourselves when we reread and revise our own passages. The consequence is both rhetorical and oddly literal, for a further attitude is struck and a new circumscription gets added to nature as new writing, or its possibility, fixes yet another horizon. Whether in writing or in the larger body of experience, the price of character's transmission comes to be incurred in the further qualification or criticism of every venture.

The costliness of critical practice consists in its tendency to turn against and shut down what feel like our most hopeful passages. For Emerson, however, the critical turn comes as a fresh skepticism rather than as the censure of a resurgent old age. It recalls what the image of the transparent eyeball momentarily forgets: that for the eye to open with any effect, it needs "a focal distance within the actual horizon of human life." The reprovals of skepticism, sterile in their own terms, lead outward to new issues and applications.

Contrary to appearances, the question following the visionary passage in "History"—"Is there somewhat overweening in this claim?"—is not the sort of rhetorical question that sardonically implies its own answer. It only announces the skeptical contraction that must follow any moment of prophecy or dilation. The reproving turn is circumspect and practical. It asks us to look around and compare our prophetic expectations with what we actually see; and if there is indeed no relation between the two, if the claim utterly belies the present fact, then Emerson vows to "reject" all he has written, "for what is the use of pretending to know what we know not?"

Of course, the way we address this question of use also rides on how we read Emerson's word "overweening." If to ween is to think optatively, to suppose or expect something yet to come, then it will take the future to show whether the most eloquent claims in "History" are merely a presumptuous conceit. In promising to reject all he has written if reality does not in some way bear him out, Emerson stakes his work on actual outcomes. Hence by questioning his claim he underwrites it (if only with his character), as must be done for all claims on the future, ordinary claims as well as more extravagant ones.

But we still haven't reached the bottom of "Then I *reject* all I have written." It seems that Emerson's rejection is a present deed as well as a promise, and that somehow it casts up the future while it also underwrites the future. In the first paragraph of the next essay, "Self-Reliance," Emerson warns us about rejecting our exceptional ideas, which can seem like baseless gleams and flashes because they are unsustained by convention: "A man should learn to detect and watch that gleam of light which flashes across his mind from within, more than the lustre of the firmament of bards and sages. Yet he dismisses without notice his thought, because it is his. In every work of genius we recognize our own rejected thoughts; they come back to us with a certain alienated majesty" (27).

Critics have found it useful to see rejection in this case as something working along the lines of Freudian repression; the "alienated majesty" of the revenant thoughts makes a fine analog to Freud's notion of the uncanny.[9] But we need a more exacting treatment of the original before we can appreciate the comparison. Emerson is talking specifically about thoughts that return in texts, thoughts that deserve to be kept *as* texts or parts of texts. These thoughts (he also calls them convictions and opinions) belong to a more worked-up stage than that of impulse and instinct: each one is already a fact, a specimen of writing, or, as Emerson says in a graphic pun, a "spontaneous impression" (*CW* 2:27). Writing journals is perhaps the best way to avoid dismissing such material; indeed, journalizing combines the invention of thoughts with the project of retaining all of them.

In writing an essay, though, even Emerson cannot have it both ways. "Reject," with its latent manual sense (think of driving nature out with a fork), smacks of a deed crucial to the drafting stage of writing, and most especially to a drafting procedure such as his in which every lecture and essay has been built up by culling the right statements from the vast stock of his own recorded thoughts. Emerson's indexing method guaranteed that all the relevant material in the journals was available to hand, and present to mind, at every moment in composing an individual essay. So what holds for any strong statement—that we hit upon it largely by rejecting or "belying" other possible statements—held in the extreme for Emerson. Every selection was underwritten by a massive deed of rejection.

"History" describes this constitutional necessity as "the fault of our rhetoric," and Emerson's essays often turn vindictively on themselves over the issue of their own partiality. This is the point of the dictum in "Nominalist and Realist": "No sentence will hold the whole truth, and the only way in which we can be just, is by giving ourselves the lie." The essays give themselves the lie out of skepticism about their individual claims, which prove fragmentary not so much in contrast to some abstract ideal of wholeness as in contrast to the parabolic repletion of the journals, where numerous other thoughts always stand ready to come forth with competing claims just as thoroughly "his own" as any of those printed in the essays. Like a compensating mood, the skepticism rises out of the writing practice itself rather than out of any detached epistemological concerns. Emerson's skepticism about what he has elected to affirm in writing reflects his persistent stake in what he has found himself compelled to reject, which is still present in the way transparent objects are present in spite of their invisibility—still present, that is, in the wholeness of practical possibility.

Now perhaps I can afford the luxury of comparisons. Will it suffice to say that the essays necessarily "repress" the full body of the journals? This would assume that the practical experiment of an essay (which must come to terms with limits of topic and generic format) is to the journals (which are a process as much as a text) what consciousness is to unconscious mnemonic systems in Freud. The comparison only works if the governing opposition between conscious and unconscious processes is replaced with a similar opposition obtaining between the built-in limitations of different enterprises within the same writing project. But Emerson's writing practice so thoroughly covers the scope of life as a whole that it seems redundant to treat its inventive, editorial, and critical features as metaphors for the machinery of some more general psychic apparatus. In this case, the practice of writing (a source, after all, for Freud's metaphors of rejection, censorship, and deferred recognition) is at least as complex as the hypothetical defense mechanisms that can be compared to it; but the practice has the compelling advantage of being something that deals concretely and manifestly with the material elements in hand. A distinguishing feature of Emerson's writing is that all the deeds and stances Freud accounts for under the rubric of the unconscious take place within a discipline "conscious" to such an extreme that no other field of activity remains for speculation.

Would it be a better analogy for "rejection," then, to say that, for Emerson, drafting already recorded thoughts for an essay is like a national election in America?[10] Whatever legitimate claims of representativeness might be made by the elected individuals, there remains, in terms of the election process, no real alternative to rejection and exclusion. The same holds true for writing. The essayist must settle for a practical compromise that can only be compensated for in the style of rejection itself. Emerson hints at something like this when he says, "He dismisses *without notice* his thought, because it is his." Under Freud's influence we read this as an unconscious deed in which the mind represses its own products without "noticing" what it does. Some such implication is surely there; yet the main sense of Emerson's idiom is of *notice* as a warning or intimation, and particularly one delivered in writing. (Given the volatile economic conditions of the 1830s and '40s, this sense of "dismisses without notice" seems especially pertinent.)

So let us say that the writer should respect the same decencies respected by a worthy employer. Let us say that if the economies of writing, the hard terms to which even essays must submit, force us to reject many of our own best thoughts, then the least we can do is give advance notice of this dismissal, to others and to ourselves. This is another way of accounting for how Emerson's style, which rejects as much as it affirms, puts the reader on notice with a consciously faulty rhetoric, where the seams between exclusive statements are scored by, or scored into, a literary character that includes notice of what has been rejected.

∾ ∾ ∾

I must return to the grounds of Emerson's rejection in the passage from "History." These have to do, he says, with "use": "for what is the use of pretending to know what we know not?" He poses similar questions of use in "Experience": "Of what use, if the brain is too cold or too hot, and the man does not care enough for results, to stimulate him to experiment, and hold him up in it?" (*CW* 3:30). And again, in "Montaigne": "What is the use of pretending to powers we have not? What is the use of pretending to assurances we have not, respecting the other life?" (*CW* 4:89).

If we take seriously the point Emerson makes in "Intellect" and elsewhere, that "every intellection is mainly prospective" (*CW* 2:197), we must grant that it is the tendency of thoughts to be somewhat overweening, to expect more than present circumstances will allow. We must also grant that skeptical backstrokes will compensate for each of our experimental claims. Flights of expectation return to earth when confronted by demands for empirical verification, since certainty must be grounded in what is present to hand. Thus against the indefinite postponements of expectation, skepticism keeps us uncomfortably awake to the questions of what we actually see and know. As with the emperor's new clothes, this often means contradicting rhetorical guises and admitting what we fail to see; hence the skeptic says, in "Montaigne," "I see plainly . . . that I do not see" (*CW* 4:89). But Emerson also says of the skeptic that "he denies out of more faith, and not less" (103).

In this spirit, I might suggest that the eruption of skepticism following the eloquence of "History" demonstrates that "pretending to know what we know not" can in fact have a use, so long as we *know* we are pretending. We use our pretensions to hold ourselves up in the expectant or experimental attitude that pursues a claim into the future and watches for its verification there. This requires discriminating between belief and "actual knowledge," even if belief thereby becomes mainly a practical means of orientation toward the future, and even if what remains to knowledge turns out to be largely a negative certainty.

Looking around us, we see that we are pre-tending, extending forward by leaning rather precariously on a faulty rhetoric—that we are expecting a future, caring greatly for it, but not yet seeing it. As Emerson writes in "Experience": "I know that the world I converse with in the city and in the farms, is not the world I *think*. I observe that difference, and shall observe it. One day, I shall know the value and law of this discrepance" (*CW* 3:48). The very fact that he relies on perception as a gauge for measuring "discrepance" affirms Emerson's confidence in plain sight and in the capacity of present reality to alert him, at least, to what "the world of thought" tends to belie.

So skepticism works as a kind of reality testing, though for practical purposes it consigns the ultimate results of its tests to the future. As I observed in my discussion of biography, Emerson recommends a similar empirical confidence as the key to understanding history: "We are always coming up with the emphatic facts of history in our own private experience, and verifying them here" (*CW* 2:6). Richard Poirier encourages us to see this as one of the many places where Emerson forecasts the outlooks of American pragmatists, particularly in their stress on the instrumental or vehicular nature of ideas about what is true.[11] An "emphatic fact," like a new classification, generates special prospects for further experience. Hence William James writes of the "leading" effect of truth concepts: "They lead us, namely, through the acts and other ideas which they instigate, into or up to, or towards other parts of experience with which we feel all the while . . . that the original ideas remain in agreement."[12]

In light of the end of "History," however, it would seem Emerson shows that ideas cannot "lead" us anywhere worthwhile unless we also rear back somewhat, doubting their guidance. For skepticism's proviso is another emphatic fact. Alert to possible discrepancies, irritated by them, the skeptical mood allows us the critical protest against our pretensions while also sending us forward to see how they work out. And indeed, this is just the practical effect the conclusion of "History" has: skepticism and common sense converge in their demand to be shown, in terms of private but communicable experience, the fact in question.

The vindictive return of local circumstance, a return we experience in skeptical self-questioning, vindicates our situation at least in this one respect: it refastens us to the terms of empirical life, which hold us now as they must hold us in the future. So grounded, "History" draws closer to its open-ended conclusion, which turns out to be the starting point for further essays.

∾ ∾ ∾

It should be clear by now that I am treating Emerson's skepticism as something different from what the word tends to mean in strictly epistemological settings. I have been looking at skepticism as a working feature of action and experience rather than as a set of doubts about what human beings can know. Epistemological skepticism, on the other hand, has concerned itself with the limits of our ability to gain certain knowledge of the nature or even the existence of objects. It may evaluate experience to question the validity of empirical truth-claims, or it may evaluate the limits of pure reason prior to experience; in either case, it judges the possibilities or conditions that pre-define any particular act of knowing anything.

Now, any reader of *Nature* and "Experience" will recall Emerson's willingness to entertain the extremest doubts of this sort, even those doubts that convert our inability to ascertain the substantial existence of nature into a Berkeleyan faith that nature exists only in the mind. Yet it is also the case that Emerson raises those doubts within a framework of further uses, uses pertaining to ends other than epistemological ones. In the "Idealism" chapter of *Nature,* for example, he almost offhandedly grants the "noble doubt . . . whether nature outwardly exists"; but then he subjects it to the criterion later made famous by pragmatists such as Peirce and James: "What difference does it make, whether Orion is up there in heaven, or some god paints the image in the firmament of the soul? The relations of parts and the end of the whole remaining the same, what is the difference?" (*CW* 1:29)

For the epistemologist, the answer to such questions makes all the difference in the world, as it defines for us what we can or cannot know about the existence of objects. Emerson makes it clear, however, that for him the difference depends on what we can *do* with the answer. As far as concerns his ability to make use of nature, the answer makes no difference: "Whether nature enjoy a substantial existence without, or is only in the apocalypse of the mind, it is alike useful and alike venerable to me. Be it what it may, it is ideal to me, so long as I cannot try the accuracy of my senses" (29). The answer to the question of the world's existence, and hence to the question of whether we can have certain knowledge of objects, makes no practical difference. At the same time, Emerson finds that a noble raising of the doubt makes a great deal of difference. Doubts, especially extreme doubts, work even better than knowledge in provoking us to try out new experience.

For Emerson, skeptical moments are biographical before they are epistemological. They befall us, as moods do, in the course of our empirical passages and endeavors. As a matter of course, they generate epistemological doubts of all sorts, but these doubts arise from within the economics of endeavor rather than as consequences of some Pyrrhonistic or Cartesian *ēpochē*. Hence Emerson opposes his skeptical doubts not to certain knowledge but to "belief," which for him appears first as a quality of engagement, a practical orientation toward the future; only by implication does it raise issues of certain knowledge.[13] As he points out in "Experience," skepticism records a descent into fragmentary immediacy, whereas belief looks forward to a prospect of the whole. Both poles of experience, however, work within a larger compensatory process of life: "Life has no memory. That which proceeds in succession might be remembered, but that which is coexistent, or ejaculated from a deeper cause, as yet far from being conscious, knows not its own tendency. So it is with us, now skeptical, or without unity, because immersed in forms and effects all seeming to be of equal yet hostile value, and now religious, whilst in the reception of spiritual law" (*CW* 3:40–41).

Skepticism looks ahead by withholding belief, working and watching for the fact to be shown. But there is no doing this without also holding hard to the evidence of the world at hand, which must ground our enterprise if only by the most chastening contradictions. This is where "our actual knowledge" falls into question, particularly if we allow Emerson's point in *Nature,* that "few adult persons can see nature." The brutal contraction of focus in the passage from "History"—"Hear the rats in the wall, see the lizard on the fence, the fungus under foot, the lichen on the log"—jars satirically against the copious beliefs previously announced in the essay. Yet the target of Emerson's satire is not belief per se, but the normal knowingness that demeans the world at hand, the careless premises or understandings that make our claims on the future (and on history) evasions of actuality rather than its deliberate pursuit. The apparent meanness of "these neighboring systems of being" draws its color not from rats and lizards but from our own even meaner presumptions about what lies presently at hand. We fail to see the facts nearest to us because we take them for granted in what we pretend to know.

"Our actual knowledge" comes off rather poorly in all this (the passage harps mercilessly on the word "know"); but the compensation is worth noting, even if it requires going beyond "History" to find it. Skepticism shuts down our grander prospects, yet it starts us on the road to more earnest vision, perhaps even to natural history, by directing our eyes to the near things we tend normally to overlook. It may be that these are rats, lizards, and lichens. Or they may be the near things Emerson invokes in "The American Scholar" when he speaks of embracing the common and sitting at the feet of the familiar: "the meal in the firkin; the milk in the pan; the ballad in the street; the news of the boat; the glance of the eye; the form and gait of the body" (*CW* 1:67).

This same proximity to common things reappears as an imperative in "The Poet," where Emerson says that "the poet names the thing because he sees it, or comes one step nearer to it than any other" (*CW* 3:13). What he there calls "the ravishment of the intellect by coming nearer to the fact" (16) is the other side to skepticism's contracted focus; it requites our painful perceptions of limit with "the plain face and suffing objects of nature, the sun, and moon, and water, and stones"—objects Emerson says ought to "fill the hands of children" (17). In "The Poet," as finally in "History," such common things make their own promises to the persistent eye, since they stand ready to furnish their parts toward a future whole: "Nothing walks, or creeps, or grows, or exists, which must not in turn arise and walk before him as exponent of his meaning" (23).

Transforming our limited objects or objectives into terms of power happens not through transcending limits but in seizing limits and turning them into instruments. But first we must squarely behold the limits by opening our eyes to near things. It is well worth the sense of loss in affirming the limits of life as our own, since they also suggest the prospect of regaining the world as a whole:

All the creatures, by pairs and by tribes, pour into his mind as into a Noah's ark, to come forth again to people a new world. This is like the stock of air for our respiration, or for the combustion of our fireplace, not a measure of gallons, but the entire atmosphere if wanted. And therefore the rich poets, as Homer, Chaucer, Shakspeare, and Raphael, have obviously no limits to their works, except the limits of their lifetime, and resemble a mirror carried through the street, ready to render an image of every created thing. (23)

Readers of *The Red and the Black* will remember this same Platonic figure of the mirror carried through the street, which Stendhal famously invokes to defend his realist practice from charges of meanness or immorality: "His mirror shows you slime, and you blame the mirror! Rather, blame the highway where the puddles stand; or rather still, blame the inspector of roads who allows the water to stagnate and the puddles to form."[14] Devotion to the hard terms of circumstances, themselves oppressive from one standpoint, liberates the novelist, as it liberates the essayist and the scientist, from the pieties of standard practice. Of course an ocean stands between Stendhal's exuberant pessimism and Emerson's affirmations of common objects. On the other hand—setting aside issues of rhetorical mood, which are purely strategic—there is no great distance between the savage invocation of lizards and lichens in "History" and the celebration of visionary premises in ordinary things in "The Poet." Nor is it far from Emerson to Thoreau's careful detailings of nature in his journals or to Whitman's even more affirming inventories in *Song of Myself,* where specimens of limit, by virtue of their nearness and commonness, can at any moment become exponents of unlimited power:

> And limitless are the leaves stiff or drooping in the fields,
> And brown ants in the little wells beneath them,
> And mossy scabs of the wormfence, and heaped stones, and elder
>   and mullen and pokeweed.

∾ ∾ ∾

Whatever uncertainties it detects, Emersonian skepticism believes in our own ability to see the self-evident. Our surprising encounters with things teach us to doubt our former approaches to things, and everything becomes more real than it was before. This is why the skeptic denies out of more faith, not less, ultimately sharing resources with his antagonistic twin, the prophet. Even an essay as given over to prophecy and revelation as "The Over-Soul" confirms this same practical confidence: "Foolish people ask you, when you have spoken what they do not wish to hear, 'How do you know it is true, and not an error of your own?' We know truth when we see it, from opinion, as we know when we are awake that we are awake" (*CW* 2:166). Seeing is believing; and though we may not, in skeptical moments, see much that merits belief, we still believe in our ability to verify the truth when we come across it. In "Montaigne," Emerson emphasizes this openness to belief as a way of distinguishing the skeptic from the mere programmatic doubter, whose practice is no less dubious than that of the uncritical believer:

> This, then, is the right ground of the skeptic, this of consideration, of selfcontaining, not at all of unbelief, not at all of universal denying, nor of universal doubting, doubting even that he doubts; least of all, of scoffing, and profligate jeering at all that is stable and good . . .
>
> Every superior mind will pass through this domain of equilibration,—I should rather say, will know how to avail himself of the checks and balances in nature, as a natural weapon against the exaggeration and formalism of bigots and blockheads. (*CW* 4:90, 97)

Skepticism finds its original in Wordsworth's obstinate questionings, not in Blake's idiot questioner. We should recall that Emerson lived in an age when established forms of common life were doubted loudly by competing eccentricities of moral and religious persuasion. It was as clear then as it is now that scoffing and credulity are the easy reflexes of extremes that meet, and that their combination parades through the age as a parody of the practical bond between self-reliant skepticism and self-reliant belief.

In his analysis of polarities such as prudence and heroism, conservative and reformer, mystic and skeptic, Emerson seems more interested in discriminating the characteristics of self-reliance than in blowing the whistle on its parodies. But some things nonetheless get exposed. In lectures such as "The Conservative" and "New England Reformers," Emerson finds that the moldy conservative and the radical reformer are alike in being poor critics of both the ordinary world and their own sacred texts. The radical's scoffing at things as they are masks a fatuous devotion to doctrine; on the other side, the conservative's shortsighted defense of things as they are masks a dismissal of further human possibility. (Note how, in describing this exposure, I am driven to employ the familiar vocabulary of motive, defense, and dissimulation with which radicals and conservatives endlessly unmask one another.) Even when he decides to fend off the claims of one camp or the other, Emerson's own skepticism in regard to both camps keeps him from falling into their defining terms. He prefers to speak of belief and skepticism in dynamic terms of compensation, action and reaction, cause and effect, or, as in the passage just cited, "the checks and balances of nature."

Emerson credits the ordinary world, the unpredictable resource we share for our verifications, with the power to undo programmatic positions, certified as they may be by fashions, movements, or institutions. Skepticism is one way of relying on the common resource of experience, which, Emerson insists, is also the place where belief finds its beginnings. Disoriented, reoriented by what skepticism exposes, the path of belief will be hard, solitary, and most often uncertain. It will also be unaccommodating to other believers and, by meeting that criterion, may prove itself worthy of real communication.

So it is that skepticism and belief sustain one another by mutual provocation. Skepticism recalls belief home to its source in perception by demanding that our expectations answer to the private yet common world of experience; but it is just as surely the case that what Emerson calls "*the universal impulse to believe*" (*CW* 3:42), which lies at the quick of both skepticism and revelation, will startle the skeptical eye with irresistible prospects. Doubts and detections of limit are not merely criticisms of established things, but fresh findings in nature. They are like the lusters in our reading or, for the naturalist, like those New World specimens that defied even the broadest of standing classifications. Without this freshness, without a perception so striking and so reliable that it outshines all prior persuasions, criticism can be nothing but censure, scoffing, or mechanical dissection.

Hence in "Circles" Emerson insists that skeptical revisions are themselves shot through with surprise, that they are beginnings as well as determinations, and that they base their doubts of old statements on thresholds of new activity. This confidence in the outcomes of skepticism resurfaces at the close of the "Reality" segment in "Experience," where Emerson declares that "out of unbeliefs a creed shall be formed" (43). He affirms it again in 1845 while gathering ideas for "Montaigne": "Skepticism profits by suggesting the grander generalization which yet remains to us (as proved by this or that anomaly) after our present religion & philosophy shall be outlived" (*JMN* 9:220). As I have mentioned, the "anomaly" is not only a discrepancy or unexplained fact within a conceptual system (though it is this too); it is first of all a positive surprise, a new perception. Pursuing its implications, seeing what the anomaly "proves," leads eventually to a "grander generalization," a further system of belief that reclassifies the facts of the old system in light of the new finding: "The new statement is always hated by the old, and to those dwelling in the old, comes like an abyss of skepticism. But the eye soon gets wonted to it, for the eye and it are effects of one cause; then its innocency and benefit appear, and, presently, all its energy spent, it pales and dwindles before the new hour" (*CW* 2:181).

Perception of anomaly, then, works as a kind of initial prophecy, the first outcropping of a more capacious prospect of the whole, which in turn prepares the field for future skepticisms. As for the natural history of the process itself, Emerson can only call it, in "Experience," "a series of which we do not know the extremes, and believe that it has none" (*CW* 3:27).

I should pause here to note that the train of thought running from "Circles" to "Montaigne" offers a striking forecast of any number of later American thinkers who have been concerned to map out revolutions in conceptual models, whether these occur in private experience or at large in intellectual history. I think not only of Thomas Kuhn's analysis of scientific revolutions, but of Peirce's famous "three categories" (Firstness, Secondness, Thirdness), which detail a process of intellectual disturbance and reorientation that strongly resembles the dynamic model presented in "Circles." A further recasting of both "Circles" and Peirce appears in the second chapter of *Pragmatism,* where James explains the meaning of pragmatism by recounting the Emersonian sequence of old belief, anomaly or surprise (James calls this "novelty," the "boiling over" of experience), and new generalization. Pressing further, it is easy to discriminate the same basic pattern in George Santayana's account of "shock" as the basis for belief in *Skepticism and Animal Faith,* in Thomas Dewey's theories of learning in *Democracy and Education,* and in Thorstein Veblen's study of economic revolution in *Imperial Germany and the Industrial Revolution.*

The line stretching from "Circles" to Kuhn's *Structure of Scientific Revolutions* comprises an American tradition that seizes the episode of new perception as a key for opening up the nature of both history and private experience. A hard look at this tradition (which is just starting to be studied *as* a tradition) would suggest that more recent European studies of historical shifts in ideology or "discursive formation" are rather less innovative than they advertise themselves to be. The idea that frameworks of value are instrumental in nature, and hence that they share the impermanence of any historical contingency, has never been much of a surprise to American thinkers. For many Europeans, on the other hand, the same idea tends to fuel even more intense fixation on the frameworks themselves, which offer endless opportunity for archaeological siftings and unmaskings of concealed motives. But Americans have characteristically been more interested in the practical outcomes of skepticism than in the accusations it affords. Following Emerson, Americans find the process of crisis and transformation—taking the path from man, not to man— to be the more compelling index to human possibility. They tend to be optimistic about skepticism because it proves so useful in getting them ahead in things.

It seems fitting that Emerson, the prime advocate of this sensibility, never rests long enough for his grand generalizations to settle into a system. Each of his statements strikes us as an anomaly, even against a context as tentative as the essay. What keeps him unsettled is his need for fresh moments of precisely focused sight, moments equally critical and creative. The essays teach us that we, as readers, need to look out for the same pivotal things.

His celebrated definition of power in "Self-Reliance," for example, pictures such a moment by suggesting both the wild flight of Milton's Satan across chaos and sharply directed patterns of optical movement such as those involved in reading. Power, Emerson says, "resides in the moment of transition from a past to a new state, in the shooting of the gulf, in the darting to an aim" (*CW* 2:40). By the terms of this passage, transitional momentum finds direction in the focal points of new objects, whether these appear as states, aims, or even things. Particular objects may be abandoned and exchanged, but they are never transcended in any categorical way. In fact, we grasp objects in their fullest nature only when we treat them as objectives for actions. Thus moments of power are both ecstatic and practical, combining the most extreme transport with the most discriminating objectivity. Power "resides" (the word suggests crossing between sides and also remaking the sides—both the limits and the arrayed meanings—of a new situation) in the vertex where lines of belief and skepticism meet before departing once again.

Such enactments occur prior to speech and writing; they occur in a solitary course of action comparable to reading, which for Emerson is where we rather diabolically discover our own critical superiority. Yet in spite of their priority and privacy, these moments furnish the basis for our ventures into communication. It must be admitted that eloquent passages of belief in speech or in writing tend not to detail such original moments (much less their original objectives) but rather to take off from them, and so inevitably to abandon or betray them. But the character of power's transactions impresses us beyond its rhetoric. For readers with a stake in originality, powerful new perception is communicated not in overt claims but in the fugitive effects of life departing from source—in cracks, forks, swerves, and backstrokes—the very faults that both skepticism and criticism find remarkable.

∾ ∾ ∾

If perception is where skepticism and belief coincide before turning away to oppose one another in the conduct of life, it stands to reason that moments of coincidence, which happen to us as solitary individuals, will always refresh our sense of where we stand in regard to others and to nature. We behold the self evident not in propositions but in the only place we can hope to find it, in the common world. Emerson's persistent devotion to "facts" is, after all, a devotion to what proves evidence to a community, though the individual bears witness to the fact alone; as he writes in "Intellect," "it is no recondite, but a simple, natural, common state, which the writer restores to you" (204). This is hardly to say that facts by themselves comprise the common world, as if circumstances alone were enough. Rather, the facts at hand offer an opportunity to start together on the way to a diverse but common realm of practice and communication, where in different ways we work together even as we work apart.

Both reading and writing depend on the most careful attention to familiar objects and experiences, facts whose nearness to our lives makes them easy to overlook and, by virtue of that nearness, most worth caring about.[15] It was Emerson's need for objects themselves, as well as his need for a unifying technique, that moved him to embrace natural history in the Jardin des Plantes. (Indeed, the vast collections he saw in Paris had been gathered to ensure that critical technique recovered what was nearest in even the most exotic objects; the naturalist's own work was to tally with the intimate workmanship in things.) Hence in "Intellect" Emerson writes: "We must learn the language of facts. The most wonderful inspirations die with their subject, if he has no hand to paint them to the senses. The ray of light passes invisible through space, and only when it falls on an object is it seen" (198–199). Connecting objects with the artist's "hand" goes beyond the standard notion that, by virtue of certain technical skills, the artist renders ideas by imitating nature. Emerson suggests that natural objects *are* the artist's hand—not only the artist's characteristic style but also his practical grip, in a fully bodily sense, on common or communicable truth.

Our starting places in facts, the places skepticism returns us to, forecast the ends of style. "Ask the fact for the form," Emerson says in "Poetry and Imagination." He extends the point in his late notebook on "Rhetoric": "Always plant your foot upon a stone. The strength of writing is to have ever a fact under you" (*TN* 2:180). And again, "Write only that which cannot be omitted. every sentence a cube, standing on its bottom, like a die, essential & immortal. leave out all the words, & put in only the things" (172). Style must show how our hands are already working in the world, turning up the hard ground of our skepticisms as well as all our premises for belief.

In slack times we do not see our hand in familiar things, but moments of realization remind us that it was our eyes, not the things and not our hands, that were closed: "Day creeps after day each full of facts—dull, strange, despised things that we cannot enough despise,—call heavy, prosaic, & desart. And presently the aroused intellect finds gold & gems in one of these scorned facts, then finds that the day of facts is a rock of diamonds, that a fact is an Epiphany of God, that on every fact of his life he should rear a temple of wonder, joy, & praise" (*JMN* 7:29).

This is one of many places in the journals where windows seem to open onto the skeptical, experimental practice of composition. Emerson collected "facts" during dry and weary times as steadily as in times of commanding energy. His special discipline demanded that he keep his hands in his work even when his eyes saw nothing worth believing. The journal passage celebrates a prospector's reward, or, to be more exact, a reward akin to that of the mineralogist, for whom one fact becomes precious when it serves as the starting place for insight that radiates into other facts and opens a new prospect of the whole.

But Emerson's passage also addresses the origins and responsibilities of higher compositions, since finally it affirms the democratic basis for essay writing, which is, at the least, a provisional kind of temple building ("Thou art Peter, and upon this rock I will build my church"). The responsibility consists in holding true to the hardness and the ordinariness, if not to the obscurity, of our original findings. We inspect our materials and, surprisingly enough, a certain adamance goes translucent; the drab day turns into "a rock of diamonds" (observe how its stony nature persists); and we recognize our hand already apparent in what we have unearthed as the groundwork for belief. We cannot forget that an unrewarded skeptical discipline first assembled the foundations. Any public frameworks of belief must recall the rather stubborn confidence that sustained the original practice and that persists in its foundations. Since this was not only our own confidence in things, but also the independent adamance *of* things, belief at that level cannot be abstracted from hard work, ordinary objects, and the solitude of the worker.

A diamond is nothing but infinite space if we forget that it is also a rock, and that as a rock it still stands for the obstacles and efforts we all endure alone. The diamond's stony nature communicates our common circumstances more heartily than the clear propositions of its facets, which are only proposed out of the original discipline. This is the sense of the famous passage about rocks and poverty in "Experience," which may be Emerson's strongest single statement of his poetics or of what, at bottom, he found most trustworthy in the practice of writing: "And we cannot say too little of our constitutional necessity of seeing things under private aspects, or saturated with our humors. And yet is the God the native of these bleak rocks. That need makes in morals the capital virtue of self-trust. We must hold hard to this poverty, however scandalous, and by more vigorous self-recoveries, after the sallies of action, possess our axis more firmly" (CW 3:46).

We read the axial possessions of this responsibility in the bare style of Emerson's sentences, which manage, like the hard terms of life on earth, to contain and call home any number of excursions into belief. And since I am talking about temples and their stony foundations, it is worth noting that something like this responsibility can be seen in the architectural tradition most consonant with Emerson's style and most consonant with its own native place: that of the meeting halls and Congregational churches on the commons of New England towns. These temples, whatever claims they entertain in regard to communities of belief, keep to the plain spirit of their foundations in bare lines and lapidary statements. In the same way, Emerson's essays, whatever their momentary flights, pass on the character of those native facts to which both skeptic and believer will doubtlessly return.

True Romance

Emerson holds that we realize the shared world in moments of vision that are, by nature, critical. Out of skepticism's discipline, we glimpse the plain foundations of common life.[16] Any more elaborate structures lie only in prospect. There is a major paradox here, since our hopes for community, and for communication, rely on our success in taking exception to every established proposal of community: "Space is ample, east and west, / But two cannot go abreast, / Cannot travel in it two" (*CW* 2:157). We plant our stake in the whole when we prove ourselves wholly independent individuals.

For Emerson, this means taking critical exception not only to the imprisoning conventions of the age but also to their shadowy twins: utopias, moralistic causes, and sentimental solutions that would redress age's disabilities with the more efficient dictates of a perfected age. The rage for a social conformity immune to serious exception vents our resentment of the one thing we have in common—that we are all bound by criticism's necessity. This is a costly condition, for it will always separate us as much as it joins us. It will not let us rest easy in devotion to doctrines and moralisms; it will not let us grow old together. Our age will always offer causes, as it were, for evading just what Emerson most celebrates in the American critical condition: its proposal that our only real chance for sharing the world lies already at hand, in the challenge of present circumstances, and that we do so strenuously, momentarily, and by ways that, from one perspective, look like perfect solitude.

This view sets Emerson far apart from those who see historical conventions and institutions, conscious or unconscious, as the only practical basis for common life. It also separates him from the Rousseauistic sentiments that believe the happy terms of human community are given by nature, only to be perverted and betrayed by social institutions. For Emerson, community, like communication, is something achieved in the original actions of individuals. Such action requires rejecting or taking exception to preestablished conventions—taking the way from man, not to man. It also requires building a new orientation in regard to new exceptions taken. Hence criticism is a necessary part of community, just as opening and focusing the eye are necessary for fresh vision.

The exceptional nature of original actions implies that for the most part, in our unexamined habitual behavior, we live in exile from the common (this much Rousseau would agree with); but Emerson also maintains that our strenuous critical moments are themselves the highest fruit of culture, that indeed their insights may foster new cultural systems and traditions of belief, even though in their own terms they exceed any formal enclosure. Because they are excessive, because they take exception, the moments when we realize the common world are moments when we are most respectful of distance, of the critical distance that unites us even as it keeps us apart. This is why Emerson's recognition that "literature is now critical" also recognizes the prospect of a literature that shares democracy's respect for the rights and responsibilities of individuals. Original deeds of writing represent the active life in a democracy; and the solitude of the democratic individual turns out to be, by nature, literary.

Emerson celebrates the critical distance or "repellency" that obtains between persons, since it attests, on one side, to the constitutional independence of character and, on the other, to a dynamic and provocative medium for communication. But Emerson also holds that communication draws its power to provoke from its address to real foundations in the common world. "Our action should rest mathematically on our substance," he says in "Character." "It is only on reality, that any power of action can be based" (*CW* 3:59).

These statements reflect the claim I have been pressing all along, and that all my attention to natural history goes to support: Emerson's work engages the actual world in the most thoroughgoing sense, aiming no less intensely than science and realist novel-writing to account for those reliable but mostly concealed realities that make up the shared world. Certainly Emerson's arguments make use of abstraction and generalization—many readers mistake this for evidence of mysticism or airy idealism—but these are means rather than ends, practices that serve the science of reality. Any rarifications produced in such practices are brought to earth by the hard materiality of Emerson's style.

Concrete achievements of style, however, cannot alter the fact that we manage to rely on reality only by aiming at it. The same optical and critical distances that hold us in solution with others also hold us apart from reality itself. This creates a problem as well as a field of opportunity, for the desire for reality is of too absolute a nature to be put off into the prospects of endless communication. "Reality is all we prize," Emerson said in his "Lectures on the Times."

> As the granite comes to the surface, and towers into the highest mountains, and, if we dig down, we find it below the superficial strata, so in all the details of our domestic or civil life, is hidden the elemental reality, which ever and anon comes to the surface, and forms the grand men, who are the leaders and examples, rather than the companions of the race. The granite is curiously concealed under a thousand formations and surfaces, under fertile soils, and grasses, and flowers, under well-manured, arable fields, and large towns and cities, but it makes the foundation of these, and is always indicating its presence by light but sure signs. (*CW* 1:182–183)

In the figure drawn out here, reality's bedrock competes with its manifold domestic and civil concealments. Granite may be stable and firm to the grip, yet these qualities seem more to describe what Emerson desires than his desire's material fulfillment. Though it may appear in grand men and distant mountains, reality becomes more concealed, more cultivated, in its nearer manifestations; it "comes barely to view in our immediate neighborhood," he goes on to say. The "slight but sure signs" by which it reveals itself in deeds of vision and communication are bound to tantalize more than satisfy. Granitic as it is, reality to some degree falls into the terms of the surface when it crops up. Nevertheless, Emerson says: "For that reality let us stand: that let us serve, and for that speak. Only as far as *that* shines through them, are these or any times worth consideration" (183).

To picture reality as a stone is to indicate that our foundations should be of a nature we can rely on in a physical, literal sense. The desire that Emerson expresses in regard to reality, the desire to close the distance between himself and it, is one he never admits in regard to other persons. He often represents it in terms of manual grasping or holding. In *Nature* he finds himself unable to "clutch" the world's beauty, which he can only witness from behind "the windows of diligence" (14). "The American Scholar" suggests a tactile, almost parental enfolding in its demand that we "embrace the common." And in "Experience" Emerson speaks far less hopefully of "that reality, for contact with which we would even pay the costly price of sons and lovers"; then he complains that, in a life of "evanescence and lubricity," where objects "slip through our fingers then when we clutch hardest," death may turn out to be the only "reality that will not dodge us" (*CW* 3:29).[17]

The best evidence of reality, it seems, is our drive to close with it, and so to abolish the constitutional remoteness in which we live, even if this means jumping the life to come. Since the terms of this critical constitution are given by perception (skepticism and fresh vision are both deeds of perception), the homesickness or lovesickness of Emerson's desire for reality is bound to threaten his practical commitment to a series of open-ended perceptions.

Perhaps this only exposes a fact that had obtained all along: that the critical conditions of the common world stand at odds with reality, which is nonetheless their foundation and only significant object. Time and experience tempt Emerson to bow to the distance itself, and to grow weary in the endless series of lessons affirming it. He addresses this weariness in "Experience," when he admits that "sleep lingers all our lifetime about our eyes, as night hovers all day in the boughs of the fir-tree. All things swim and glitter. Our life is not so much threatened as our perception" (*CW* 3:27).

Let me pursue this last point: that if reality is all we prize, and if perception holds us off from it even while revealing "slight but sure signs," then perception itself falls into jeopardy. To do so, it is important to rework the old philosophical anxiety that worries about perception as a more or less reliable mediator, perhaps an obstacle, in regard to apprehending a separate reality. While Emerson follows Goethe and Coleridge in affirming the active, creative nature of perception (as opposed to Locke's passively received "impressions"), he also accepts the skeptical rule, implicit in Locke and explicit in Hume, that puts literal reality out of reach and that instead finds our claims on the real to be based on "belief," which inheres in a certain "quality" of perceptions. Once this concession is made, we become less anxious about our objects, real or unreal, than about how well we can manage the deed of seeing them. And whether as cause or consequence, this deed in turn depends on how well we can manage to believe in them.

Perception is a process of life, not just an epistemological vehicle;

as such it falls prey to all the hazards of youth and age. By the same token, reality is bound intimately into perceptual activity—it suggests itself in *senses* of something freestanding and absolute—and so any real effect must make its appearance within terms of a perceptual life prone to illusions, temperamental distortions, serial displacements, superficies, and subjectiveness.

One would expect reality to appear in contradistinction to these "lords of life" (or lords of perception), but "Experience" lists reality as yet another in their company, cropping up among them in fragmentary glimpses, indicating itself in surprises and fugitive effects. As critics have noted, in no other essay does Emerson's point of view seem so thoroughly locked into the terms and limits of empiricism.[18] Nevertheless, or perhaps for just this reason, "Experience" shows him craving reality (just what empiricism asks us to set aside) as intensely as Socrates craves it: his decidedly un-Socratic insistence on perception does not make the craving go away; it only puts it in keener perspective.

There are many words in Emerson's journals and essays that also occupy the high place held in "Experience" by the philosophical term "reality." Instinct, spontaneity, God, cause, source, self, life, youth, absolute or supreme nature, force, light—Emerson is always ready to call these real. Yet all these interchangeable names speak in one way or another for the work of an inner drive; they seem to apply more specifically to what lies behind acts of perception than to what lies before us in the objects we perceive. If such names imply an aim or direction for the enterprise of opening the eye, it lies along the way of what Emerson calls "reception," which entails opening ourselves to things, but with an eye first to what they provoke from our own secret resources. These are resources of activity and invention, and are always constructive at least in some provisional way.

"Our thinking is a pious reception," Emerson says in "Intellect" (*CW* 2:195), where he accounts for "intellect receptive" as a whole range of organizing capabilities, including perception, spontaneous insight, classification, and that natural-historical process of detachment by which objects are "eviscerated of care" and "offered for science" (194). Like the open formats at the Jardin des Plantes, "intellect receptive" both furnishes and organizes the mind's museum, which for Emerson coincides with the museum of writing: "Each truth that a writer acquires, is a lantern which he turns full on what facts and thoughts lay already in his mind, and behold, all the mats and rubbish which had littered his garret, become precious" (197). I have discussed how Emerson founded his writing project in the plan for just this sort of transformational reception, which appears as a method common to both life and composition.

I have also suggested that such reception demands a certain sacrifice on the part of its objects: they yield their natural uniqueness to insights and techniques that deal only in their natural history. This involves no small sacrifice on the the part of the naturalist himself. In his writings before "Experience," Emerson is more than willing to affirm that the prices of his receptive practice are repaid in reception itself. He confidently declares, in "Intellect," that "who leaves all, receives more. This is as true intellectually, as morally" (203). And in "The Over-Soul," we find a cool prediction of the caducous leaves of "Experience": "The things we now esteem fixed, shall, one by one, detach themselves, like ripe fruit, from our experience, and fall. The wind shall blow them none knows whither" (163).

Such stoic pronouncements seem fitting so long as we hold fast solely to the instigating power of instinct, cause, self, or youth. By virtue of such devotion we should always be throwing ourselves ahead of things, leaving old attachments behind, relying on nothing but the forward transition. "Circles" celebrates just this receptive practice: "In nature, every moment is new; the past is always swallowed and forgotten; the coming only is sacred. Nothing is secure but life, transition, the energizing spirit" (189).

But the affirmations of "Circles" are not those of "Experience," which acknowledges a reliance that often gets submerged, perhaps taken for granted, in the earlier work. "Experience" takes account of the fact that devotion to source depends on faith in a destination; and also that, in one sense or another, we need the destination to strike us as firmly as the source. This reliance has as much to do with our objects as with our own resources; it learns as much from perception as from instinct.

Indeed, the differing qualities of our perceptions of objects—some things seem much more real than others—teach the very practical lesson that our receptive work depends on confidence in some further objective or aim. Reception must admit that it relies on some reality in the world, something that serves as both foundation and ultimate aim. Our critical constitution by itself is not enough to provide the firm, reliable sense of an objective. As Emerson complains, there is no *getting* in simply receiving: "All I know is reception; I am and I have: but I do not get, and when I have fancied I had gotten anything, I found I did not" (*CW* 3:48).

With this point I come to the reason why "Experience" dwells on the word "reality," with all its designations of an objective, believed-in world, rather than on any of Emerson's more wonted terms of instinct and reception. "Experience" explores our need to engage just the power that all those receptive terms name, but with the vitally added sense of an objective or practical purpose. This can only be suggested in the form of what empirical life most distinctly offers us: objects. In other words, "Experience" essays our reliance on an objective, our need not only to open ourselves to reality, but to close with it. To do this, the essay does not need to probe beyond the empirical format of reception; instead it probes into the foundations assumed by reception.

Disturbingly enough, this returns us to a place where we confront the sacrifices originally entailed by our reception. There we learn that our drive for contact with reality—the drive that inspires all receptive practices—resembles our desire to come close to or close our arms on our dearest human objects, which above all things feel most real. The utter uniqueness of these objects (I denote human beings with this cold optical term because the essay insists on it) instructs our drive for reality in just the way that these objects correspond to, and in a real sense bring to life, our own sense of utter uniqueness. Unfortunately, the desire to close with a dear object becomes most acute, and most capable of representing our drive for reality—for "the sharp peaks and edges of truth"—when the object in question has been lost forever. In this case, it becomes clear that belief in our own real ends resembles, relies on, but then (as experience will have it) does not finally coincide with belief in the objects we have loved, which inevitably "detach themselves."

The final separation of these two beliefs—our real belief in others and belief in our own real ends—repeats a pattern special to America, where origins always get turned loose from their destinations. In "Experience," the fact that these two beliefs first do and then finally do not coincide makes for an account balanced between extreme hope and extreme despair, the contest of which generates the special experiment of the essay.

The chief example of such a dear but lost object is of course Emerson's son, Waldo, who died of scarlet fever in 1842, two years before the publication of "Experience." Waldo's death was the latest twist in Emerson's sad pattern of losing those dearest to him, a pattern already defined by the losses of his first wife and his brothers, Edward and Charles. Critics who write on "Experience" turn inevitably to this pattern of bereavement, and many point to some element of difference in Waldo's death. The difference, for me, has to do with the question of Emerson's real aim or object, which has fallen into jeopardy in the essay. After each of those earlier deaths, Emerson had found strong compensation in new objects. Following Ellen's death in 1831, it had come in the discovery of his work; his remarriage to Lydia Jackson and his closer relationship with Charles were important secondary compensations. After Charles's death in 1836, Emerson was given Waldo's birth five months later, as well as the energy and fresh perceptions needed to finish *Nature*. New accomplishment in writing and new attachments to others were always twined together in Emerson's recuperations from devastating loss: the brilliance of his literary recoveries makes it easy to forget that, for him, death was made up for with human affection as well as with stronger work.

Accordingly, the object of his work and the object of his love could resemble each other to the point of coincidence, if not full identification. In June 1836, shortly after Charles's death and in the middle of Lydia's pregnancy, Emerson was looking ahead to his own child's arrival when he wrote that "infancy is the perpetual messiah which comes into the arms of these lost beings & pleads with them to return to paradise" (*JMN* 5:181; *CW* 1:42). The compensatory cast of this sentence gives a practical edge to the old Wordsworthian idealization of infancy; for the expected infant will not only bring the old plea of sublime reminiscence, but also a reason for returning to health and balance, which means regaining a sense of hopeful prospects.

Grieving for Charles, Emerson had lamented, "Miserable is my own prospect from whom my friend is taken" (*JMN* 5:151); but soon after Waldo's birth he wrote, "I think Hope should be painted with an infant on her arm" (257). His vision of Waldo as a resurrection of the hope that had died with Charles was solemnized when old Ezra Ripley, Emerson's step-grandfather, baptized the new child in "the selfsame robe in which twentyseven years ago my brother Charles was baptised" (324). Surely this human reward was part of what Emerson spoke of, at the end of "Compensation," when he wrote: "We cannot part with our friends. We cannot let our angels go. We do not see that they only go out, that archangels may come in" (*CW* 2:72). Later, the naming of Emerson's second child, Ellen, and his fourth, Edward, continued the pattern in which he identified compensation for the deaths of previous "friends" in the births of children as well as in new powers of work.

In "Experience," the death of a firstborn child raises this pattern to a second, harder point of challenge; for here the deep compensation of life for life seems itself capable of dying in some final way, even though a train of more superficial substitutions keeps on ringing through the register of perception: "Dream delivers us to dream, and there is no end to illusion" (*CW* 3:30). "The secret of the illusoriness," Emerson later adds, "is in the necessity of a succession of moods or objects."

In contrast to Emerson's loss of his dearest object, it is the dry irony of perception's automatic continuance, needing no hope of an end to close on, that finally presents the most dangerous threat to perception in "Experience." Meaningful perception relies on hope, on the sense of an aim beyond its instruments. Without a hopeful aim there can be no progress, but only static succession, "a series of which we do not know the extremes, and believe that it has none." Or as Coleridge wrote, "Work without hope draws nectar in a sieve, / And hope without an object cannot live."[19]

I come back, then, to the place in "Experience" where Emerson speaks of "the reality, for contact with which, we would even pay the costly price of sons and lovers," while in the same breath he admits that "souls never touch their objects" (*CW* 3:29). The contradiction between the desire of the first phrase and what seems the iron prohibition of the second once again raises the old question: How much can perception avail in respect to reality?

In thinking about Emerson's concept of transparency, I determined that perception works economically, through precise exchanges of objects and media. The rules of exchange are set by a natural constitution dictating that nothing is got for nothing; and Emerson made sense of the deep losses in his own biography by appealing to this same compensatory equation. He brooded over this feature of life—that new perceptions are paid for with old objects—long before "Experience." And a journal entry of 1846 shows him still considering the issue in no less extreme terms: "Ah, a new perception avails much & always costs something. One perception costs me my orchard, another my wife, another my caste or social connexion, and another my body, & we are content to pay these prices" (*JMN* 9:436).

Emerson experiments with the notion that he might be perceiving himself right out of the world, even out of his life; but it only seems so because he does not indicate what new perception "avails" for. Certainly new perception avails for nothing unless it repays us with better if not closer purchases on reality. To say that we are "content" to be dying for those better purchases is one way to express the double sense of fullness and craving that informs the situation. "Experience" prepares us for this answer, because it displaces the question of reality into an issue of serial realization. Like death, its near relation, reality works instrumentally at some virtual point within the perceptual series, not outside it.

But the compensatory equation is too perfectly balanced to account for the fact that reality remains an aim beyond both the objects seen and the costs absorbed, while still somehow consisting intimately in the work of seeing. As Emerson elsewhere protests, "The soul is not a compensation, but a life" (*CW* 2:70). Something vitally important seems left over in Emerson's naming of "that reality, for contact with which we *would even pay* the costly price of sons and lovers." The phrase stumps us. What is it that drives Emerson, in a passage treating the death of his son, to reaffirm an offer the nature of experience proves to be starkly gratuitous? Like similar passages in *Nature,* "Compensation," and "Circles," this moment from "Experience" documents the fact that Emerson has paid just such costly prices in full measure, regardless of his willingness to do so. There is something *extra* in his offer to pay again what he already pays, something unaccountable in regard to either costs or benefits.

We can only suspect that this extraordinary offer makes up Emerson's strongest address to reality; for reality's intimate remoteness corresponds to what seems the gratuitousness or grace of his offer to pay costly prices all over again. As if in spontaneous but distant communication with reality, the painful offer orients us toward the future, which is also something extra beyond the full ledger of present perception. "Our life seems not present, so much as prospective," the essay declares at one point, "not for the affairs on which it is wasted, but as a hint of this vast-flowing vigor" (*CW* 3:42).

Emerson's offer, "we would even pay," can only sound ironic in regard to the present; but it is earnest in respect to the future. I lift the word "earnest" from a passage already quoted from "The Over-Soul," where Emerson says that the soul "dwells in the earnest experience of the common day" (*CW* 2:172). Earnest experience pays down on future purchases by drawing on resources it is surprised to find available. (Robert Frost uses the word in a similar way in his sonnet "Mowing," where as a harvester he seeks a true response to "the earnest love that laid the swale in rows," the work of an earlier season that initially plowed and sowed the poetic ground at hand.) Emerson's earnest offer to pay again what he has already paid—an offer he makes in writing, which is also something exceptional in regard to ordinary experience—prepares the ground of reality that will give rise to new perception. This may not give him title to reality, but it gives him a vital stake in it—in other words, a stake in the future.

"Experience" teaches us to look out for reality as a promise incipient in compelling perceptions. It can crop up in surprises, spontaneous actions, and disasters. Other times, it appears as the luster of "expectation" reflected in objects; in practical terms, this means the sense in which objects are pregnant with our own future activity. Emerson saw the most moving of these lusters in other people, but they only led him on, like his own best thoughts, along the way of further and better work: "Thus journeys the mighty Ideal before us; it was never known to fall into the rear. No man ever came to an experience which was satiating, but his good is tidings of a better. Onward and onward!" (*CW* 3:43).

To find these words encouraging, we have to imagine ourselves engaged in a curious sort of pursuit, less like quests for a Grail or a golden fleece than like the questionable progress of the self-propelling contraption pictured when we speak of hitching our wagon to a star or hoisting ourselves by our bootstraps. The onward trick of reality gets exposed in "Experience" as a kind of remote pulley or come-along, not pristinely separate but somehow extending from us, and hence journeying before us, and along with us, as part of the instrumental process by which we advance through one perception to the next.

Such a view may well seem to strip the onward journey of its romance, inducing even more of the somnolence with which "Experience" keeps struggling. After all, if our ultimate aim is reality (and

for Emerson it is, in spite of everything), there must be terrible weariness in the thought that reality is mainly the prescription of more
work already written into our horizons. The saving realizations in
"Experience," however, take heart from the idea that reality, in all its
aloofness, belongs to us as our own, and that somehow we keep it up,
look after it, by bringing new work into the world.

Stanley Cavell has described "Experience" as Emerson's meditation on being a father, both of children and of essays.[20] Cavell's insight
gains fuller scope when we consider that Emerson's aim, reality, also
turns out to be authorized, furthered if not fathered, by Emerson's
essay, which ends not only with the promise of further work but with
a nod to the fact that earnest work is already, in the very luster of its
promise, being done:

> And the true romance which the world exists to realize, will be the
> transformation of genius into practical power. (*CW* 3:49).

Here, in one of Emerson's most astonishing phrases, reality turns
into a transitive verb, though in the infinitive mood. "True romance"
comes first, however: affirmation of the world's existence and its possible realizings comes subordinately, almost offhandedly. This is a
surprise, considering how slippery the question of reality and the
world's existence has been throughout the essay—"Let us treat the
men and women well: treat them as if they were real: perhaps they
are" (35).

As the joke shows, "Experience" never denies the weary intangi-
bility of the question of reality, which Emerson is nevertheless driven
to pose and re-pose. But "true romance," which suggests a performed
truth such as that of marriage rather than any certainty of knowledge,
finally gives him the basis for overlooking the question. The force of
his final sentence comes to bear in his intriguing conjugation of romance with practical transformation, an avowal that takes place over
and above all questions of existence and reality. The sentence does
not say that romance will explain, instigate, or attend the transformation: the romance will *be* the transformation. The world exists to
make rather than to find; all romantic distances and deferrals, the
stagecraft of reality-hunting, will abide in the work being done. Of
course the old sense of unacted desire in romance does remain, as
Emerson after all sets his copula in the future tense. So in an impor-

tant way this is a romance yet to be consummated. But the truth vouched for in Emerson's promise, that genius will transform into "practical power," proclaims the harnessing of energy for work, not energy's mere liberation from constraint, and that means work toward even further realization. Thus, in Emerson's rich syntax, the infinitive "to realize" seems to come forward again into the clear space of conclusion laid open by that final word "power": practical power is the power to realize, to understand and to make things real. Emerson's phrase, in the work it performs, calls the world back into existence as a place for dwelling "in the earnest experience of the common day." Like the American West, which for Emerson is the image of both reality and true romance, it will be a place made in practical transformations that never stop looking ahead.

Notes

Index

Notes

Introduction

1. Timothy Dwight, *Travels in New England and New York,* ed. Barbara Miller Solomon (Cambridge, Mass.: Harvard University Press, 1969), vol. 2, pp. 98–99. Dwight alludes to Aeneas's pilgrimage to the rocky temple of Apollo at Delos.

2. Charles Lyell, *A Second Visit to the United States of North America* (London, 1849), vol. 1, pp. 67–73.

3. Thomas Cole's diary entry for October 6, 1828, in Catherine H. Campbell, "Two's Company: The Diaries of Thomas Cole and Henry Cheever Pratt on Their Walk through Crawford Notch, 1828," *Historical New Hampshire* 33 (1978): 325. Cole's famous canvas *The Notch of the White Mountains* hangs in the National Gallery in Washington. For a review of Cole's and other painters' treatments of the White Mountains, see University Art Galleries, University of New Hampshire, *The White Mountains: Place and Perceptions,* exhibition catalog (Hanover: University Press of New England, 1980). The integrated vision Cole records at the opening of the Notch gives way to other feelings as he goes farther. He finds himself horrified at the site of the great avalanche that had destroyed the Willey family two years earlier. For yet another treatment of the Notch and the Willey disaster, see Nathaniel Hawthorne's tale "The Ambitious Guest."

4. William Cullen Bryant, "To Cole, the Painter, Departing for Europe," in *Poems* (New York, 1854), vol. 2, pp. 14–15.

5. See Frederick W. Kilbourne, *Chronicles of the White Mountains* (New York, 1916; reprint, Bowie, Md.: Heritage Books, 1978), pp. 25–27, 70–100.

6. "The Prairies," in Bryant, *Poems,* vol. 2, p. 23.

7. The biographical and theological aspects of Emerson's rejection of the ministry have received many extended treatments. Few critics have paid more than passing attention, however, to the actual "hour of decision" during his trip to the mountains. See Richard Grusin, *Transcendentalist Hermeneutics: Institutional Authority and the Higher Criticism* (Durham, N.C.: Duke University Press, 1991), pp. 45–46.

8. Emerson had toured the same area with Ellen Tucker, then his fiancée, in October 1829. See *JMN* 3:159–162. For ease of reading, I have normalized some of Emerson's spellings in passages from this source. I have also omitted some of his deletions as indicated by the editors.

9. Cited in Ralph L. Rusk, *The Life of Ralph Waldo Emerson* (New York: Charles Scribner's Sons, 1949), pp. 161–162.

10. Thomas Carlyle, "Corn-Law Rhymes," in *Critical and Miscellaneous Essays* (London, 1899; reprint, New York: AMS Press, 1969), vol. 3, p. 143. (Page citations are to the reprint edition.)

1. Ruins in the Eye

This chapter includes revised versions of essays previously published in *Raritan* (winter 1990) and *Studies in Romanticism* (summer 1991).

1. Cleanth Brooks, "The Organic Theory of Poetry," in *Literature and Belief: English Institute Essays, 1957,* ed. M. H. Abrams (New York: Columbia University Press, 1958), p. 63.

2. Samuel Taylor Coleridge, *The Statesman's Manual,* ed. R. J. White, in *The Collected Works of Samuel Taylor Coleridge,* ed. Kathleen Coburn (Princeton, N.J.: Princeton University Press, 1969–), vol. 6, p. 30.

3. By definition, whole texts can never be symbolic in the synecdochic sense Coleridge insists upon; only fragments can be symbolic. Thomas McFarland anticipates this point: "The inescapable fact is that the symbol as such is always jagged, is always a fragment incomplete in itself" (*Romanticism and the Forms of Ruin: Wordsworth, Coleridge, and Modalities of Fragmentation* [Princeton, N.J.: Princeton University Press, 1981], p. 27).

4. Marjorie Levinson has attempted to classify the various types of "Romantic fragment poems" by analyzing the relation, posed by particular poetic fragments, between the fragmentary texts and the "ideal (abstract and extrinsic) wholes" that they project (*The Romantic Fragment Poem: A Critique of a Form* [Chapel Hill: North Carolina University Press, 1986], p. 27).

5. Samuel Taylor Coleridge, *Biographia Literaria,* ed. James Engell and W. Jackson Bate, in *Collected Works,* vol. 7, bk. 2, p. 13 (hereafter cited parenthetically in the text by book and page number).

6. This fragmentation becomes especially pronounced at the conclusion of the discussion of Wordsworth in chapter 22 of *Biographia Literaria,* where Coleridge strings together a medley of poetic extracts "most manifesting" the faculty of "imaginative power." In addition to the sequence of cited passages, Coleridge offers a page index to other "striking" places in Wordsworth's poems.

7. It is worth recalling that Coleridge first undertook *Biographia Literaria* as a preface to *Sibylline Leaves,* on the order of Wordsworth's preface to *Lyrical*

Ballads. The sheer contrast in bulk between Coleridge's critical volume and his volume of poems says a great deal about how the conditions he establishes for literary production outweigh the products themselves.

8. The purely ideal magnum opus is customarily distinguished from the collection of manuscript fragments known as the *Opus Maximum.* Thomas McFarland, who is editing the Princeton edition of the *Opus Maximum,* writes of those manuscripts that, "though written with the idea of the larger whole in view, they are actually merely the residuum of Coleridge's conception, and, if one wishes to play further with paradox, it may be said that they actually have no greater claim to being thought of as elements in the *magnum opus* than does, say, the *Aids to Reflection*" (*Romanticism,* pp. 355–356).

9. Ibid., p. 343.

10. When Coleridge, for example, introduces the "Essays on the Principles of Method," which form the penultimate section of the 1818 edition of *The Friend,* he explains that he has added the section in order to "fulfil the original scope of The Friend"; and yet in the same breath he characterizes the "Essays" as "preparatory steps" and as "the necessary introduction" to the truly systematic text that would surely follow (*The Friend,* ed. Barbara E. Rooke, in *Collected Works,* vol. 4, bk. 1, pp. 445–446). *The Friend*'s "original scope," even as it is "fulfilled," turns out to be only "preparatory."

11. McFarland, *Romanticism,* p. 349.

12. Though it does not discuss Coleridge, Philippe Lacoue-Labarthe and Jean-Luc Nancy's *The Literary Absolute: The Theory of Literature in German Romanticism,* trans. Philip Barnard and Cheryl Lester (Albany: State University of New York Press, 1988), helps to make an important distinction between the fragmentary texts of Coleridge and the fragmentary mode of Novalis, Jean Paul, and the Schlegels. Both Coleridge and the German Romantics produced their fragments within an epistemological condition that, according to Lacoue-Labarthe and Nancy, made systematic exposition of reality impossible. But whereas the Germans relied on fragmentary form as an effective mode of presenting an active and dialectical subject that had become unpresentable in terms of any completed text, Coleridge insists that his fragments have full meaning *only* in regard to a literally completable systematic text.

13. Coleridge, *Statesman's Manual,* p. 30.

14. Paul de Man, "The Rhetoric of Temporality," in *Blindness and Insight,* 2nd ed. (Minneapolis: University of Minnesota Press, 1983), p. 192.

15. Among the numerous discussions of the *Statesman's Manual* passage and de Man's attack upon it, that of Stephen Knapp, in *Personification and the Sublime: Milton to Coleridge* (Cambridge, Mass.: Harvard University Press, 1985), stands closest to my account. Taking issue with de Man, Knapp finds the Coleridgean symbol to be a "medium" leading into "a world of expec-

tations, practices, and acts" (p. 17). I would qualify Knapp's pragmatic reading by insisting that the realm of poetic activity mediated by the symbol remains, for Coleridge, a peculiarly *textual* domain of meaning. Coleridge's choice of the Gospel of John as a paradigm for the magnum opus suggests that the *logos* of the *Logosophia* will be both material text and active meaning.

16. In *Aids to Reflection,* Coleridge accounts for "abstraction" as one of the "proper Functions of the Understanding." The process of understanding "may be reduced to three acts, all depending on and supposing a previous impression on the senses." The first of these acts is the "appropriation of our Attention" by the "*total impression*" of a perceptual whole. The next act is that of "Abstraction, or the voluntary withholding of the Attention" as we "reflect exclusively" on those components of the total impression we recall having noticed in previous total impressions. Through abstraction, attention is "drawn away from" the present impression even as we *ex*tract fragments of that impression in order to compare them with objects of memory; a fragmented memory has substituted for the present perceptual whole. The final step in the process of understanding, "Generalization," consists in cognitive "use" of the abstracted, isolated components of the previous total impression (again, they have been tallied, through "reflection," with previously abstracted components of perceptual wholes) as "*common characters,* by virtue of which the several objects are referred to one and the same sort" (*Aids to Reflection,* ed. John Beer, in *Collected Works,* vol. 9, pp. 224–225).

17. John Locke, *An Essay Concerning Human Understanding,* ed. Alexander Campbell Fraser (New York: Dover, 1959), vol. 2, pp. 16–17. The entire third part of the *Essay,* "Of Words," treats linguistic formation as a matter of classification. Locke emphasizes the "arbitrary" relation between words and objects. In regard to the "mixed mode" (a collection of ideas making "one complex idea"), he argues that "it is the mind that combines several scattered independent ideas into one complex idea; and, by the common name it gives them, makes them the essence of a certain species, without regulating itself by any connexion they have in nature" (p. 45).

18. Coleridge to James Gilman, November 10, 1816, *Collected Letters of Samuel Taylor Coleridge,* ed. Earl Leslie Griggs (Oxford: Oxford University Press, 1956–1971), vol. 4, p. 689.

19. William Blake, *Jerusalem* 15:14–20, in *The Poetry and Prose of William Blake,* ed. David V. Erdman (New York: Doubleday, 1970), p. 159.

20. Rudolph Carnap, *The Logical Structure of the World and Pseudoproblems in Philosophy,* trans. Rolf A. George (Berkeley: University of California Press, 1967), p. 63. Carnap means "whole" not in Coleridge's sense, but in the sense of what Coleridge calls an "aggregate": "The character of a whole or a collection (or of an 'aggregate') has been erroneously connected with the concept of a set ever since its inception" (ibid.). Carnap follows Frege and

Russell on this point. Throughout this chapter I refer to "classes" instead of the corresponding mathematical term "sets."

21. Coleridge's knowledge of medieval philosophy would have anticipated for him many of the precepts of twentieth-century theories of classes. He devoted the whole summer of 1801 to studying the work of Duns Scotus, who elaborately refutes the Thomist and Augustinian class-logic that presumes to establish hierarchical continuity in the material world. Scotus's attack rests on his perception that individual, species, and genus are entirely discontinuous realms. Emile Bréhier notes that "if Augustinianism affirmed continuity in being *and therefore* continuity in knowledge, and Thomism continuity in being *but* discontinuity in knowledge, the doctrine of Scotus might be formulated: discontinuity in being *and* discontinuity in knowledge" (*The Middle Ages and the Renaissance,* trans. Wade Baskin [Chicago: University of Chicago Press, 1967], p. 184).

22. De Man, "Rhetoric," p. 207.

23. B. L. Packer, *Emerson's Fall: A New Interpretation of the Major Essays* (New York: Continuum, 1982), pp. 72–84.

24. Leonardo da Vinci, *The Notebooks of Leonardo da Vinci,* trans. and ed. Edward MacCurdy (New York: Reynal and Hitchcock, 1938), p. 254.

25. Cited by Joseph Anthony Mazzeo, *Medieval Cultural Tradition in Dante's Comedy* (1960; reprint, New York: Greenwood Press, 1977), p. 90. (Page citations are to the reprint edition.)

26. Among the many critical accounts of the transparent eyeball passage from *Nature,* see especially Harold Bloom, *Figures of Capable Imagination* (New York: Seabury Press, 1976), pp. 48–51, and *Agon: Towards a Theory of Revisionism* (New York: Oxford University Press, 1982), pp. 166–169; James M. Cox, "R. W. Emerson: The Circles of the Eye," in *Emerson: Prophecy, Metamorphosis, and Influence; Selected Papers from the English Institute,* ed. David Levin (New York: Columbia University Press, 1975), pp. 57–81; Richard Poirier, *The Renewal of Literature: Emersonian Reflections* (New York: Random House, 1987), p. 202; David Van Leer, *Emerson's Epistemology: The Argument of the Essays* (Cambridge: Cambridge University Press, 1986), pp. 20–25, 51–53.

27. *Oxford Latin Dictionary* notes the rather late metonymic transfer of meaning from "service in fulfillment of obligation" to "body of officials or their department" (*s.v.* "officium," 6b). The next metonymic step, in English, gives us the place where officials work.

28. Parmenides frag. 8, in G. S. Kirk and J. E. Raven, *The Presocratic Philosophers: A Critical History with a Selection of Texts* (Cambridge: Cambridge University Press, 1957), p. 276.

29. Herman Melville, *Moby-Dick, or The Whale,* ed. Alfred Kazin (Boston: Houghton Mifflin, 1956), p. 163.

2. The Emerson Museum

This chapter contains revised versions of essays previously published in *Representations* (fall 1992) and *Prospects* (1994).

1. The Muséum d'Histoire Naturelle (commonly called the Jardin des Plantes) was formally created in 1793 as the combination of three prerevolutionary institutions: the Jardin du Roi; the Cabinet du Roi; and the Ménagerie du Roi. When Emerson visited the Muséum in 1833, he viewed mineral collections laid out by René-Just Haüy (1743–1822); the menagerie and zoological cabinets had been arranged mainly by Georges Cuvier (1769–1832), though parts of the mammal collections followed the classifications of Etienne Geoffroy Saint-Hilaire (1772–1844). The collection of shells, which Emerson remembers in *Nature,* was set up by Jean-Baptiste Lamarck (1744–1829). Finally, the botanical gardens and herbaria exhibits were organized according to the system of Antoine-Laurent de Jussieu (1748–1836). Because of the publicity offered by the displayed collections, there was strong competition (most notably between Cuvier and Geoffroy) for control over the various cabinets. See Dorinda Outram, *Georges Cuvier: Vocation, Science, and Authority in Post-Revolutionary France* (Manchester: Manchester University Press, 1984), pp. 161–188.

2. Cited in Outram, *Georges Cuvier,* p. 251 n. 84.

3. Henry David Thoreau, *Walden,* ed. J. Lyndon Shanley (Princeton, N.J.: Princeton University Press, 1971), p. 210.

4. Most of Emerson's critics and biographers note the importance of his experience in the Jardin des Plantes, and several have examined its consequences or intellectual content. See H. H. Clark, "Emerson and Science," *Philological Quarterly* 10 (1931): 225–260; David Robinson, "Emerson's Natural Theology and the Paris Naturalists: Towards a Theory of Animated Nature," *Journal of the History of Ideas* 41 (1980): 69–88; B. L. Packer, *Emerson's Fall: A New Interpretation of the Major Essays* (New York: Continuum, 1982), pp. 41–48; Leon Chai, *The Romantic Foundations of the American Renaissance* (Ithaca, N.Y.: Cornell University Press, 1987), pp. 141–150; Elizabeth A. Dant, "Composing the World: Emerson and the Cabinet of Natural History," *Nineteenth-Century Literature* 44 (1989): 18–44.

5. Before the incorporation of the hilly *labyrinthe,* the best view of the grounds was to be had at the lowest spot, as one entered through the front gate near the Seine. From there, wrote the Muséum's historian, J.-P.-F. Deleuze, "one sees the Cabinet of Natural History, which occupies the width of the Jardin and appears to rise above two enclosures, one of which is the seed-nursery and the other is a broad square lake, dug at an incline to the level of the river and ringed with shrubs on its sides. To the right and left are the two great avenues of lindens" (*Histoire et description du Muséum Royal*

d'Histoire Naturelle [Paris, 1823], vol. 1, p. 193; unless otherwise noted, translations are mine).

6. Louis Agassiz, *An Essay on Classification,* ed. Edward Lurie (Cambridge, Mass.: Harvard University Press, 1962), p. 9.

7. My treatment of the Muséum, concerned as it is with the "look" of the whole place to the amateur, emphasizes the more Aristotelian classificatory theories of Cuvier somewhat at the expense of protoevolutionist classifiers like Lamarck and Geoffroy, whose work was also in evidence among the Muséum displays. I stress the paradigmatic centrality of Cuvier not only because of his relative dominance over the Muséum's public image but also because his belief in the essential reality of hierarchical classes was accommodated "naturally" by the representational techniques of natural history museums. On Cuvier's fusion of exact comparative anatomy with hierarchical classification, see Ernst Mayr, *The Growth of Biological Thought: Diversity, Evolution, and Inheritance* (Cambridge, Mass.: Harvard University Press, 1982), pp. 182–184, 367–371.

8. "The German erudition" would include not only eighteenth-century philology but the "higher criticism" devoted to biblical study. Both hermeneutic disciplines proved that "superhuman" texts were products of cultural traditions, built up over time. For discussion of the impact of the higher criticism on Americans such as Emerson, see Julie Ellison, *Emerson's Romantic Style* (Princeton, N.J.: Princeton University Press, 1984), pp. 42–45; Barbara Packer, "Origin and Authority: Emerson and the Higher Criticism," in *Reconstructing American Literary History,* ed. Sacvan Bercovitch (Cambridge, Mass.: Harvard University Press, 1986), pp. 67–92; Richard Grusin, *Transcendentalist Hermeneutics: Institutional Authority and the Higher Criticism of the Bible* (Durham, N.C.: Duke University Press, 1991).

9. Toby A. Appel, in *The Cuvier-Geoffroy Debate: French Biology in the Decades before Darwin* (New York: Oxford University Press, 1987), notes that "Cuvier could expound the text of *Le règne animal* through the very halls of the Muséum, as the vertebrates were arranged according to his classificatory scheme" (p. 36).

10. Baron Georges Cuvier, *The Animal Kingdom, Arranged in Conformity with its Organization,* trans. H. M'Murtrie (New York, 1831), vol. 1, p. 159.

11. Deleuze, *Histoire,* vol. 2, p. 663.

12. "Catalogue des préparations anatomiques laissées dans le Cabinet d'Anatomie Comparée du Muséum d'Histoire Naturelle par G. Cuvier," *Nouvelles annales du Muséum d'Histoire Naturelle* 2 (1833): 417–508.

13. Michel Foucault, *The Order of Things: An Archaeology of the Human Sciences* (New York: Vintage Books, 1970), pp. 267–268.

14. In *Methods of Natural History* (Boston: Ticknor and Fields, 1863),

Agassiz celebrates his teacher Cuvier as the founder of comparative anatomy. Agassiz explains: "With this new principle as the basis of investigation, it was no longer enough for the naturalist to know a certain number of features of a certain number of animals,—he must penetrate deep enough into their organization to find the secret of their internal structure. Till he can do this, he is like the traveller in a strange city, who looks on the exterior of edifices entirely new to him, but knows nothing of the plan of their internal structure. To be able to read in the finished structure the plan on which the whole is built is now essential to every naturalist" (pp. 9–10). For Agassiz, the plan uncovered by comparative anatomy precedes the visible organism both historically and ontologically. The plan offers an "inside" that is not merely internal to the living creature but comes before it and occupies a realm of reality independent from it. Penetrating inside the creature, then, is also penetrating *beyond* it.

15. Samuel Taylor Coleridge, *The Friend,* ed. Barbara E. Rooke, in *The Collected Works of Samuel Taylor Coleridge,* ed. Kathleen Coburn (Princeton, N.J.: Princeton University Press, 1969–), vol. 4, bk. 1, pp. 497–498.

16. Ibid., pp. 457, 451.

17. Henry James, "Ralph Waldo Emerson" (1887), in *Henry James: Literary Criticism; Essays on Literature, American Writers, English Writers,* ed. Leon Edel (New York: Library of America, 1984), p. 252.

18. Alexis de Tocqueville, *Democracy in America,* trans. Henry Reeve; rev. Frances Bowen; rev. and ed. Phillips Bradley (New York: Alfred A. Knopf, 1980), vol. 2, p. 26.

19. See Packer, *Emerson's Fall,* pp. 85–88. The idea that literary life in New England was empty or puerile before the major writers of the American Renaissance reflects the power of those writers, but it is not a fair assessment of the milieu in which they worked. Lawrence Buell, in *New England Literary Culture: From Revolution through Renaissance* (Cambridge: Cambridge University Press, 1986), notes that the crowded literary scene of the first two decades of the century makes it "progressively harder to tell who the really important New England authors are" (p. 43). Buell points out that the impact of major figures such as Emerson has tended to narrow views of the preexisting field. It may be objected that Buell is speaking of quantity rather than quality. But no one can discount the achievement of William Cullen Bryant, who was well known by the time Emerson began his major work. Even leaving the rest of the pre-Transcendentalist literary scene aside, Bryant's was a towering contribution to the national literature. (Whitman, for example, called Bryant the greatest poet of the century.) Emerson had strongly mixed feelings about Bryant, ranking him with Milton and Burns in 1835 (*JMN* 5:16), and then in 1837 putting him in a list of "American genuises" who "all lack nerve & dagger" (7:200). In any case, to find limitations in American liter-

ature before 1836 is one thing; but to say with Emerson and the Europeans that American literary life was empty or bare is at best a useful fabrication.

20. On the influx of New World botanical specimens, see A. G. Morton, *History of Botanical Science: An Account of the Development of Botany from Ancient Times to the Present Day* (London and New York: Academic Press, 1981), p. 118. Mayr (*Growth of Biological Thought,* pp. 165–166) blames the considerable lag of zoological science behind botany at least in part on the fact that an adequate means of preserving animal specimens was not found until the development of arsenic preparation in the 1750s. Since the Renaissance, on the other hand, botanists had been possessed of herbaria or specimen books containing pressed and dried plants. "Most of Linnaeus' descriptions of non-Swedish plants," Mayr writes, "were made from herbarium specimens." Like the entries in a journal, herbarium specimens were selected, classified, and rearranged into a systematic text, to be presented in a book or folio that would treat the species as paragraphs or pages (quite literally, "leaves") and the genera as pages or chapters. Foucault notes how Linnaeus wished, in his botanical catalogs, "that the order of the description, its division into paragraphs, and even its typological modules, should reproduce the form of the plant itself" (*Order of Things,* p. 135).

21. The earliest botanical gardens were those established at Padua, Pisa, and Florence by 1546. Their quadrilateral layouts reflected the notion that the flora of all four corners of the earth could be represented in a single, systematically composed garden, a latter-day Garden of Eden. See John Prest, *The Garden of Eden: The Botanic Garden and the Re-Creation of Paradise* (New Haven, Conn.: Yale University Press, 1981). See also Morton, *History of Botanical Science,* pp. 15–64.

22. Deleuze, *Histoire,* vol. 1, p. 60.

23. The best expressions of Emerson's grand encyclopedic hopes are to be found in the dedications to his fifteen-volume "Wide World" series (1820–1824). At the opening of "Wide World 6," for example, Emerson drapes his own work in millennial colors: "Two thousand years have passed, and the mighty progress of improvement & civilization have been forming the force which shall reveal Nature to Man. To roll about the outskirts of this Mystery and ascertain and describe its pleasing wonders—be this the journey of my Wideworld. The *Hand* shall come;—I traced its outlines in the mists of the morning" (*JMN* 1:115).

24. Thomas Carlyle, "Novalis," in *Critical and Miscellaneous Essays* (London, 1899; reprint, New York: AMS Press, 1969), vol. 2, p. 28.

25. "Nature is a swamp, on whose purlieus we see prismatic dewdrops, but her interiors are terrific" (*JMN* 13:450). Compare this statement to its opposite in another journal entry, where nature is "without depth but with

innumerable lateral spaces . . . Nature has only the thickness of a shingle or a slate; we come straight to the extremes: but sideways & at unawares the present moment opens into other moods & moments, rich, prolific, leading onward without end" (9:68).

26. Thoreau, *Walden*, p. 243.

27. Elizabeth Palmer Peabody's account of Alcott's school in Boston puts journal writing at the heart of the curriculum: "Mr. Alcott presents this exercise as a means of self-inspection and self-knowledge, enabling the writers to give unity to their own being, by bringing all outward facts into relation with their individuality, and gathering up fragments which would otherwise be lost" (*Record of a School: Exemplifying the General Principles of Spiritual Culture*, 2nd ed. [Boston, 1836; reprint, New York: Arno Press and New York Times, 1969], p. xxvi; page citations are to the reprint edition).

28. Jeremy Bentham, *Chrestomathia*, in *A Bentham Reader*, ed. Mary Peter Mack (New York: Pegasus Books, 1969), p. 273.

29. Deleuze, *Histoire*, vol. 1, p. 233.

30. René Desfontaines, *Tableau de l'école de botanique du Jardin du Roi*, 2nd ed. (Paris, 1815). "This little book," Desfontaines explains, "is particularly meant to facilitate correspondence with foreigners, to indicate to them the plants which they can acquire and those with which they can enrich the Jardin through reciprocal exchange" (p. v).

31. Deleuze, *Histoire*, vol. 1, p. 232.

32. Each living specimen in the systematically arranged parterres carried a placard detailing its place in the invisible hierarchy of conceptual forms. As Deleuze describes them, these texts were synopses of the "history" of each plant: "All the plants are labelled: the largest labels, the red ones, at once indicate the classes and the families; after that comes the label of the genus, which is placed over the first species of each genus; finally, the labels of the species, on the first line of which is the initial letter of the genus and the classical Latin name, and on the second line the French name, and on the third line the indication of the country where the plant grows naturally, with signs marking if it is an annual, perennial, or ligneous, if it grows in open ground, or in plantations, or in a greenhouse. Above many of these labels one sees a stripe colored red, green, yellow, blue, or black, meant to indicate whether the plant is used for medicine, in domestic economy or in the arts, if it is sought after for a garden ornament, or if it is poisonous" (*Histoire*, vol. 1, p. 231).

33. Lawrence Rosenwald, in *Emerson and the Art of the Diary* (New York: Oxford University Press, 1988), pp. 53–57, also discusses the relation of Emerson's indexing activity to his reconception of the journalizing project in the years 1833–1834.

34. By contrast with the eighty-two index topics of journal "A," the 144

pages of journal "Q" (March 1832–November 1833) are given only seventeen index topics, most of which can only be uncertainly located. Almost no index topics were given to the five pocket-size notebooks Emerson kept during his European tour. Nine of Emerson's book-length indexes are collected in *JMN* 12. A copy of "Index Major" appears in *Emerson's Workshop*, ed. Kenneth Walter Cameron (Hartford: Transcendental Books, 1964), vol. 2.

35. Cuvier, *Animal Kingdom*, p. 5. "This scaffolding of divisions," Cuvier adds, works as "a sort of dictionary, in which we proceed from the properties of things to arrive at their names; being the reverse of the common ones, in which we proceed from the name to arrive at the property." Once the system was codified and made available in textbooks like *The Animal Kingdom* or Jussieu's *Genera Plantarum,* the amateur, or the explorer, could "find" the natural locus of an unidentified specimen by working "down" through the classificatory register, recognizing first more general characters to locate class and order, then more specific characters to locate family and genus.

36. In spite of obvious differences between Jussieu's and Cuvier's classificatory models (Jussieu organized the plants in a continuous series while Cuvier conceived his *embranchements* as discontinuous), the Muséum publicized them as united advocates of the "natural method": "Cuvier did for zoology what Jussieu had done for botany, in establishing, according to natural relations indicated by invariable characters, a classification which was universally adopted" (Deleuze, *Histoire*, vol. 1, p. 145). See Foucault's discussion of the distinction between "system" and "method" in eighteenth-century natural classification (*Order of Things*, pp. 138–145).

37. Ernst Robert Curtius, *European Literature and the Latin Middle Ages,* trans. Willard R. Trask (New York, 1948), pp. 319–326.

38. See Foucault's discussion of plant signatures (*Order of Things*, pp. 25–30).

39. Agassiz, *Essay on Classification,* p. 9.

40. Foucault, *Order of Things*, p. 136.

41. "History" in the sense of its Greek root—that is, as a systematic description of a fully present subject, rather than as an account of past circumstances survived into the nineteenth century only in the term "natural history." The treatment of history in the Muséum, since it emphasized construction rather than objective, irreversible process, was bound to favor spatial over temporal terms of conception. (This was also the case in my consideration of Coleridge's symbol.) Myra Jehlen, in *American Incarnation: The Individual, the Nation, and the Continent* (Cambridge, Mass.: Harvard University Press, 1986), observes a general tendency in American thought to treat temporal matters spatially, as a constant field of possibility rather than a historical process (pp. 6–12). For provocative further discussion of the spatializing tendencies in American thought, see Philip Fisher, "Democratic

Social Space: Whitman, Melville, and the Promise of American Transparency," *Representations* 24 (fall 1988): 60–101.

42. As he awaited his ship's departure on September 6, 1833, Emerson wrote, "I like my book about nature & wish I knew where & how I ought to live" (*JMN* 4:237).

43. In 1790, the officers of the Jardin du Roi, threatened with severe budgetary cutbacks, successfully defended the institution before the National Assembly by depicting the Jardin as the embodiment of philosophical principles (particularly those of Buffon) congenial to the Revolution. The Jardin was reorganized on an egalitarian basis in 1793; the committee proposing the new order concluded, "It is thus, Messieurs, that the Jardin des Plantes, transformed into a veritable *Muséum d'histoire naturelle,* could soon become a sort of metropolis for all the sciences useful to agriculture, commerce, and the arts" (cited by Appel in his summary of the history of the Muséum; *Cuvier-Geoffroy Debate,* pp. 16–18). Outram also discusses the "utopic" function of the Muséum in Cuvier's Paris (*Georges Cuvier,* pp. 183–184).

44. Georges Cuvier, *Tableau élementaire de l'histoire naturelle des animaux* (Paris, Year 6 [1798]). Cuvier compiled this abridgment of his classificatory system for use as a textbook in public education. His preface opens by pointing out that the study of natural history has been "substituted for those parts of the old curriculum which are no longer in accord with the principles of republican government" (p. v).

45. Ibid., pp. xi–xii.

46. Cuvier, *Animal Kingdom,* p. xv.

47. Edward Everett, "On the Importance of Scientific Knowledge to Practical Men, and on the Encouragements to Its Pursuit," in *Orations and Speeches on Various Occasions,* 4th ed. (Boston: Little, Brown, 1856), vol. 1, p. 268.

48. Ibid., p. 273.

49. Louis Agassiz, *Contributions to the Natural History of the United States of America* (Boston: Little, Brown 1857–1862; reprint, Arno Press, 1978), vol. 1, p. x.

50. Agassiz published his *Essay on Classification* as a separate volume in 1859, the same year that Darwin's *Origin of Species* first appeared. Despite the almost immediate ascendancy of Darwin's theory, Agassiz bitterly insisted on his Cuvierian framework until his death in 1873.

51. Carl Bode notes that one of the first acts of the Concord Lyceum, on its founding in 1829, was a resolve to obtain " 'a cabinet of minerals, a library, and an apparatus for illustrating the sciences' " (*The American Lyceum: Town Meeting of the Mind* [New York: Oxford University Press, 1956], p. 189). See also Ralph S. Bates, *Scientific Societies in the United States,* 2nd ed. (New York: Columbia University Press, 1958). William Ellery Channing noted in his 1841 lecture on "The Present Age" that "lyceums spring up in almost every village

for the purpose of mutual aid in the study of natural history" (*The Works of William Ellery Channing, D.D.* [Boston: American Unitarian Association, 1898], p. 160).

52. Channing, *Works,* pp. 160, 161.

53. Ibid., p. 160.

54. Ibid., p. 161.

55. Cuvier, *Tableau,* p. xii.

56. Bliss Perry makes this connection in *Emerson Today* (Princeton, N.J.: Princeton University Press, 1931), pp. 40–47.

57. Darwin's impact on the novel has been penetratingly discussed by Gillian Beer, in *Darwin's Plots: Evolutionary Narrative in Darwin, George Eliot, and Nineteenth-Century Fiction* (London: Routledge and Kegan Paul, 1983), and by George Levine, in *Darwin and the Novelists: Patterns of Science in Victorian Fiction* (Cambridge, Mass.: Harvard University Press, 1988). There are no comparable studies, however, of the influence of pre-Darwinian natural history on nineteenth-century novels.

58. Honoré de Balzac, *La comédie humaine,* ed. Pierre Citron (Paris: Editions du Seuil, 1965), vol. 1, p. 51.

59. Stendhal, *The Red and the Black,* trans. Lloyd C. Parks (New York: Signet Classics, 1970), p. 439. In his essay in *Mimesis* on French realism, Erich Auerbach notes that the boredom Julien Sorel finds in the Hôtel de la Mole expresses how "the inadequately implemented attempt which the Bourbon regime made to restore conditions long since made obsolete by events, creates, among its adherents, an atmosphere of pure convention, of limitation, of constraint, and lack of freedom, against which the intelligence and good will of the persons involved are powerless" (*Mimesis: The Representation of Reality in Western Literature,* trans. Willard R. Trask [Princeton, N.J.: Princeton University Press, 1968], p. 456). The Bourbon Restoration had produced an incongruous state of things: energies unleashed by the Revolution of 1789 were constrained for a period within resurrected, yet fully superseded, forms. In Auerbach's estimate, this circumstance generated a kind of crisis of ennui—the *besoin d'occupation,* perhaps, that worried Cuvier—for the upper classes prior to the Revolution of 1830, a crisis Stendhal relied on as the framework for much of the action in *The Red and the Black.* But it should not be forgotten that, although industrialization on the scale of Britain's and New England's would not take hold in France until the Second Empire, the French market economy was burgeoning at the period of Emerson's visit, producing new configurations of power and supplanting old ones.

60. Cuvier, *Animal Kingdom,* pp. xv–xvi.

61. Adolphe Quételet, *A Treatise on Man and the Development of His Faculties* [*or, an Essay in Social Physics*] (Edinburgh, 1842; reprint, Gainesville, Fla.: Scholars' Facsimiles and Reprints, 1969), p. 9. Emerson read this translation

in 1845. For discussion of Quételet's impact on the new science of statistics, see Stephen M. Stigler, *The History of Statistics: The Measurement of Uncertainty before 1900* (Cambridge, Mass.: Harvard University Press, 1986), pp. 161–220.

62. Quételet, *Treatise*, p. 5

63. Ibid., p. 8.

64. Karl Marx, *Grundrisse: Foundations of the Critique of Political Economy*, trans. Martin Nicholas (New York: Vintage Books, 1973), pp. 156–157.

65. Thomas Carlyle, "Signs of the Times" (1829), in *The Philosophy of Manufactures: Early Debates over Industrialism in the United States*, ed. Michael Brewster Folsom and Steven D. Lubar (Cambridge, Mass.: MIT Press, 1982), p. 274. Among the many literary historians who discuss nineteenth-century "mechanism," see Leo Marx, *The Machine in the Garden: Technology and the Pastoral Ideal in America* (New York: Oxford University Press, 1964); Carolyn Porter, *Seeing and Being: The Plight of the Participant Observer in Emerson, James, Adams, and Faulkner* (Middletown, Conn.: Wesleyan University Press, 1981); and Michael Gilmore, *American Romanticism and the Marketplace* (Chicago: University of Chicago Press, 1985).

66. Marx, *Grundrisse*, p. 157.

67. Karl Marx, *Capital: A Critique of Political Economy*, trans. Samuel Moore and Edward Aveling (New York: Modern Library, 1906), p. 83.

68. Outram, *Georges Cuvier*, pp. 184–188.

69. Walter Benjamin, *Charles Baudelaire: A Lyric Poet in the Era of High Capitalism*, trans. Harry Zohn (London: NLB, 1973), pp. 35–66.

70. Alexis de Tocqueville to Louis de Kergorlay, June 20, 1831, *Selected Letters on Politics and Society*, ed. Roger Boesche, trans. James Toupin and Roger Boesche (Berkeley: University of California Press, 1985), p. 81.

71. "There is now an obvious tendency to treat with indifference all the ideas that can stir society, whether right or wrong, noble or base. Everyone seems to agree in considering the government of his country *sicut res inter alios acta* [as one thing that is done among others]. Everyone is focusing more and more on individual interest . . . It is not a healthy and virile repose. It is a sort of apoplectic torpor" (Tocqueville to Eugène Stoffels, January 12, 1833), *Selected Letters*, p. 81.

72. The arcades were the places, Benjamin observes, where the flâneur felt most "at home." Aside from Benjamin, my information on arcades, and in particular on the Passages des Panoramas, derives primarily from Johann Friedrich Geist, *Arcades: The History of a Building Type* (Cambridge, Mass.: MIT Press, 1983), pp. 464–476. See also Margaret MacKeith, *The History and Conservation of Shopping Arcades* (London: Mansell Publishing, 1986). For discussion of Benjamin's *Passagenwerke*, his grand, unfinished project that took the *passages* as its central metaphor, see Susan Buck-Morss, *The Dialectics of Seeing: Walter Benjamin and the Arcades* (Cambridge, Mass.: MIT Press, 1989).

73. Cited in Benjamin, *Charles Baudelaire,* pp. 37, 158.

74. Outram, drawing from Benjamin's discussion of the arcades, points to the utopian sensibility shared by the Muséum and the arcades (*Georges Cuvier,* pp. 183–186).

75. Emile Zola, *Nana* (New York: Harper and Bros., 1957), p. 220.

76. Ellison (*Emerson's Romantic Style,* pp. 160–194) explores this ideal of transition both as a feature of Emerson's style and as one of his means of conceptualizing the project of writing.

3. Life's Writing

1. For this passage I cite the more emphatic first-edition text of Emerson's *Essays* (Boston: James Munroe and Company, 1841), pp. 4–5.

2. Freud, whose attack on the priority of conscious thought depended on picturing consciousness on the order of a detached "sense-organ," also asserted that thought (a certain portion of which becomes available to consciousness) maintains what Emerson would call a "pious" stance toward the work of perception. The essay "Negation" is one of several places where Freud describes thought as "an experimental action, a kind of groping forward" through available ideas. The ego learns this "technique," Freud says, from the ongoing unconscious work of perception: "For upon our hypoth esis perception is not a merely passive process; we believe rather that the ego periodically sends out small amounts of cathectic energy into the perceptual system and by their means samples the external stimuli, and after each groping advance draws back again" (*General Psychological Theory: Papers on Metapsychology,* ed. Philip Rieff [New York: Collier Books, 1963], p. 216). So for Freud as well as as for Emerson, perception has a hands-on dimension that works ahead of the realm of conscious oversight, which retrospectively inhilits perceptual activity with its own version of probing, procrastinating "reception."

3. For David Hume, believable ideas are those that most strongly imitate the quality of perceptions, which are suffered passively: *"Our belief is more properly an act of the sensitive, than of the cognitive part of our natures"* (*A Treatise of Human Nature,* ed. Ernest C. Mossner [London: Penguin Books, 1969], p. 234; Hume's emphasis). Belief in an idea renders it "strong and lively," so that it "approaches in some measure to an immediate impression" (p. 145). For discussion of Emerson's early reading of Hume, see Evelyn Barish, *Emerson: The Roots of Prophecy* (Princeton, N.J.: Princeton University Press, 1989), pp. 99–115.

4. Richard Poirier's discussions of labor in Frost's poetry bear strongly on this point; see *Robert Frost: The Work of Knowing* (New York: Oxford University Press, 1977).

5. In his extended meditation on this phrase in the introduction to *Poetry and Pragmatism* (Cambridge, Mass.: Harvard University Press, 1992), Richard Poirier describes how the soul's becoming binds it to an entirely prospective future identity: "Note that 'the soul' is first named as if, with its definite article, it were an entity; note, too, that its realization as an entity is immediately and forever delayed, its presence transferred to an ever elusive future, with the word *'becomes.'* The soul never 'becomes' a thing or a text; it exists in the action of becoming" (p. 28). This is the same dynamic sense of Emersonian identity that Nietzsche must have loved. I merely complement Poirier's discussion with the point that Emerson's dynamism, whatever its occasionally nihilistic overtones, also restores the common world of material nature. This is in keeping with Poirier's own discussions of the work of writing as he finds it in other places in Emerson, Frost, and James. Picturing the soul as something essentially *at work* on any number of objects does not remove it from nature; on the contrary, it brings it into more intimate contact with nature.

6. Friedrich Wilhelm Nietzsche, "The Twilight of the Idols," in *The Portable Nietzsche*, trans. and ed. Walter Kaufmann (New York: Viking Press, 1954), p. 522.

7. Here again I cite the first-edition text of *Essays,* p. 127. Emerson's thinner revision of the passage appears in *CW* 2:90.

8. Nietzsche and Freud both divest the instinctual realm of all moral attributes, instead treating moral structures as historical conditions generated by instinct's struggle to satisfy itself in action. For both writers, though, the fact that moral categories become seen as historical contingencies (or as accrued structures of restraint) does not alter the basic Prometheanism of their views on instinct and the will to power. But it is also true that Freud (at least after his 1915 essay on narcissism) found himself compelled to admit that the categories of spontaneous drive and inhibiting defense are not so easily isolated from each other, and that the force of resistance turns out to be as primary—indeed, as instinctual—as the instincts it sets itself against. Emerson's arguments, which also tend to historicize and destabilize particular moral categories, often resemble moments in Nietzsche and Freud, but Emerson derives his arguments from a different strain of inquiry.

9. A masterful account of the vicissitudes of this moral paradigm may be found in Lionel Trilling's *Sincerity and Authenticity* (Cambridge, Mass.: Harvard University Press, 1972).

10. Kenneth Burke's systematic demolition of the old pieties toward motives (Burke resolves motives into strategies of symbolic action) has helped to consummate the pragmatic devaluating of intentions that Emerson began. Starting in his 1935 masterpiece *Permanence and Change* (3rd ed. [Berkeley: University of California Press, 1984]), Burke effectively removes motives

from their supposed sources in personal history and relocates them in the realm of interpersonal activity, a discursive realm Emerson would identify as nature. With his famous argument that "motives are shorthand terms for situations," Burke makes it impossible to speak of literal motives in Freud's biologistic sense. Instead, Burke treats motives as ready-made strategies on the interpreter's part for meeting and making the character of another's actions or statements. Motives lead not into personality but into the scene of their imputation, a scene that exercises the ideological framework of the imputer, who uses motives as ways of placing character within the framework. Burke argues that modern experience, in which multiple interpretive frameworks appear simultaneously, is thus bound to be preoccupied with (and perhaps paralyzed by) unresolvable questions of motives.

11. The sentimental picture of domestic life as an island of purity in an otherwise immoral or amoral world was a strong one in the antebellum period. It represents another turn in the ancient distinction between domestic and public spheres that classical thought explores in great detail; see Hannah Arendt, *The Human Condition* (Chicago: University of Chicago Press, 1958), pp. 22–135. But whereas the classical *oikos* was ruled by patriarchal dictate, the nineteenth-century middle-class home was supposedly the domain of the mother. The best account of this transformation, and of its consequences both for women and for literature, remains Ann Douglas's study *The Feminization of American Culture* (New York: Knopf, 1977). Following Hawthorne and Melville, Douglas finds dark implications for literature in this distinction. Other critics have seen the sentimental domestic sphere as a place of new power for women, and as an opportunity for protopolitical transformations of gender relations in literature as well as in political and religious life. These latter views tend toward a programmatic overvaluing of the sentimental literature of the period.

4. Practical Power

1. The phrase "In Nature, nothing can be given, all things are sold" was a favorite of Emerson's. Its original is in Xenophon: "The gods demand of us toil as the price of all good things" (*Memorabilia* 2.1.20, trans. E. C. Marchant [Cambridge, Mass.: Harvard University Press, 1923]). Emerson found a more trenchant version of the phrase in Montaigne's essay "That We Taste Nothing Pure": "Pleasure chews and grinds us; according to the old Greek verse, which says that *the gods sell us all the goods they give us;* that is to say, that they give us nothing pure and perfect, and that we do not purchase but at the price of some evil" (*The Essays of Michel Eyquem de Montaigne*, trans. Charles Cotton, ed. W. Carew Hazlitt [Chicago: Encyclopaedia Britannica, 1952], p. 326; emphasis added).

2. Emerson had recently finished his lecture course "Human Culture" when he made this complaint to Carlyle in May 1838. At that moment, he was open-endedly inventing materials in his journals for future work. The way his journal writing looked to him then—antagonistic to whole form because of an excess of assertion in every part—forecast the style of the essays to come.

3. In January of 1830, Emerson began a careful reading of Marie Joseph de Gérando's *Histoire comparée des systèmes de philosophie* (Paris, 1822–1823). The journals show that he was particularly taken by Gérando's study of the pre-Socratic philosophers. He seized on Thales' assertion that "the essence of the soul is motion," but added that a system based on motion alone begs the presence of a primal impelling force, a "first principle" (*JMN* 3:363). Gérando's account of Thales' pupil Anaximander was more wholly satisfying to Emerson, for Anaximander's doctrine seemed to connect the dynamic interplay of the elements with exactly the sort of "first principle" lacking in his master's theory: "Anaximandre voulut rendre cette démonstration plus rigoureuse, il en scruta les fundemens; il se trouva de la sort conduit à lui donner un principe d'un ordre nouveau, un principe absolu et entierement metaphysique: *rien ne se fait de rien*" (vol. 1, p. 349). Emerson noted the passage in his journal: "Anaximander made this his maxim *Nothing can come of nothing*. And De G. says this was the pivot upon which long Greek philosophy turned" (*JMN* 3:364). The underlined phrase, which might as easily have been taken from Aristotle, Epicurus, Lucretius, or the village market, stayed in Emerson's mind. It accorded with a notion that had possessed him, he claimed in "Compensation," since he was a boy. In the same journal he rendered it in Latin—"Ex nihilo nil fit" (*JMN* 3:368)—as if further to dignify the term's authority.

4. Friedrich Wilhelm Nietzsche, *The Will to Power*, trans. Walter Kaufmann and R. J. Hollingdale, ed. Walter Kaufmann (New York: Random House, 1967), p. 339.

5. Thomas Carlyle, *Sartor Resartus*, in *The Works of Thomas Carlyle*, centenary ed. (1896; reprint, New York: AMS Press, 1969), vol. 1, p. 50.

6. "Primal repression" is one of Freud's most mysterious metapsychological ideas. Something like it seems to be at work all the way from the description of neuronic structures in the 1895 *Project*, to the essays on infant sexuality and narcissism, to the cosmology of *Beyond the Pleasure Principle*. Perhaps the most one can say is that primal repression is an event of antagonism or "anticathexis" practically connate with any impelling force of instinct or external stimulation.

7. Matthew Arnold, "The Function of Criticism at the Present Time," in *The Complete Prose Works of Matthew Arnold*, ed. R. H. Super (Ann Arbor: University of Michigan Press, 1960–1977), vol. 3, pp. 270, 285.

8. I cite the first edition of *Essays* (Boston: James Munroe, 1841), p. 235. The 1847 edition cuts the first sentence, and replaces "serene, impersonal, perfect" with "vital, consecrating, celestial."

9. In several of his discussions of poetic influence, Harold Bloom brings this moment from "Self-Reliance" into prominence by treating it as an account of a psychic process comparable to repression. He manages to do so without diminishing the unique power of either Emerson or Freud, for Bloom invokes Freud as another visionary critic rather as a code for explanation. See especially *Agon: Towards a Theory of Revisionism* (New York: Oxford University Press, 1982), pp. 169–172.

10. This comparison in some ways corresponds to the analogy with Freud, but it leaves no room for personal motives. Freud himself, in his discussion of condensation in dreams, uses the metaphor of an election to describe the way dreams get put together: "A dream is constructed . . . by the whole mass of dream-thoughts being submitted to a sort of manipulative process in which those elements which have the most numerous and strongest supports acquire the right of entry into the dream-content—in a manner analogous to election by *scrutin de liste*" (*The Interpretation of Dreams,* ed. and trans. James Strachey [New York: Avon Books, 1965], p. 318).

11. Emerson's stress on empirical verification, along with its consequences for American pragmatists, is a major concern in two books by Richard Poirier, *The Renewal of Literature: Emersonian Reflections* (New York: Random House, 1987) and *Poetry and Pragmatism* (Cambridge, Mass.: Harvard University Press, 1992). For further discussion of Emerson's founding place among American pragmatists, see Cornel West, *The American Evasion of Philosophy: A Genealogy of Pragmatism* (Madison: University of Wisconsin Press, 1989) and Russell B. Goodman, *American Philosophy and the Romantic Tradition* (Cambridge: Cambridge University Press, 1990).

12. William James, *"Pragmatism" and "The Meaning of Truth"* (Cambridge, Mass.: Harvard University Press, 1975), p. 97. Though Charles Sanders Peirce concerns himself with logical as well as empirical verification, he anticipates James when he finds that a "guiding principle" ("almost any fact can be a guiding principle") is a "habit" that leads us forward experimentally: "[Its] truth depends on the validity of the inferences which the habit determines; and such a formula is called a *guiding principle* of inference" ("The Fixation of Belief," in *Selected Writings,* ed. Philip P. Wiener [New York: Dover Publications, 1958], pp. 96–97).

13. By claiming that Emerson's skepticism pertains to practices and events rather than to epistemology, I am suggesting that, in a major sense, he leaves the epistemological field to Hume, Kant, and other worthy contenders. This is not to discount the rich epistemological implications of Emerson's skepticism as explored by Stanley Cavell and David Van Leer; it is merely to point

out that his skepticism arises as an issue of practice rather than as an address to longstanding epistemological problems. Skepticism, with all its epistemological implications, is something that *happens* in the course of Emerson's work. As such it is a stance to be described alongside other stances; but skepticism itself is not for Emerson a position *from which* to give a definitive account of one thing or another.

14. Stendhal, *The Red and the Black,* trans. Lloyd C. Parks (New York: Signet Classics, 1970), p. 359.

15. In 1835, before Charles's death and as he was at work on *Nature,* Emerson admitted that this reliance on material objects was an essential, indeed involuntary, feature of his compositional practice: "Charles wonders that I don't become sick at the stomach over my poor journal yet is obdurate habit callous even to contempt. I must scribble on if it were only to say in confirmation of Oegger's doctrine that I believe I never take a step in thought when engaged in conversation without some material symbol of my proposition figuring itself incipiently at the same time. My sentence often ends in a babble from a vain effort to represent that picture in words" (*JMN* 5:77; see also *CW* 1:20). His own characteristic practice led Emerson to agree with Guillaume Oegger's assertion that words derive from our uses of material things. This is reflected not only in the "Language" section of *Nature,* but also in Emerson's advice to Carlyle to make his words "one with things" (*CEC,* 99).

16. The general sense of my argument in this section owes much to Stanley Cavell's suggestion, in his study *In Quest of the Ordinary: Lines of Skepticism and Romanticism* (Chicago: University of Chicago Press, 1988), that Emerson and Thoreau seek "the prize of the ordinary" (p. 4). Cavell persuasively brings these American writers into line with Heidegger and the analytic tradition in philosophy.

17. See Cavell's discussion of Emerson's "clutching" in *This New Yet Unapproachable America: Lectures after Emerson after Wittgenstein* (Albuquerque, N.M.: Living Batch Press, 1989), pp. 86, 108.

18. See B. L. Packer, *Emerson's Fall: A New Interpretation of the Major Essays* (New York: Continuum, 1982), pp. 157–162.

19. Samuel Taylor Coleridge, "Work without Hope," in *Samuel Taylor Coleridge,* ed. H. J. Jackson (New York: Oxford University Press, 1985), p. 139.

20. Cavell, *Unapproachable America,* pp. 77–118.

Index

Abstraction: in allegory, 34, 37–39; Coleridge on, 262n16. *See also* Classification; Remove

Action, 15–17, 67–68, 106, 241, 244–245; as abandonment, 11–12, 83; in Coleridge, 40; spontaneous, 172; as becoming, 184–185; vs. intention, 190, 192; and domestic life, 194–201; and heroism, 195–196

Adams, John Quincy, 132

Aeschylus, 211

Agassiz, Louis, 85, 87, 113, 125–126, 163, 164, 169; *Contributions to the Natural History of the United States of America*, 134; *Essay on Classification*, 65–66, 102–103

Alcott, Bronson, 113

Anaximander, 206

Anti-Masonry, 137–138

Arnold, Matthew, 219–220

Authority, 3, 10, 74–75, 110, 111; and biography, 174; and character, 193

Balzac, Honoré de, 140–142, 158; *Comédie humaine*, 140

Bartholomew of Bologna, 43

Benjamin, Walter, 157

Bentham, Jeremy, 115

Biography, 20, 170–184, 194, 198; vs. history, 170, 175, 178, 181, 192; as writing, 179–180, 190, 209. *See also* Experience; History

Blake, William, 36, 72, 151, 176, 221, 237; *The Book of Urizen*, 38

Bloom, Harold, 90

Boston Natural History Society, 60, 134

Botanical gardens, 98, 131. *See also* Muséum d'Histoire Naturelle; Natural history

Brooks, Cleanth, 22–23, 24

Bryant, William Cullen, 4–5

Buffon, George Louis Leclerc de, 123, 140

Burke, Kenneth, 274–275n10

Carlyle, Thomas, 94, 107, 174, 190, 206, 219; Emerson's first visit with, 15, 69, 90; on Novalis, 104; on Emerson, 208–209; "Corn Law Rhymes," 13, 14; *The French Revolution*, 196; *On Heroes and Hero-Worship*, 170; *Sartor Resartus*, 214; "Signs of the Times," 152

Carnap, Rudolph, 36–37

Cavell, Stanley, 147, 255

Catastrophe, 2, 14, 18, 220–221, 254. *See also* Death, Emerson's responses to; Geology

Cézanne, Paul, 156

Channing, William Ellery, 9; "The Present Age," 134–137

Character, 180, 185–194, 199–200, 227, 228; graphic sense of, 185–186; and style, 186–189; vs. personality, 188–190; as nature, 189. *See also* Biography

Classification: natural, 35, 59–60, 65–66, 75–79, 83–84, 122–123, 125–126; Emerson and, 67, 119–122, 169–170; and life, 85–86; development of,

279

Sense of wholeness
Calm, solitude
miracle of self & nature
Love of peacetime alone

Is rain
Dan's presence
Down can
Sunny weather
Being trapped - painters, etc.